AUSCHWITZ-BIRKENAU

From Hell To Hope?

SIMON BELL

Text copyright © 2017 Simon Bell

All rights reserved.
Printed in the United States of America.
No part of this book may be reproduced, or stored in a retrieval system, or transmitted in any form or by any means, electronic, mechanical, photocopying, recording, or otherwise, without express written permission of the publisher.

ABOUT THE AUTHOR

Simon Bell is a first-time author who feels duty-bound to add a small contribution to the knowledge and understanding of what we now refer to as 'the Holocaust', and to be able to put into print some thoughts and observations about lessons that need to be learnt. Simon is a retired mental health nurse with over 37 years of National Health Service experience. The first 15 years of his career were spent working in hospitals, and included – in old asylum care – looking after severely damaged, elderly survivors of the war in Europe and the Holocaust. These shadows of humanity had eyes that appeared not to see, but had tormented minds that sadly knew and saw too much. That instilled a long-held interest not just in the Holocaust but in the consequences of all hatred and discrimination. For nearly 22 years he worked with mentally- disordered offenders, and has dealt with most types of criminal behaviour, witnessed the consequences of crime, and dealt with those who have experienced the extremes of personal trauma. Aside from a clinical role, he also helped to deliver training to a range of mental health and other disciplines in helping them to understand and deal with patients who have experienced childhood and adult sexual abuse. In the summer of 2016 Simon retired. He is now studying for an MA in Second World War Studies: Conflict-Societies- Holocaust.

SIMON BELL

Simon prides himself on not having any formal allegiance to religious or political parties or groups. He is however, dedicated to challenging intolerance and hatred in all of its forms, and seeking to ensure that those who might be targeted or oppressed are supported and cared for. He has been fortunate to have visited Auschwitz-Birkenau on a number of occasions, as well as other sites in Poland, and to have spent time meeting and exchanging correspondence with survivors and scholars, historians and others who share his interest. He does not pray, but he wishes and hopes for a better, more tolerant, and more caring world.

DEDICATIONS

This book is dedicated firstly and most importantly to all who suffered, died, and survived during the Holocaust; and to those who have suffered in the far too many genocides and acts of intolerance that have happened since that time. It is dedicated to the fortitude, strength, humility, and resolve of those survivors who are still with us, who pledge their lives to educating and informing future generations by their willingness to share incredibly personal accounts of trauma that are beyond the comprehension of most people. Without these people the Holocaust becomes a series of pictures, or words on a page, or the remains of buildings at former camps. It becomes an event in human history the sheer magnitude of which could be lost in translation. Without them we are open to the outrageous and shameful challenges of Holocaust deniers; but those who dismiss history cannot argue with the living memory of survivor accounts. It is dedicated to present and future generations who are entrusted with honouring and remembering what happened so that we can honestly and passionately not just say, "Never again," but we can pledge ourselves to act always in the name of decency and care for our fellow human beings.

It is dedicated to good folk - irrespective of religion, or lack of such belief; or political affiliation, or country of origin, or language, or skin colour, or gender, or sexuality, or any other definable otherness - who care about fellow human beings, and want to make a difference. It is dedicated to some incredibly special people that I have been fortunate to know in a professional and personal capacity who have left me time and time again with feelings of positive hope for now and the future.

ACKNOWLEDGEMENTS

Thanks to the staff at *Auschwitz-Birkenau State Museum* in Oświęcim in Poland. On each visit I have found the staff to be helpful, courteous, knowledgeable, and invaluable. It is those staff whose efforts maintain the site of the camps to ensure that history lives on in the grounds, space, and physical ruins; and in the fantastic but moving educational environments.

I am grateful to the staff at Beth Shalom, The National Holocaust Centre in Laxton, near Newark, Nottinghamshire, England. In particular, I thank the many guest-speakers – survivors - who have indulged me with their time, and have shared their stories with me and others.

I am grateful to friends, associates, colleagues, scholars and historians who have supported me through this project and helped nurture the need to put thoughts on paper. I particularly need to thank Jessica Clark and Debbie Callahan-Sepper for their encouragement and shared passion. I also thank Rainer Hoess, a man dedicated to challenging intolerance; who has brought honour back to his family name, and has shared with me his time, knowledge, and patience. I am honoured and privileged to call Rainer a friend. I am fortunate to have met and got to know survivors of this, one of the darkest periods in human history.

I cannot write this book without offering personal thanks to Kitty Hart- Moxon. You are an inspirational woman, and I feel humbled and honoured to know you and to have your friendship.

There is a 'Holocaust industry' that at times is deserving of criticism. Some within that industry seek personal gain, esteem, kudos, and profit. Such a criticism cannot justly be directed at those work at and run *Auschwitz-Birkenau*. I have witnessed first-hand the immense pressure of the world's press and those in high office being brought to bear at Auschwitz. It was clear that the needs of survivors and their loved ones were being given the highest level of priority by the museum staff at all levels.

I would like to thank my wife Bev and my sons Josh and Ben above all. Not many wives accept a husband travelling hundreds of miles just to talk to someone or tolerate him researching endlessly from a houseful of Holocaust related material. Without their support this book would never have happened.

CONTENTS

About The Author	v
Dedications	vii
Acknowledgements	ix
Foreword	xiii
Introduction	xv
Chapter One - A Very Personal Perspective	1
Chapter Two - The Jews and the Roma in Germany	11
Chapter Three - Hitler, Mein Kampf, and the Rise of The Nazis	18
Chapter Four - Creators and Exponents of The Final Solution	39
Chapter Five - A History of Auschwitz and its Brutality	100
Chapter Six - The Germans, Racism, Anti-Semitism and Complicity	119
Chapter Seven - Jewish Resistance – Lessons in Courage	130
Chapter Eight - Survivor Accounts	147
Chapter Nine - Could it Happen Again?	217
Chapter Ten - Reflections and Hope	252
Chapter Eleven - Auschwitz-Birkenau Today	258
Chapter Twelve - Anniversary of the Liberation	262
Epilogue	275

(All Photographs By Simon Bell)

FOREWORD

'Three generations have missed out on Holocaust Education since WORLD WAR II, and I believe this may have contributed to the numerous genocides these past 70 years. It seems that little has been learned from history. The Holocaust did not begin in the gas chambers - it started with words: it was a gradual process, but the warning signs were ignored. We need to learn from the past that catastrophic events occur when communities become divided, and there is no solidarity.

It is vital to educate each generation who need to understand the warning signs, the failures that allowed prejudice, discrimination and persecution that lead to vast programmes of mass-slaughter that affected the whole world. We cannot predict the future, and because the Holocaust occurred once it could happen again. We do not know who will be targeted next, or where or when it could take place.'

Kitty Hart-Moxon, OBE
July 2015

INTRODUCTION

"No one is born hating another person because of the colour of his skin, or his background, or his religion. People must learn to hate, and if they can learn to hate, they can be taught to love, for love comes more naturally to the human heart than its opposite."

Nelson Mandela

On 27th January 1945 forces from the Soviet Union liberated the camps that made up the vast and sprawling complex of Auschwitz. They found scenes of barbarity, cruelty, devastation, deprivation, death, and carnage beyond the wildest imaginations of even the most battle hardened troops. Elsewhere across Europe other concentration and death camps were liberated by allied military personnel. The images of that time are etched into the psyche of modern history. Few then could comprehend man's capacity for cruelty, or that a people could try to eradicate fellow human beings from the face of the earth due solely to their faith or a perception of their race.

Since 2001 the date of the liberation of Auschwitz has been known as *Holocaust Memorial Day* in the UK. It commemorates not only the events of the Holocaust but also the genocides in Cambodia, Rwanda, Bosnia and Darfur. Elsewhere around the world this date is known as the *International Holocaust Remembrance Day.*

27th January is a time for reflection on the dangerous consequences of intolerance and hate. It is a time to remember the death and suffering brought about in circumstances most of us will not experience and that few of us today can truly understand.

The Holocaust is gradually fading away in history due to the passage of time. Many of the concentration and extermination camps have been destroyed, and the land that they once occupied has been built on or reclaimed by nature. Some are marked by memorials or small museums. Those camps that remain, such as Auschwitz, are living museums, but for many visitors the harsh reality of what occurred there is difficult to grasp. The survivors of Auschwitz and other camps are becoming fewer in number. They are all elderly now. In time they will be lost to us. Many will take the memories of what they experienced with them to the grave. Some have shared their stories with close confidants. Some were too damaged by what happened to ever be able to communicate their distress to others. Some, thankfully, have seen it as a duty and honour to tell the world in books, lectures, film, and television documentaries, so that they can help to ensure that we never forget what took place across much of continental Europe during the years of the Nazi regime.

On 27th January 2015 the world commemorated the seventieth anniversary of the liberation of Auschwitz. It was a particularly poignant anniversary as it was the last significant date that many Holocaust survivors were able to acknowledge and contribute to, during the memorial events around the world. Approximately three hundred survivors actually attended the commemoration at Auschwitz – the site of their suffering – and for some this was to be their first or their final visit.

Much has been written about the Holocaust in the years since 1945. The world is a more informed place, and hatred is challenged both morally and legally. But since 1945 there have been further genocides, and at any given time people are being slaughtered in brutal wars for no other reason than their differences from those that oppress them. We must strive to learn from the past, to challenge hate and oppression, and to always ensure that no matter what, we never forget. This book is intended as a small contribution to those ideals.

There will be no images in this book of emaciated inmates, striped uniforms, piles of bodies, or pictures of stern and hard-faced Nazis. The grainy black and white photographs or films of Auschwitz and other camps can be easily accessed elsewhere. Old images suggest a bygone time, or history as events from long ago, and of little relevance to us today. The reality when one visits Auschwitz is that it happened in real time, in living memory, in full colour, in three dimensions, in the solid and palpable form of life and death, of suffering and fear, of earth, of bricks, of wood, of railway lines, and of cattle trucks. The barrack blocks are there to be seen and felt. The ground walked upon is the same ground on which millions trod before life was cruelly stubbed out. The remains of gas chambers and crematoria occupy the vision and mind of those privileged to visit. This place - this site of utter brutality - is real. It is not a history lesson, the contents of a book, or a television documentary.

Visitors today become part of the past. History becomes part of them. By breathing the air of Auschwitz one shares the molecules and essence of those who were there in harsher times. Survivors of the Holocaust see the place as it was then, not as it is now.

To understand, and hopefully to learn from the past, one has to listen, and read, and watch, and actively use the human capacity for imagination. Only then can the magnitude of what Auschwitz symbolises be truly appreciated. This book is largely a work of reflection, based on the impact on one person visiting the death camp, years after the events that made the small Polish town of Oświęcim notorious in human history. The pictures of today, and the words that fill these pages, are intended to help others to appreciate and understand not just mankind's capacity for horror, but also the necessity of mankind to learn from the past.

It is our obligation – our responsibility – to those who were at Auschwitz, to ensure that lessons are truly learnt. The duty to contribute to the knowledge of others becomes absolute. Those who embark on this journey in a search for fame or an enhanced reputation, or for financial gain, have missed the point. The reasons for researching, and writing, and informing others are simple – it is because we must, and failure to do so is an insult to history. In the summer of 2014 I decided that it was time to put words on paper, from my perspective. So here they, humbly, are.

CHAPTER ONE
A VERY PERSONAL PERSPECTIVE

In 1981 I started my career in mental health care when I gained employment at a large psychiatric hospital. I had been fortunate to work there briefly the year before as a visiting student nurse. Like all purpose-built Victorian asylums it was typical of its type. Constructed outside of the local population centre this imposing red brick building was set back in expansive and grand wooded grounds. Several hundred patients were housed within its walls and many, if not most of them, were what were classed as 'long stay'. These were people for whom the hospital had been home for many years, and in some cases, for many decades. Some had long-term mental illnesses such as schizophrenia, many were learning disabled, many were demented, and a small number were there because of juvenile delinquent behaviour decades before, or even for the 'illness' of giving birth out of wedlock in less enlightened times.

It was an institution with fixed, rigid routines which were meant to control behaviour (though that was never said at the time). Hygiene would be attended to at set times of day; bathing would be permitted once a week according to a rota; clothing was issued from a store-room; food was given at set times, and cigarettes and treats were dispensed by staff rather than being the property of the patients. Violence was commonplace. Abuse of patients by patients, including sexual exploitation, was almost an accepted and tolerated norm, and true dignity was not a concept readily promoted.

The treatments of that time, particularly for schizophrenia, were in truth wholly ineffective. Symptoms were not alleviated, and the side effects from the toxic volumes of medication were horrendous. Mental health care then worked very much within a medical model of diagnosis, symptoms, and chemical treatment. Institutionalizing patients was a means to achieve the smooth running of wards. The staff cared of course, and always tried to do their best for patients, but they worked in a system that by today's standards was barbaric, and removed much of the dignity human beings in hospital should expect. And although I was passionate about doing the best for people, and to my knowledge never harmed anyone, I too was part of that system.

We had little concept at that time about the causes of mental illness over and above some largely almost mythical biological model that suggested chemical imbalances and genetic predisposition. We certainly had no real idea of trauma, and how that contributes significantly to poor mental health.

Amongst the long-stay patients were elderly men (mainly) and some elderly women, of German and Eastern European origin. In truth they were only in their late 50s, or their 60s and 70s, but to a young man barely turned 20 they were ancient. That perception was not helped by the culture of the hospital. The clothes issued to patients were charitable gifts of second-hand property. They were the clothes of old people, and gave these relatively young patients a bearing that added years to their given age. These people had lived through the horrors of the war in Eastern Europe, and some were Holocaust survivors. We knew this, but the relevance of their experiences and the impact of that on their illnesses, mental disorders, and behaviour was not something we ever considered - and I have no idea why. In hindsight it was obvious: they had vivid and distressing visual and auditory hallucinations; they had nightmares which would cause them to scream out in terror; they were fearful of others; they would fight over food and drink; they hoarded and bartered anything that could be used to trade. We would find small stacks of food, cigarettes, and tobacco hidden in bedding or the lining of clothes.

Today we would recognise their presentation and symptoms as being the result of institutionalisation, and a background of overwhelming trauma. Indeed, in the years since then I have cared for people who have survived other genocides, and we know full well that the trauma experiences are what cause their mental health problems. We address the trauma with therapy, and if required give medication to alleviate symptoms. Today we see the entirety of the individual rather than just a person with a mental illness. Hindsight is wonderful, but I so wish the attitudes towards mental health problems we have now had existed then. I wish even more that I had elements of my middle- aged questioning mind at that time so that I could have done more for those people who deserved, absolutely, the most compassionate care available. I cannot turn back the clock. But I can do something now, and I am dedicated to that cause.

I have been fortunate to visit Auschwitz-Birkenau in the baking heat of summer and in the bitter cold of a Polish winter. For many today, visiting the camps is merely part of some 'bucket list', or a thing to do when taking a break in Krakow. For me it was a personal mission, a pilgrimage, homage, and a duty to go. And it is a duty I intend to fulfil again.

There is a myth - possibly well meant, possibly promoted to suggest an added grimness, and possibly based on a genuine perception. The myth is that when one visits Auschwitz-Birkenau one is immediately aware that there are no birds. Much as this myth is compelling it is not true. In summer, Auschwitz-Birkenau is remarkably alive with plant life, grass, insects, and of course birds. One tends not to notice them because one is overwhelmed by the enormity of what one sees, and what the camp signifies. It is impossible to enter a place designed and run solely for slave labour, for suffering, and ultimately as a place of industrial murder, and not be emotionally absorbed by the reality of where one is and where one is walking. The average human mind, when faced with this place, has no time to observe wildlife. But the wildlife is there, and its existence can be a reassurance that even at a site of bestial horror and cruelty, in time, life re-emerges and some form of normality prevails.

Auschwitz I with its *Arbeit Macht Frei* (work makes you free) sign over the gate has an immediate familiarity to the visitor with even a basic knowledge of the Holocaust. It has abundant and imposing brick barracks, the ever-present barbed wire, and the all-seeing guard towers. It is not a place of hope. In many ways today it is a living museum and the blocks house educational displays and artefacts. There are of course the huge collections of a personal nature: hundreds of suitcases, toys, shoes, artificial limbs, shaving equipment and the shocking room full of human hair – tonnes of it, removed from inmates with the intention of making socks, shirts and blankets for soldiers on the Eastern Front. And each lock of hair, and every personal belonging, represents a person whose life was taken in brutal circumstances at the behest of a regime hell-bent on erasing a whole population from the face of the earth. There are places of torture and execution. There is the block where Mengele and his colleagues conducted barbaric experiments, and betrayed every ethic of the medical and nursing professions. And of course there is the wholly intact gas chamber in which many thousands of innocents died and were cremated.

Nearby, in an irony not lost on me, is the grand property where Camp Commandant Rudolf Hoess (also spelt Höss), and his family lived in luxury only a few yards from where the most inhuman activities were occurring. In that mansion some bizarre and surreal version of familial normality was enacted, whilst the smells and sounds of cruelty, suffering and death wafted over. And next to the gas chamber is the gallows from which Hoess was fittingly hanged – in sight of one of his shocking creations.

Auschwitz II, or Birkenau, is to me a more distressing place. As one walks through the arch of the guard tower at the gate one is immediately taken back to every film, photograph, article and personal account one has seen. The ugly vastness of Birkenau is breath-taking. Remains of barracks stretch beyond the range of sight. Each pile of stones is evidence of a building that housed thousands in cramped conditions of unbelievable suffering. Strolling alongside the rail lines of the ramp one is aware that one is stepping in the same place where millions trod before being taken to their deaths, or being selected for the slower death of incarceration, disease and forced labour. Each footstep for me is a step in someone else's shoes. I envisage the transports arriving - the bemused and terrified occupants emerging starved and uncertain; the fear they would have experienced with the shouting, the dogs, the beatings, and the search lights; the anxiety of looking at this strange and vast place with its hundreds of barracks, barbed wire, towers, and occupants of shuffling, emaciated inmates; the terror and uncertainty of selection; the distress at being separated from loved ones, and not knowing what was going to happen to them or yourself; the belief – totally human in its origin – that things could not be too bad after what had been experienced before, and that the oddness of the orders to march left or right, to be separated by age and gender, to leave belongings in a pile, to strip and be shaved, to don camp-issue clothes, and to shower to remove lice, all made sense.

A short walk from the selection ramp and one reaches the remains of the gas chambers and crematoria. For me the large and grand official memorial fades as I see only these places, these constructions of death and human destruction. It matters not whether 1.5 million or 2 million or 3 million died here. The specifics of numbers become mere details to argue about rather than the reality of industrial-scale slaughter. What matters is that our fellow human beings were killed for no other reason than hatred of their faith, their ethnicity, their politics, their sexuality, their gender, their age, or their perceived infirmity. The killing at this and other camps was wrong then, and will always be wrong. The gas chambers and crematoria, even in a state of ruin, are sites where humanity demonstrated an evil beyond most people's comprehension. As I stand by them I feel I breathe in the same air that those who were murdered did, before their oxygen was taken away in moments of terror.

Nearby are the pits of human ash. *Human ash?* The ash was stored awaiting disposal. Some was dumped in nearby ponds and meadows. There was so much of it that the Nazis ran out of a means of disposal - each microscopic grain, a speck of a person, born from love, and with hope for life, but with that love and hope snuffed out pointlessly and brutally. Some were burned in the open air because the crematoria could not cope with the volume of work. Some – perhaps in excess of 40,000 – were burned alive!

The barracks on either side are stark environments that stand now as a permanent reminder of how people not selected for immediate death were treated: bunk upon bunk, toilets without dignity, mud or dust depending on the season, and bitter cold, or sweltering heat. As a fit, able-bodied and healthy man, I struggled to cope with the winter cold, and I was dressed appropriately for the weather. I cannot comprehend how inmates in the camp, dressed only in pyjamas and clogs, starved, diseased, wounded, weak, mentally damaged, exhausted and terrified, coped. And yet many did cope, and worked as ordered, and rebelled, and survived with a fortitude that will always humble me.

I have no religious conviction. I lost no relatives in the Holocaust. I have not personally been targeted for racial or religious hatred. But I am a human being. I believe that we all bleed the same red blood, that we breathe the same air, and that we all want to live our lives comfortably, love and raise our children safely, and reach old age believing that we have done our best. I hate no one. I will disagree passionately with people and their causes, particularly those that seek to harm, belittle, scapegoat, or endanger others, but personally I cannot hate.

I am honoured to have cared for survivors. And even if, in hindsight, I did not deliver the best care compared to today's standards, I did try; and I honour those people in my memory and in my attitude today. I have read, watched, heard, and absorbed numerous accounts of the Holocaust and other genocides. I have tried to understand the thinking and bizarre logic that led the Nazis to come to power, and that led people from other nations to actively and enthusiastically join in their hateful and cruel activities. I have been privileged to meet survivors who dedicate their lives to educating and informing. Each survivor I have met has humbled me. A sad reality is that those who survived the 'Holocaust' (from the Greek -'whole burning') are elderly now. Slowly their numbers will diminish, and we will no longer have first-hand access to their personal accounts. The bricks and mortar, the space, and the physical environment of Auschwitz-Birkenau may be there for generations yet to come. The lessons of what happened there and elsewhere are the responsibility of those of us who live today. We are entrusted with that, and we are the duty-bound custodians of history, tasked with ensuring that we never forget, and we always remember the lessons.

I class myself as neither a scholar nor an historian in any classic or formal sense that those roles would normally be defined. I am a nurse, a husband, a dad, a man who cares, and a person who wants to make a difference. I freely admit to being passionate in my need to challenge intolerance in all of its forms, and wanting to try, in some small way, to make part of the world a bit better, even if that is only through encouraging others to think and consider a little bit before they leap to opinions or condemnation of others. This book in no way intends to add greatly to the histories and scholarly works that have already been written. It certainly does not seek to compete with or to challenge the abundant survivor accounts available in book shops, online, in film, or that can still be heard in person. The accounts of survivors – those who were there, who experienced the horror and cruelty – are the most powerful and relevant accounts. We must value every word, and cherish the privilege that they have chosen to share with this, and later generations, their stories. We must learn from them, and never forget the circumstances that resulted in millions dying and suffering in Auschwitz-Birkenau and elsewhere in the Holocaust. It is hoped that this book will contribute to the understanding of Auschwitz, particularly for students and those new to the subject, and that they too will develop a passion to honour the history of those who suffered, died, and survived throughout this dark and shameful period of human existence.

I was raised by decent parents in a loving and generally tolerant home and community. I would describe my parents as right of centre in their political thinking, and from traditional conservatism in their world view. Both would seek to avoid causing deliberate harm or offence to others, but they were from a time when casual racism was considered the norm and socially acceptable.

For reasons I cannot explain I instinctively railed against the far right from an early age. In the mid-1970s the National Front were prominent in the UK, and whilst they did not enjoy electoral success, their mark – in the form of graffiti - was seen everywhere. And the attitudes they espoused would slip easily off the tongue of otherwise supposedly decent people. At that time racial hatred in the UK was directed towards people of West Indian and Asian origin. But there was also a tendency to mock other races or nationalities, and Jewish jokes were acceptable in the classroom and the workplace. This never sat comfortably with me, and as I have matured in years, and hopefully in mentality, I have become increasingly determined to stand up to intolerance in any form it takes. It is still astonishing that in this day and age we can hate or scapegoat others purely because of their race, religion, language, culture, or country of origin, when the horrors of Europe's past are still alive in the memory of survivors. It is astonishing that even in sport there is a need for a 'Kick It Out' anti-racism campaign, because black footballers routinely have to suffer 'monkey' chants. Or that it is considered acceptable 'banter' for supporters of Tottenham Hotspur, an English football club with a traditional Jewish following, to suffer other fans making hissing noises in reference to gas chambers.

In my own home town of Shrewsbury in Shropshire in England the local Muslim community applied (thankfully with success) to convert a vacant premises they had purchased, into a prayer and cultural centre. During the planning process this building was picketed regularly by far right protesters. When challenged to explain what their objection was the reply was chillingly simple – "We don't want *them* here." It was reassuring that the prevailing local opinion was in favour of this centre, but the attitude of the far right protesters was, sadly, not an isolated view.

And what of those elderly patients? They moved on to community care and hopefully to a better life. I presume most if not all are no longer with us. Years of asylum care would have taken its toll on their general health. But we can honour them too by dedicating ourselves to fight hatred and intolerance in all of its forms.

***

CHAPTER TWO
THE JEWS AND THE ROMA IN GERMANY

There is evidence of Jewish history in Germany dating back to the fourth century A.D. Jews actually migrated to Germany and elsewhere in Europe during the time of the Roman Empire, and their existence in the continent pre- dated Christianity's arrival. By the eighth century Jewish communities were flourishing amongst the tribes along the Rhine in what is now Germany. By the time Christianity became established Jews were living in harmony with their neighbours. They spoke the old Germanic languages, could hold public office, and could work in all trades and industries. There was no real unification of the many German tribes at the time, but eventually a loose confederation was formed that became known as 'the Kingdom of Germany'.

In the eighth-ninth centuries, Charlemagne united most of Western Europe, and Germany became part of the Holy Roman Empire. As a result of this the Roman Catholic Church emerged as a powerful force across Europe. Roman Catholicism suggested that the Jews were a rejected people. The church formally suggested that Jews should be shunned economically and socially, in line with the Theodosian Code of the fifth century. This suggestion was largely rejected in Germany.

Jews in Germany acquired a reputation as reliable merchants, and as such were popular because of the goods they could provide. What may be seen as the golden age for Jews in Western Europe ended on 26 November 1095 when Pope Urban II appealed for Christians to help liberate Jerusalem from Muslim Turks. The Pope's appeal led to the First Crusade. The long-established and comparative harmony and cooperation between Christians and Jews ceased. Jews became viewed increasingly as outsiders, and rumours abounded that they were allied to the Muslims. The Christian Crusaders would routinely massacre whole Jewish communities when en route to the Holy Land.

Jewish life, and the communities the Jews lived in and amongst, changed after the First Crusade. They no longer had an exclusive role as traders and merchants. They became increasingly subjugated by the church. They established roles as moneylenders, which did not help to improve their popularity. Jews were prohibited from holding public office or from interacting with Christians. They became unable to wander around towns and cities without facing threats and physical attack. This led the Jewish communities to establish ghetto areas where they could safely live together. The collective, self- imposed isolation of Jews led to the development of 'Yiddish' - a mix of Hebrew and medieval German dialects.

The thirteenth century saw the advent of the Inquisition. Jews became included amongst those deemed to be heretics. They were accused of killing children for ritual purposes, host desecration, and poisoning wells during the Black Death (plague) in the fourteenth century. They were repeatedly forced out of towns and communities throughout this period and through the Reformation. Martin Luther failed to convert Jews, and denounced them, which resulted in further hostility and violence.

Each German city granted Jews certain rights, defined what taxes should be paid, and defined where Jews could live. This actually afforded Jews some protection but they effectively became the property of a local ruler. Jews still occupied trades as merchants and moneylenders. Unfortunately as majority Christian populations became crowded out of key industries the consequence was violence against Jews and expulsion from that area. This resulted in Jews wandering around Europe. By the late fifteenth century most Jews had moved to Eastern Europe and were mainly to be found in the area now known as Poland.

The status of Jews began to improve in the seventeenth century, and they became more valued by the rulers of Germany. As a result Jews developed into a more urban and professional community. They even took part in the 'Year of Revolution' in 1848, and afterwards were granted full citizenship.

By the late nineteenth and early twentieth century anti-Semitism in Germany became more common. This increased after World War I, but Jews maintained equality and their rights until Hitler and the Nazis came to power in 1933. Hitler made no secret of his anti-Semitism, and referred to it in detail in *Mein Kampf*. In 1935 the Nuremberg Laws defined Judaism in terms of race, rather than religion, and led to the withdrawal of citizenship rights for all Jews in Germany. In 1936 Austria was annexed. On 9th November 1938 the notorious event known as 'Kristallnacht' (night of the broken glass) occurred in which Jewish businesses, homes and synagogues were attacked and destroyed. At least 91 Jews were killed in the attacks, and approximately 30,000 were arrested and incarcerated in concentration camps. Jewish homes, hospitals, and schools were ransacked, as the attackers demolished buildings with sledgehammers. It is estimated that over 1,000 synagogues were burned, and well over 7,000 Jewish businesses were destroyed or damaged. Those Jews who could do so began to leave Germany after Kristallnacht, and in the ten months that followed that night approximately 115,000 fled the Third Reich. Some of the children were placed on 'Kindertransports' to the UK.

In March 1941 Hitler ordered the 'Final Solution' to the Jewish Question. The immediate impact was that all Jews were forced to wear yellow stars on their clothes, were moved to ghettos, and then began to be moved to concentration camps for forced labour or extermination. On 20 January 1942 the Berlin-Wannsee Conference, chaired by Reinhard Heydrich, with minutes taken by Adolf Eichmann, identified the estimated number of Jews in Europe, and formulated the plans for their extermination in camps such as Auschwitz- Birkenau. By 19 May 1943 Germany was declared 'Judenrein', or free of Jews. In reality some 19,000 Jews survived the war in Germany.

There is not a huge body of history about the 'Roma', or 'Gypsy' population. In part this is due to their being a people who did not traditionally maintain written records. Estimates of the number of Roma killed in the Holocaust vary from a conservative 200,000 up to a possible total of 500,000 – 600,000. Proportionately, the Roma suffered more losses than any other group apart from the Jews.

The Roma have their origins in India from where they began to wander in the late Middle-Ages. Why they left their original homeland is not known. The word 'gypsy' comes from an old misconception that they were of Egyptian heritage. Eventually the Roma arrived in Europe.

Technically the Roma are an Aryan people (in the same way that modern Iranians are). This caused problems for the Nazi interpretation of racial stereotyping as it did not conform to the perception of Germans as Aryan. The Roma were perceived as being 'non-persons', 'a-socials', 'labour-shy', and of foreign blood.

AUSCHWITZ-BIRKENAU

The Nuremberg Laws of 1935, which excluded Jews from aspects of German life and citizenship, were amended to include the Roma, and from as early as 1936 Roma were being sent to concentration camps. At a conference on 30th January 1940 a decision was reached to expel all Roma from Germany, and relocate them in occupied Poland, where they were often placed in the already overcrowded Jewish ghettos.

Initially, Himmler wanted to exempt two tribes of Roma from death, and merely wanted to sterilise them. On 16th October 1942 Himmler ordered that all Roma should be sent to concentration camps. Most were sent to the Gypsy Camp at Auschwitz-Birkenau, which initially received 20,000 Roma from Germany and the occupied territories. The majority were gassed. Those Roma in Poland who were not sent to Auschwitz or the other death camps were shot on the spot. It is not known with certainty how many were shot. The 1943 Citizenship Law in Germany did not mention the Roma because they were not expected to exist much longer.

From 1942 the Roma were sent mainly to Auschwitz. Many were subjected to the medical experiments of Dr Mengele and his colleagues. The Gypsy Camp was liquidated on 6th August 1944. Some occupants were sent to other camps. It is estimated that approximately 3,000 remained and were gassed.

Former Auschwitz Commandant Rudolf Hoess discussed the Gypsies in his autobiography written in captivity before he was executed: 'In 1942, however, an order was given that all Gypsy-type persons on German territory, including Gypsy half-castes, were to be arrested and transported to Auschwitz, irrespective of sex or age. The only exceptions were those who had been officially recognised as pure-blooded members of the two main tribes.' He goes on to state, 'I cannot say how many Gypsies, including half-castes were in Auschwitz. I only know that they completely filled one section of the camp designed to hold 10,000.' (Others estimate 16,000.) He detailed how poor the conditions were, including the inability to provide proper food for the children. Hoess describes a visit from Himmler: 'In July 1942 the Reichsführer SS visited the camp. I took him all over the Gypsy camp. He made a most thorough inspection of everything, noting the overcrowded barrack-huts, the unhygienic conditions, and the crammed hospital building. He saw those who were sick with infectious diseases, and the children suffering from 'Noma' (a form of cancerous growth, normally fatal, and usually found on the face, as a result of starvation and physical disability), which always made me shudder, since it reminded me of leprosy, and of the lepers I had seen in Palestine – their little bodies wasted away, with gaping holes in their cheeks big enough for a man to see through - a slow putrification of the whole body. He noted the mortality rate which was relatively low in comparison with that of the camp as a whole. The child mortality rate, however, was extraordinarily high. I do not believe that many new-born babies survived more than a few weeks. He saw it all, in detail, and as it really was – and he ordered me to destroy them. Those capable of work were first to be separated from the others, as with the Jews.'

It is timely to recall that Hoess here is also discussing children he had been tasked to incarcerate who had been living in desperate conditions that he and the Nazis had created. He adds, 'The Gypsies capable of work were transferred to another camp. About 4,000 Gypsies were left by August 1944, and these had to go into the gas chambers. Up to that moment, they were unaware of what was in store for them. They first realised what was happening when they made their way, barrack-hut by barrack-hut, towards Crematorium I. It was not easy to drive them into the gas chambers. I myself did not see it, but Schwarzhuber (a Commander of the Protective Camp Birkenau) told me that it was more difficult than any previous mass destruction of Jews, and it was particularly hard on him, because he knew almost everyone of them individually, and had been on good terms with them. They were by their nature as trusting as children.' (Rudolf Hoess, Commandant of Auschwitz pp 124-127)

    The Roma have existed in Europe for hundreds of years, sometimes on the periphery of the main society. The near elimination of the Roma by the Nazis is a fact rarely mentioned or acknowledged in the history of the Holocaust. It is a fact that is very much a part of the history of Auschwitz.

***

CHAPTER THREE
HITLER, *MEIN KAMPF*,
AND THE RISE OF THE NAZIS

'National Socialism', or Nazism, was not created solely by one man, but it became the political and power vehicle of one man and his ideas. Without Hitler it is unlikely there would have been a Nazi Germany. Of course, many others were involved in the creation of the Nationalsozialistische Deutsche Arbeiterpartei (NSDAP) - the National Socialist German Workers Party (called the 'Nazi Party', based on the German pronunciation and abbreviation). The Nazis were among a number of popular and violent movements to emerge in Germany amidst the chaos after the First World War. Germany was a country in financial ruin due to the punitive obligations placed on it by the victorious countries of the 1914 to 1918 conflict.

Many of the territories previously thought of as German were now under the control of others. Many people of German heritage and with German as a first language were now no longer part of what they would regard as their own country; and the German population was aware that they had been forcibly detached from their brethren by the punishments inflicted in defeat. The German currency collapsed in the midst of a worldwide recession and the

AUSCHWITZ-BIRKENAU

economy became crippled from hyper-inflation. The monarchy had been removed. There were millions of former soldiers who had returned from war to a land of chaos, and who found themselves in Germany wondering what they had fought, suffered, and lost comrades for. Many movements and political groups attempted to fill the void, including communists, socialists, anarchists and the far right. The German borders and hinterlands were explosive and violent. Various Freikorps were established and made up of former soldiers who perceived themselves as fulfilling a patriotic duty. They fought to maintain some form of order and security for a state that was banned from having any more than an essential military capability. The Freikorps were an unofficial force that was welcomed by regional and national government when it suited, but that could be disowned just as quickly.

In all of this upheaval and chaos was to emerge a young man of Austrian birth – Adolf Hitler. Much of what is known, or accepted knowledge of Hitler's early life has been gleaned from *Mein Kampf*, of which more detail will be referred to later. This was a combination of autobiography and political thoughts written during a period of imprisonment in 1924. It was released in two volumes in 1925 and 1926. It is an important work that explains the thoughts and reasoning of a man whose influence and hatred brought unparalleled destruction to Europe and much of the world. It is a book that is roundly condemned by many. Some feel it should be banned, and never again be published. Its existence is crucial – however distasteful the views expressed within it – in helping people today to better understand Hitler and the birth of Nazism in the 1920s. More will be referred to of *Mein Kampf* in due course, but first to Hitler himself.

Hitler was born on 20 April 1989 in Braunau am Inn, Austria, the son of Alois Schickelgruber Hitler, aged 52 and his younger third wife Klara Poelzl. There were five other children from the marriage, but only Adolf and a sister reached adulthood. His father had two other children from his second marriage. He was apparently a resentful, discontented, and moody child with an unstable temper. He had a poor relationship with his father who was a strict disciplinarian, but he doted on his mother. Most accounts suggest that Hitler had very little affection for his father who was reputed to have beaten him regularly. He was, however, devoted to his mother. In *Mein Kampf* Hitler referred to his parents somewhat idealistically, though ironically – 'My father, a dutiful civil servant, my mother giving all her being to the household, and devoted above all to us children in eternal, loving care.' (*Mein Kampf* p. 4)

Hitler's mother died from cancer in December 1908. This was to have a major impact on her son. He was educated during four years at the Realschule in Linz, where he went at the behest of his father. Hitler intimates in *Mein Kampf* that he was not happy with going to Realschule but '… one day it became clear to me that I would become a painter, an artist. There was no doubt as to my talent for drawing: it had been one of my father's reasons for sending me to the Realschule, but never in all the world would it have occurred to him to give me professional training in this direction.' (*Mein Kampf* pp 8 & 9)

Hitler left the Realschule aged 16. In October 1907 he moved to Vienna where he would live until 1913. His perception of his artistic abilities was higher than others had of him. Hitler had high opinions of his own artistic abilities, and applied to attend the Viennese Academy of Fine Arts, but much to his annoyance he was rejected. He spent the next five years in Vienna: it was an uncomfortable and unhappy time. He survived by selling paintings, and doing low-level jobs. He invariably stayed in men-only hostels, often with fellow labourers, whose views, behaviour and attitudes he disapproved of. During this period he developed a hatred for Marxists, Jews, Liberalism and the Habsburg monarchy. He studied the thoughts of Karl Lueger, which helped to develop his views on anti-Semitism and the purity of Germanic blood. He also studied the work of Lanz von Liebensfels and Goerg von Schoenerer from whom he learned about the idea of the 'eternal Jew' as the symbol for all chaos, corruption, and the destruction of culture, politics and the economy. He saw the press, prostitution, syphilis, capitalism, Marxism, democracy and pacifism as being part of a Jewish conspiracy to undermine the German nation and the purity of what he had come to see as the Aryan race. It is possible some of his thoughts on prostitution and syphilis may have been due to catching that infection from a sex worker in Vienna.

In May 1913, feeling disillusioned with Vienna, Hitler moved to Munich. In August 1914 he joined the Sixteenth Bavarian Infantry Regiment and saw service as a despatch rider. He received the Iron Cross (First Class) for bravery but did not rise above the rank of Lance Corporal. He was wounded twice in action. He was also gassed just four weeks before the end of the war and spent three months in hospital in Pomerania, in part because he had been temporarily blinded. As he recovered he developed an intense anger about the failed German revolution of 1918. He became convinced that fate had chosen him to rescue Germany from the wrongs of the Treaty of Versailles, Bolsheviks, Social Democrats and Jews.

In the summer of 1919, Hitler was assigned by the Reichswehr (German defence) to a role that effectively involved spying on the various political parties that had emerged in post-revolutionary Munich. In this role Hitler was sent to investigate a small nationalist group called the 'German Workers Party'. In September 1919 he joined the party, which at the time only had about forty members. He changed its name to Nationalsozialistische Deutsche Arbeiterpartei (NSDAP, or National Socialist German Workers Party) which became shortened to the Nazi Party, and by July 1921 Hitler had appointed himself as the party chairman.

Hitler discovered that he had a gift for oratory. It was Hitler too, who gave the party the swastika symbol. In *Mein Kampf* Hitler explains the origins and design of the Swastika which has become the most potent visual symbol of Nazism. He states: "Unlike the bourgeois politicians, I have, in our movement, always upheld the standpoint that it is a true good fortune for the German nation to have lost the old flag. What the republic does beneath its flag, can remain indifferent to us. But from the bottom of our hearts we should thank Fate for having been gracious enough to preserve the most glorious war flag of all times from being used as a bedsheet for the most shameful prostitution. The present day Reich, which sells itself and its citizens, must never be permitted to fly the black, white, and red flag of honour and heroes.

As long as the November disgrace endures, let it bear its own outer covering and not try to steal this like everything else from a more honourable past. Let our bourgeois politicians remind their conscience that anyone who desires the black, white, and red flag for this state is burglarising our past. Truly, the former flag was suited only to the former Reich, just as God be praised and thanked, the Republic chose one suited to it. This was also the reason why we National Socialists could have seen no expressive symbol of our own activity in hoisting the old flag. For we do not desire to awaken from death the old Reich that perished through its own errors, but to build a new state. The movement which today fights Marxism with this aim must therefore bear the symbol of the new state in its very flag. The question of the new flag – that is its appearance – occupied us intensely in those days. From all sides came suggestions, which for the most part it must be admitted were more well- intentioned than successful. For the new flag had to be equally a symbol of our own struggle, since on the other hand it was expected to be highly effective as a poster. Anyone who has to concern himself much with the masses will recognise these apparent trifles to be very important matters. An effective insignia can in hundreds of thousands of cases give the first impetus towards interest in a movement. For this reason we had to reject all suggestions of identifying our movement through a white flag of the old state, or, more correctly, with those feeble parties whose sole political aim was the restoration of past conditions, as was proposed by many quarters. Besides, white is not a stirring colour. It is suitable for chaste virgins' clubs, but not for world- changing movements in a revolutionary epoch. Black was also suggested: in itself suitable for the present period, it contained nothing, however, that could in any way be interpreted as a picture of the will of our movement. Finally, this colour was not a stirring enough effect either. White and blue were out of the question despite their wonderful aesthetic effect, for these were the colours of an individual German state, and of an orientation towards particularistic narrow-mindedness which unfortunately did not enjoy the best reputation. Here too, moreover, it could have been hard to find any reference to our movement. The same applied to black and white. Black, red, and gold were in themselves out of the question. So were black, white, and red, for the reasons already mentioned, at least in their previous composition? In effect, to be sure, this colour combination stands high above all others. It is the most brilliant harmony in existence. I myself always came out for the retention of the old colours, not only because as a soldier they are to me the holiest thing I know, but because also in their aesthetic effect they are by far the most compatible with my feeling. Nevertheless, I was obliged to reject without exception the numerous designs which poured in from the circles of the young movement, and which for the most part had drawn the swastika into the old flag. I myself – as Leader – did not want to come out publicly at once with my own design, since after all it was possible that another should produce one just as good or perhaps even better. Actually a dentist from Starnberg did deliver a design that was not bad at all, and, incidentally, was quite close to my own, having only the one fault that a swastika with curved legs was composed onto a white disk. I myself, meanwhile, after innumerable attempts, had laid down a final form; a flag with a red background, a white disk, and a black swastika in the middle. After long trials I also found a definite proportion between the size of the flag and the size of the white disk, as well as the shape and thickness of the swastika. And this remained final." (*Mein Kampf* pp. 450-452)

The translator's notes in *Mein Kampf* state: 'The Swastika, on account of its alleged Aryan origins in ancient India, had been used by German extremist nationalist organisations both in Germany and Austria since the 1890s. It was introduced into the Nazi Party in August 1919 by the dentist, Friedrich Krohn, owner of a large private library much used by Hitler, member of various extremist organisations before 1914, and founder of a Nazi local group. He left the Nazi Party in 1921 in protest against Hitler's dominance.' (*Mein Kampf* p. 451)

Hitler elaborates further on the use of this symbolism: "Along the same lines arm-bands were immediately ordered for the monitor detachments, a red band, likewise with the white disk and black swastika. The party insignia was also designed along the same lines: a white disk on a red field, with the swastika in the middle. A Munich goldsmith by the name of Fuss furnished the first usable design, which was kept." (*Mein Kampf* p. 452) Hitler writes about the first use of the swastika in public in the summer of 1920, and how it had the effect of a burning torch for the movement. He adds: "And a symbol it really is! Not only that the unique colours which all of us so passionately love, and which once won so much honour for the German people, attest our veneration for the past; they were also the best embodiment of the movement's will. As National Socialists, we see our programme in our flag. In red we see the social idea of the movement, in white the nationalistic idea, in the swastika the mission of the struggle for the victory of the Aryan man, and by the same token, the victory of the idea of the creative work, which as such always has been and always will be anti-Semitic. Two years later, when the monitor troop had long since become a Sturm-Abteiling (storm section), embracing many thousands of men, it seemed necessary to give this armed organisation a special symbol of victory: the standard. This, too, I designed myself and then gave it to a loyal old party comrade, master goldsmith Gahr, for execution. Since then the standard is among the symbols and battle signs of the National Socialist struggle." (Mein Kampf pp. 452-453)

By November 1921 he was the 'Führer', or leader of the party which now had about 3,000 members. He organised brutal groups to keep order at party meetings and to break up or disrupt meetings of other parties. One of these groups became the 'Sturmabteilung' (SA) or stormtroopers, organised by Captain Ernst Rohm. Hitler's personal bodyguard was made up of members of the Schutzstaffel, or SS.

Hitler focused his speeches and propaganda on the wrongs of the Treaty of Versailles, the 'criminals' of the German November revolution in 1918, Marxists, and Jews. In February 1920 the NSDAP announced a twenty-five point programme that included the exclusion of Jews from the Volk community, and the myth of Aryan racial supremacy. It also promoted extreme nationalism, with socialist ideas of profit-sharing. Hitler's first writings from this time stressed the idea of 'anti-Semitism of reason' which must lead 'to the systematic combating and elimination of Jewish privileges. Its ultimate goal must implacably be the total removal of the Jews.'

In November 1923 Hitler became convinced that the Weimar Republic was on the verge of collapse. Hitler, together with General Ludendorff and some local nationalist groups, sought to overthrow the Bavarian government in Munich in what has since become known as the 'Munich Beer-Hall Putsch'. Hitler and his mob burst into a Munich beer hall. He fired his pistol into the ceiling, and announced that he was now in charge of a new provisional government that was going to lead a revolution against Berlin. Hitler and Ludendorff, along with about three thousand men, then marched through Munich. They were met with determined resistance by the police who opened fire. Sixteen people died in the failed putsch, and Hitler and several others were arrested.

He stood trial in February 1924, but used the trial as a political platform. A speech to the court included 'pronounce us guilty a thousand times over. The Goddess of the eternal court of history will smile and tear to pieces the State Prosecutor's submission and the court's verdict for she acquits us.' Hitler was found guilty, and sentenced to five years' imprisonment, but he only served nine months before being released.

During that nine month period he dictated *Mein Kampf* (*My Struggle*) to his loyal colleague Rudolf Hess. In the preface to *Mein Kampf*, Adolf Hitler sets out his stall:

'On April 1, 1924, I entered upon my prison term in the fortress of Landsberg am Lech, as sentenced by the People's Court in Munich on that day. Thus, after years of uninterrupted work, an opportunity was for the first time offered me to embark upon a task which many had demanded and which I myself felt

to be worthwhile for the movement. I decided to set forth, in two volumes, the aims of our movement, and also to draw a picture of its development. From this it will be possible to learn more than from any purely doctrinaire treatise. At the same time, I have had occasion to give an account of my own development, in so far as this is necessary for the understanding of the first as well as the second volume, and in so far as it may serve to destroy the foul legends about my person dished up in the Jewish press. I do not address this work to strangers, but to those adherents of the movement who belong to it with their hearts, and whose intelligence is eager for a more penetrating enlightenment. I know that men are won over less by the written than by the spoken word, that every great movement on this earth owes its growth to great orators and not to great writers. Nevertheless, for a doctrine to be disseminated uniformly and coherently, its basic elements must be set down for all time. To this end I wish to contribute these two volumes as foundation stones in our common edifice.'
(*Mein Kampf, Preface*)

Mein Kampf is a book to be studied because it is necessary for an understanding of Hitler, and the way he perceived himself, his homeland, his fellow citizens and those he considered to be his enemies. *Mein Kampf* is in part autobiography, in part political thoughts and theories, and in part some form of bizarre self-promotion in which Hitler portrays himself in a Messianic role as the potential saviour of Germany. It is not an easy read. It is a book laden with hate and anger. It leaves no doubt as to Hitler's attitude towards some of his fellow human beings. He refers casually and rabidly to his anti-Semitism, and to his ideas on the purity of the Aryan race. It is also a difficult read due to the poor style of writing (some of which may be due to translation) in which he moves at times illogically from theme to theme. It is a tome in excess of six hundred pages, much of which is rambling in nature, and merely emphasises the irrational attitudes of its author. To refer here in detail to the contents of *Mein Kampf* – a book many believe should be banned – would take up too much space, and would divert away from the purpose of a work largely intended as a reflective piece about suffering, fortitude and hope.

Hitler was open in his racist and anti-Semitic attitudes. He made no attempt to disguise his feelings about Jews and other supposed enemies. It is of use to see his own words as these best explain the thinking of a man whose hatred led to the industrial extermination of millions, and the deaths of many more in a conflict that involved many countries. Early in *Mein Kampf* Hitler reflects on the faults and problems of Social Democracy:

'Meanwhile I had learned to understand the connection between this doctrine of destruction and the nature of a people of which, up to that time, I had known next to nothing. *Only a knowledge of the Jews provides the key with which to comprehend the inner, and consequently real, aims of Social Democracy* (Hitler's italics). The erroneous conceptions of the aim and meaning of this party fall from our eyes like veils, once we know this people, and from the fog and mist of social phrases rises the leering grimace of Marxism.' (*Mein Kampf* p. 47)

It is notable how easily Hitler manages to associate Social Democrats, Jews and Marxists in a way that suggests either a direct link, or that they are one and the same. Hitler makes some form of effort to explain how his attitudes to Jews developed:

'Today it is difficult, if not impossible, for me to say when the word 'Jew' first gave me ground for special thoughts. At home I do not remember having heard the word during my father's life-time. I believe that the old gentleman would have regarded any special emphasis on this term as cultural backwardness. In the course of his life he had arrived at more or less cosmopolitan views which, despite his pronounced national sentiments, not only remained intact, but also affected me to some extent. Likewise at school I found no occasion which could have led me to change this inherited picture. At the Realschule to be sure, I did meet one Jewish boy who was treated by all of us with caution, but only because various experiences led us to doubt his discretion and we did not particularly trust him; but neither I nor the others had any thoughts on the matter. Not until my fourteenth or fifteenth year did I begin to come across the word 'Jew' with any frequency, partly in connection with political discussions. This filled me with a mild distaste, and I could not rid myself of an unpleasant feeling that always came over me whenever religious quarrels occurred in my presence.' (*Mein Kampf* pp. 47-48).

Still, at this stage of reflection, there is no hint of the hatred that would come to so dominate Hitler's thinking. While he was living in Vienna he became aware of anti-Semitic newspapers, but somewhat ironically Hitler viewed these as being unworthy of 'a nation of culture'. His observations about Jews when he considered his early life were not hostile, but his dislike and distrust of them gradually becomes more evident:

'Once as I was strolling through the Inner City, I suddenly encountered an apparition in a black kaftan and black hair locks. Is this a Jew? was my first thought. For sure they had not looked like that in Linz. I observed the man furtively and cautiously, but the longer I stared at this foreign face, scrutinising feature for feature, the more my first question assumed a new form: Is this a German? As always in such cases, I now began to try to relieve my doubts by books. For a few hellers I bought the first anti-Semitic pamphlets of my life. Unfortunately, they all proceeded from the supposition that in principle the reader knew or even understood the Jewish question to a certain degree. Besides the tone for the most part was such that doubts again arose in me, due in part to the dull and amazingly unscientific arguments favouring the thesis.' *(Mein Kampf* p. 52)

Hitler intimates here that his own views are scientific, or carefully considered. He continued to elaborate on his theme and rationale: 'Yet I could no longer very well doubt that the objects of my study were not Germans of special religion, but a people in themselves; for since I had begun to concern myself with this question and to take cognisance of the Jews, Vienna appeared to me in a different light than before. Wherever I went, I began to see Jews, and the more I saw, the more sharply they became distinguished in my eyes from the rest of humanity ... among them was a great movement, quite extensive in Vienna, which came out sharply in confirmation of the national character of the Jews: this was the Zionists.' He distinguished between what he saw as liberal Jews and Zionists, with the latter particularly provoking his disdain: 'Later I often grew sick to my stomach from the smell of these kaftan-wearers. Added to this, there was their unclean dress, and their generally unheroic appearance.' He added, 'Was there any form of filth or profligacy, particularly in cultural life, without at least one Jew involved in it?' (*Mein Kampf* pp 52-53)

Hitler viewed the Social Democratic press as being dominated by Jews from the publishers down, which may later have had some bearing on the removal of a free press in Nazi Germany. He saw the Jews as being linked to trade unions and Marxism. He suggested that there was a defined link between Jews and both prostitution and white-slave traffic: 'The relation of the Jew to prostitution and, even more, to the white-slave traffic, could be studied in Vienna as perhaps in no other city of Western Europe, with the possible exception of the Southern French ports. If you walked at night through the streets and alleys of Leopoldstadt, at every step you witnessed proceedings which remained concealed from the majority of German people until the War gave the soldiers on the eastern front occasion to see similar things, or, better expressed, forced them to see them.' (*Mein Kampf* p. 55).

Hitler had a strong belief that Jews sought the destruction of Germany. He stated, somewhat nonsensically in *Mein Kampf* that:

'Little interest, as England, from a British state viewpoint, may have in a further annihilation of Germany that of the international stock exchange Jews in such a development is great. The cleavage between the official, or better expressed, the traditional, British statesmanship and the controlling Jewish stock exchange powers is nowhere better shown than in their different position on the question of British foreign policy. *Jewish finance in opposition to the interests of the British state welfare desires not only the complete economic annihilation of Germany, but also her complete political enslavement*(Hilter's italics). The internationalisation of our German economy – that is, the appropriation of German labour power by Jewish world finance – can be completely carried out only in a politically Bolshevist state. But if Marxist shock troops of international Jewish stock exchange capital are to break the back of the German national state for good and all, this can only be done with friendly aid from outside. The armies of France must, therefore, besiege the German state structure until the Reich, inwardly exhausted, succumbs to the Bolshevistic shock troop of international Jewish world finance.' He adds in italics '*And so the Jew today is the greater agitator for the complete destruction of Germany. Wherever in the world we read of attacks against Germany, Jews are their fabricators, just as in peacetime and during the War the press of the Jewish stock exchange and Marxists systematically stirred up hatred against Germany until state after state abandoned neutrality and renouncing the true interests of the peoples, entered the service of the World War coalition.*' He elaborates in a further confirmation of his belief in a great Jewish conspiracy 'The Jewish train of thought in all this is clear. The

Bolshevisation of Germany – that is, the extermination of the national Jewish intelligentsia to make possible the sweating of the German working class under the yoke of Jewish world finance – is conceived only as a preliminary to the further extension of this Jewish tendency of world conquest. As often in history, Germany is the great pivot in the mighty struggle. If our people and our state become the victim of these blood-thirsty and avaricious Jewish tyrants of nations, the whole earth will into the snares of this octopus; if Germany frees herself from this embrace, this greatest of dangers to nations may be regarded as broken for the whole world.' (*Mein Kampf* pp. 567-568)

The Nazi ideal of Germany as an Aryan nation, with a need for racial purity, became a cornerstone for many of the brutal policies so often associated with that regime. Hitler wrote in detail of his belief in the natural flaws associated with breeding between weak and strong individuals and the concepts of natural selection and survival of the fittest. The Nazis hijacked Darwinism to their own ends and were strong believers in eugenics as a variant on Darwinian theories of natural selection. As Hitler wrote:

'No more than Nature desires the mating of weaker with stronger individuals, even less does she desire the blending of a higher with a lower race, since, if she did, her whole work of higher breeding, over perhaps hundreds of thousands of years, might be ruined with one blow. Historical experience offers countless proofs of this. It shows with terrifying clarity that in every mingling of Aryan blood with that of lower peoples the result was the end of the cultured people. North America, whose population consists in by far the largest part of Germanic elements who mixed but little with the lower coloured peoples, shows a different humanity and culture from Central and South America, where the predominantly Latin immigrants often mixed with the aborigines on a large scale. By this one example, we can clearly and distinctly recognise the effect of racial mixture. The Germanic inhabitant of the American continent, who has remained racially pure and unmixed, rose to be master of the continent; he will remain master as long as he does not fall victim to defilement of the blood.

The result of all racial crossing is therefore in brief always the following:
a. Lowering the level of the higher race;
b. Physical and intellectual regression and hence the beginning of a slowly but surely progressing sickness.' (*Mein Kampf* p. 260)

In these few excerpts from *Mein Kampf* (which should ideally be read in its entirety rather than from selected and selective passages) Hitler's anti-Semitism can be seen to develop from a mild or moderate dislike and distrust, to a rabid hatred and a belief in a worldwide Jewish conspiracy involving international finance, Bolshevism, and other countries. And not only is that conspiracy seen as being hell-bent on destroying Germany but Hitler suggests or implies that Germany has some duty to achieve 'victory'. He also makes no attempts to conceal his views on racial purity. We must remember that *Mein Kampf* was written in 1923, and first published in 1925 – ten years and eight years before Hitler came to power – so the ideas expressed within in it were not secret or unknown when he was elected. And when, after the war, Germans claimed ignorance of the anti-Semitic policies of the Nazis, it is worth bearing in mind that between eight and nine million copies of *Mein Kampf* were sold during the twenty years of Hitler's lifetime from publication until his suicide.

Following his release from prison Hitler became aware that a change of approach was needed. He considered the failure of the Beer-Hall Putsch, and decided that never again would he face weapons of the state unless he was in charge. His abilities as a political tactician came to the fore. He realised that he could not gain power just through force, but needed a combination of legal subversion of the Weimar Constitution, the building of a mass movement, and the use of paramilitary strength and street level terror campaigns. Assisted by Göring and Goebbels he began the process of reassembling his followers, and rebuilding the Nazi movement. In January 1925 the ban on the Nazi Party was lifted, and Hitler was permitted to speak in public again. He soon succeeded in extending his appeal beyond Bavaria and became popular with both the right and the left of politics.

In the election of 1928 the Nazis only won 12 seats. The escalating problems associated with the Great Depression increased Hitler's popularity with those who felt threatened by the economic collapse of Germany. His appeal stretched across classes and professions. By 1929 he was beginning to win over industrialists, nationalists, conservatives and many in the army. Assisted in this process by press tycoon Alfred Hugenberg he was able to get extensive popular national exposure. As unemployment and uncertainty became worse Hitler was able to play on national resentments, feelings of revolt, and the German's perception that they needed strong leadership. He was able to present himself as being the only possible saviour of the nation.

By the 1930 election the Nazi vote increased from 810,000 to 6,409,000 (18.3 percent of the total vote), and they gained 107 seats in the Reichstag. The Nazis, and in particular Hitler, gained significant support from major industrialists. In February 1932 Hitler was granted German citizenship. In the elections of July 1932 the Nazis emerged as the largest political party, with 14,000,000 votes (37.3 percent) and 230 seats. In November 1932 their support was reduced to 11 million votes, or 196 seats. Hitler's quest for power was helped by conservative politicians, led by

Franz von Papen, who persuaded President von Hindenburg to nominate Hitler as Reich Chancellor on 30 January 1933. A fire at the Reichstag on 27 February 1933 (possibly arranged by Hermann Göring) gave Hitler the pretext for a totalitarian, one-party state. The last free and democratic elections in March 1933 secured Hitler total power. By July 1933 Hitler had ousted conservatives from government. He also abolished free trade unions, and eliminated communists, Social Democrats and Jews from political life. A policy of sending political opponents to concentration camps began.

In June 1934 Hitler destroyed the SA leadership of his former ally Ernst Rohm. Hitler had become the undisputed dictator of Germany. By August 1934 – following the death of von Hindenburg – Hitler united the positions of Fuhrer and Chancellor, ensuring that he held all the main powers of the state. This would prevent anyone from challenging his position. He did allow Himmler, Goebbels and Göring to establish their own areas of power, but they remained subservient to him. Over the next four years he gained popular national and international political successes. In 1935 he abandoned the Treaty of Versailles, and began the process of rebuilding the army by conscripting five times as many soldiers as Germany had been permitted. He persuaded Great Britain to allow Germany an increase in naval building. He built up the strength of the Luftwaffe. In March 1936 Germany occupied the demilitarised area of the Rhineland. Germany also supplied military aid and support to Franco's fascist forces, leading to his taking control of Spain in 1939. Germany's rearmament programme led to full employment and an increase in general production. In 1938 Hitler took personal control of the armed forces. In the same year Germany agreed the 'Anschluss' with Austria and the liberation (or invasion) of the Sudetanland in what was Czechoslovakia.

On 1st September 1939 Germany invaded Poland and the blitzkrieg attack ensured that country was overrun in less than a month. Poland's defeat was assured by the invasion from the east, a few days later, by Soviet forces. The country was divided into a German annexed region, the General Government under German control, and the east occupied by the Soviets. Hitler justified this and other actions as being necessary to provide 'lebensraum', or living space, for German citizens. German forces soon invaded, and rapidly conquered Denmark, Norway, Holland, Belgium, Luxemburg and France. The planned invasion of England failed after the defeat of the Luftwaffe by the RAF in the Battle of Britain. Hitler turned his attentions to the Balkans, North Africa, Greece, Crete and Yugoslavia.

On 22nd June 1941 German forces invaded the Soviet Union in what Hitler anticipated would be a rapid victory against the lesser Bolshevik forces. He grossly underestimated the size, resilience, and military capabilities of the Red Army, the vastness of the country, and the extremes of the Russian winter. Initial military successes soon turned to losses. More defeats followed. In January 1943 the German Sixth Army surrendered, Mussolini was beaten, and the allies invaded Italy. Rommel's forces lost at El Alamein, and North Africa fell to British and US forces. German air power crumbled, and the allies were able to bomb major cities and industrial targets at will. The Soviet forces were having increased success, and began to progress rapidly westward. On 6th June 1944 over one million allied military personnel took part in the landings on the coast of Normandy. The writing was on the wall for Germany. On 20th July 1944 an assassination attempt was made on Hitler. The ringleaders were identified and executed – the footage of the executions was shown to Hitler.

AUSCHWITZ-BIRKENAU

On 19th March 1945, as impending defeat became obvious, Hitler ordered the destruction of German industry, communications, and transport systems. His narcissistic and nihilistic belief was that if he could not survive, then neither should Germany survive.

On 29th April 1945 Hitler married his long-term mistress Eva Braun. On 30 April he and Eva Braun took cyanide capsules in a suicide pact and Hitler shot himself in the mouth. Their bodies were burned in the garden of the Reich Chancellery in Berlin.

Hitler's last *'Political Testament'*, dictated on 29 April 1945, hours before he took his own life, says much about the mind-set of a man who had spent almost his entire existence preoccupied by anger and hate:

'More than thirty years have passed since I contributed my modest strength in 1914 as a volunteer in the First World War, which was forced upon the Reich. In these three decades only love and loyalty to my people have guided me in my thinking, my actions and my life. They gave me the strength to make the difficult decisions, such as have never before confronted mortal man. I have used up my time, my working strength and my health in these three decades. It is untrue that I or anybody else in Germany wanted war in 1939 .... But nor have I left any doubt that if the nations of Europe are once more to be treated only as collections of stocks and shares of these international conspirators in money and finance, then those who carry the real guilt for the murderous struggle, this people will also be held responsible: the Jews! I have further left no one in doubt that this time it will not be only millions of children of Europeans of the Aryan peoples who will starve to death, not only millions of grown men who will suffer death, and not only hundreds of thousands of women and children who will be burned and bombed to death in the cities, without those who are really responsible also having to atone for their crime, even if by more humane means .... But before everything else I call upon the leadership of the nation and those who follow it to observe the racial laws most carefully, to fight mercilessly against the poisoners of all the peoples of the world, international Jewry.'

Those Generals and others, who knew months beforehand that the war was lost, had been acutely aware of how the world would judge them. At Auschwitz, the gas chambers and crematoria were blown up, and efforts were made to destroy records of the horror that had occurred. Elsewhere, Nazis tried to get rid of evidence of their crimes. Yet Hitler, knowing the end was close, maintained his hateful defiance to the last. There is no final expression of contrition or regret - merely an instruction that the fight against the Jews of the world must continue. The statement speaks volumes about the intractable nature of Hitler's thinking.

CHAPTER FOUR
CREATORS AND EXPONENTS OF THE FINAL SOLUTION

To understand Auschwitz-Birkenau, and what the Nazis referred to as the 'Final Solution of the Jewish question in Europe', it is necessary to know a little about some of the key individuals involved. These individuals are only part of the greater picture. For the entirety of this plan to eradicate an entire population of 11 million people from Europe needed much more than a few senior Nazis. It needed the active and enthusiastic involvement and participation of many, not just in Germany, but in all countries that were occupied. To put this into perspective, some facts are needed to understand the huge numbers of people involved. Not everyone who supported the Nazis in Germany was a war criminal, but in the 1933 election over 17 million people voted for the Nazis. In the same year the membership of the Nazi party was 2 million.

By 1945, the party membership had increased to 8 million, but there may have been a degree of social expectation and coercion involved. German forces during World War II involved service by some 15 million men. Following the war, about 5000 individuals were prosecuted by the allies. Another 40,000 were tried in Poland. By 1989, in what was West Germany, 105,000 people had been investigated, of whom 6,000 were convicted. Yet, at the main Nuremberg Trials, there were only 24 defendants. These figures do not take into account the collaborators in occupied lands, and those of other nationalities who were actively involved in the brutality of Nazi crimes against fellow citizens. The numbers are enormous, and show that the activities of the Nazi regime involved a sizeable minority, if not a majority, of the German population (and those in occupied lands) either agreeing wholeheartedly with the policies of government, or being complicit through action or inaction.

A common assumption about perpetrators of genocide (not just the Holocaust) is that they must have been mentally ill, or psychopathic. Of the defendants at the Nuremberg Trial only Rudolf Hess was believed to have been mentally ill, and it is likely some of his mental health problems developed, or at least manifested in captivity, even if there were some indicators of eccentricity before his detention. The World Health Organisation *ICD-10 Classification of Mental and Behavioural Disorders*, defines a psychopath as a personality disorder. There are various sub-criteria of personality disorder that this could apply to. The most appropriate definition is 'Dissocial Personality Disorder' as this encompasses other relevant personality disorders. A Dissocial Personality Disorder is defined as being characterised by:

(a) *Callous unconcern for the feelings of others;*
(b) *Gross and persistent attitude of irresponsibility and disregard for social norms, rules and obligations;*
(c) *Incapacity to maintain enduring relationships, though having no difficulty in establishing them;*
(d) *Very low tolerance to frustration and a low threshold for discharge of aggression, including violence;*

(e) Incapacity to experience guilt or to profit from experience, particularly punishment;
(f) Marked proneness to blame others, or to offer plausible rationalisations, for the behaviour that has brought the patient into conflict with society.
There may be persistent irritability as an associated feature. Conduct disorder during childhood and adolescence, though not invariably present, may further support the diagnosis. This diagnosis includes amoral, antisocial, asocial, psychopathic, and sociopathic personality disorder.
(**World Health Organisation ICD-10 Classification of Mental and Behavioural Disorders**).

It could be argued that many of the activities of those involved in the Holocaust were psychopathic. They certainly entailed cruel acts, with a callous disregard for the suffering and distress inflicted on others. But were the perpetrators truly psychopathic within any formal diagnostic criteria? They may or may not have been. They complied with the rules of the society they lived in, even if those rules did not adhere to the norms of many other societies. They were dutiful civil servants and soldiers. They maintained relationships. They could be caring, devoted, and loving within their family and social networks. Of course, many psychopaths function well in society, and may appear to be normal. It would be easy (perhaps preferable) if their behaviour could be attributed to some illness or mental disturbance. By seeking a medical condition to explain behaviour, society hopes to find an excuse for the unspeakable.

The defendants at Nuremberg were assessed by court-appointed psychiatrists. US Army Psychiatrist Dr Leon Goldensohn assessed Rudolf Hoess, Commandant of Auschwitz, and stated in a letter dated 20th May 1946: 'His character is that of an amoral psychopath, which in itself and correlated with his personal development history, indicates a dearth of parental love and unconscious hostility towards the father. Secondly, there is the influence of National Socialism, which enabled the sadistic psychopath to commit unprecedented inhumanities in a framework of apparent social and political respectability.' He added: 'In summary, this man has no moral or ethical standards: his reaction to the mass murders of which he is charged, is apathetic.' (Thomas Harding, Hanns and Rudolf *The German Jew and the Hunt for the Kommandant of Auschwitz*, pp. 256-256)

With serial killers, rapists, murderers, child-abusers and others it is often assumed that they must be mad, or mentally disturbed. Whilst it is certainly true that some offenders have mental health problems, it is also true that most who commit crime do not do so in response to mental illness. Other factors are present, including substance misuse, greed, control, desire, disrespect, disdain, selfishness, or thoughtlessness. Many offenders have mental health issues (as opposed to illness), and some have mental health needs (as opposed to a treatable condition). Many will come from difficult and traumatic backgrounds, with abuse and neglect as features of childhood. Many are poorly educated, and are socially dysfunctional. There is a range of factors that contribute to individuals becoming offenders, and many of those are linked to life-experiences, and dependence on drugs and alcohol.

The author has dealt with several thousand suspects, defendants, and offenders over a 20-year-period of work in the criminal justice system. The factors that led to many of those people becoming involved in crime are many, and varied, but there are common features linked to upbringing and development. With violent offenders, the profile remains largely consistent with only a few exceptions. Most will be male, and from the majority ethnic and cultural population of the area they live in. They will come from broken or unstable home environments. One or both parents may have had multiple partners. They will have witnessed domestic abuse in their formative years. They will have experienced some or all forms of child abuse (physical, emotional, sexual, and neglect). They will have had social services and police involvement with their family in childhood. They may have spent time in care, or been subject to child-protection protocols. They will have had an incomplete education, with marked disciplinary, behavioural, or conduct problems. They may have struggled to take or pass exams. They will not have attended further or higher education. They will have few vocational skills, with a limited, inconsistent and unstable employment history. They will be heterosexual (mainly), but will struggle to maintain relationships. They may have a number of children by different partners, but have little involvement in the lives of those children. Their sexual relationships will have been brief, and marred by infidelity and violence. They will have commenced drug and alcohol abuse at an early age with peers. They will have had an early onset of lower level criminality that gradually escalated through the youth justice system to the adult justice system.

When one looks at those involved in perpetrating the Holocaust one is struck by the relative normality of their development, and personal histories. Some, of course, had experienced the horrors of the First World War, but that alone does not explain how they became so cruel. Many others across Europe and the British Empire (and US forces) had experienced the same war, but did not go on to commit genocide. Of course, Germany lost the war, and many felt aggrieved by that defeat, and subsequent sanctions. But neither does that explain the Holocaust. Germany was crippled by the Great Depression, but many other countries were too. Europe in the years immediately following the war was a place of political upheaval, and major social change. In Russia, the communists had taken control and created the Soviet Union. Germany had undergone its own revolution, but the political opposites of left and right were still in conflict. It is probable many things combined to create the fuel for the fires of rage that engulfed Germany and were unleashed across the continent. What is clear, though, is that madness, in any classic or diagnosable sense, was not the reason for the slaughter that followed.

Each of the following individuals has been the subject of detailed and well-recorded studies. There will not be an attempt here to give a full biographical history of these people but a brief summary will help the reader to understand some of the main individuals involved in the perpetuation of hate, the hostility towards others, the greed of war, and the total disregard for human life that led to the Holocaust. It must be stressed that the Nazi leadership alone does not bear sole responsibility. They came to power on a popular vote due to policies that many in Germany supported. The anti-Semitism of the Nazis was not disguised or concealed, and indeed in Hitler's *Mein Kampf* he was extremely open in his disdain for, and hatred of Jews. The anti-Semitic policies of the Nazis were accepted because they concurred with the established thinking of many in Germany.

As the Germans invaded and controlled other countries these were policies that did not meet with popular mass-resistance. Indeed, many in Europe actively colluded and cooperated with the Germans and led local and national policies of isolation, control, oppression, cruelty, killing, and the transportation to concentration and death camps. The Germans estimated there were 11 million Jews in Europe. Conservative accepted estimates are that at least 6 million Jews were killed in the Holocaust. That could not have happened without the active and enthusiastic involvement of the majority populations in those countries the Germans invaded. The Nazi leadership, the Nazi party members, the various branches of the German military, the police, and the security services are of course important, but they could not have succeeded without the help of others. Nonetheless, some individuals are worth looking at in isolation. Hitler was of course the unquestioned leader of Nazi Germany but he alone did not create the hate and criminality that led that barbarous regime to aggression and wholesale slaughter of fellow human beings.

Heinrich Himmler

Heinrich Luitpold Himmler was born in Munich on 7 October 1900. He is known as the leader or Reichsführer of the Schutzstaffel (SS). His father was Gebhard; his mother was Anna Maria. He had two brothers. He was named after his godfather Prince Heinrich of Bavaria, who was a student of Himmler's father. Himmler was described as a good student at school with marked academic prowess. He was not good at physical activity due to poor health. At the outbreak of the First World War Himmler was too young for military service. In December 1917, his father used his royal connections to get Himmler enlisted as an officer cadet with the reserve battalion of the 11th Bavarian Regiment. By the time the war ended in November 1918 Himmler was still in training. After the war he completed his education, and then from 1919 until 1922 he studied agronomy at Munich Technische Hochschule. Like many Germans at the time, Himmler had always held anti-Semitic beliefs. He joined the anti-Semitic group Reichskriegsflagge which confirmed, reaffirmed, and reinforced his beliefs.

In August 1922 Himmler joined the newly formed Nazi Party. He was involved in the Beer Hall Putsch – Hitler's unsuccessful attempt to seize power in Munich. Himmler was not convicted of any crime. In 1924, Himmler joined the 'Schutzstaffel', or SS. He was appointed Deputy Reichsführer-SS in September 1927. In 1929, Himmler assumed the position of Reichsführer-SS. He organised SS participation in the Nuremberg Rallies. By 1933, the SS had 52,000 members and Himmler was already insisting on strict racial purity and proof that members were Aryan.

In March 1933, Himmler set up the first Nazi concentration camp at Dachau. He appointed Theodor Eicke to run the camp. Eicke was a convicted criminal, and ardent Nazi. He established the blueprint and model for how other camps should be run, including uniforms for prisoners, isolation, corporal punishment, work details, and summary executions to ensure obedience with the regime. The camps initially housed political opponents, but soon progressed to include criminals and vagrants. In 1937, a decree by Hitler allowed for the incarceration of all 'undesirables', including Jews, Gypsies, Communists, and those deemed to be 'impure', or 'subhuman'.

Himmler was involved in helping engineer the pretext for invading Poland. It was actually known as 'Aktion Himmler', (or 'Operation Himmler'). German soldiers – dressed as Poles – launched attacks and skirmishes against Germany. The result was part of the rationale for the invasion and the start of World War Two.

On 21st June 1941, just before the invasion of the Soviet Union, Himmler commissioned 'Generalplan Ost' ('General Plan East'). The report or plan was completed in July 1942. It suggested that 31 million people in Eastern Europe and the Baltic states should be moved further east to provide space for 10 million Germans. Himmler estimated that 20 to 30 million Slavs and Jews would die in the process through conflict, starvation, or disease. There is a cold- blooded and callous disregard for the sanctity of human life in this plan. Modern military parlance refers to 'collateral damage', but Himmler contemplated, expected and planned for human losses on a level beyond comprehension.

In spring 1941 Himmler ordered that ten concentration camps should be built. In January 1942 Reinhard Heydrich chaired the Berlin-Wannsee Conference about the Final Solution to the Jewish Question. At this meeting, the estimated number of Jews in Europe was given as about 11 million and discussions took place regarding how to exterminate them. Hitler placed Himmler in charge of that plan. In June 1942, Heydrich was assassinated by members of the Czech army in exile. Severe reprisals were ordered by Himmler, with many thousands being executed. The transportation and killing of Jews increased under what was known as 'Aktion Reinhard' or 'Operation Reinhard'.

Himmler was one of the main architects and engineers of the Holocaust. He held strong anti-Semitic beliefs and concurred with the Nazis' racist ideologies. He believed strongly in the version of eugenics much misrepresented by the Germans, and his agricultural background was a major factor in the idea of selective breeding, and the creation of the master race. Children in the lands invaded were effectively kidnapped, and forced into adoption by German families, if they were believed to have strong Aryan characteristics. SS officers were encouraged to breed, to further enhance the promotion of this racially pure vision of a greater Germany.

On 4th October 1943, at a meeting with SS officials, Himmler gave what has become known as 'The Posen Speech'. The power and vitriol of this speech is palpable, even when read rather than being heard:

'I want to also mention a very difficult subject ... before you, with complete candour. It should be discussed amongst us, yet nevertheless, we will never speak about it in public. Just as we did not hesitate on June

30th to carry out our duty as ordered, and stand comrades who had failed against the wall and shoot them -- about which we have never spoken, and never will speak. That was, thank God, a kind of tact natural to us, a foregone conclusion of that tact, that we have never conversed about it amongst ourselves, never spoken about it, everyone ... shuddered, and everyone was clear that the next time, he would do the same thing again, if it were commanded and necessary. I am talking about the evacuation of the Jews, the extermination of the Jewish people. It is one of those things that is easily said. "The Jewish people is being exterminated," every Party member will tell you, "perfectly clear, it's part of our plans, we're eliminating the Jews, exterminating them, a small matter". And then along they all come, all the 80 million upright Germans, and each one has his decent Jew. They say: all the others are swine, but here is a first-class Jew. And none of them has seen it, has endured it. Most of you will know what it means when 100 bodies lie together, when 500 are there or when there are 1000. And ... to have seen this through and -- with the exception of human weakness -- to have remained decent, has made us hard and is a page of glory never mentioned and never to be mentioned. Because we know how difficult things would be, if today in every city during the bomb attacks, the burdens of war and the privations, we still had Jews as secret saboteurs, agitators and instigators. We would probably be at the same stage as 16/17, if the Jews still resided in the body of the German people. We have taken away the riches that they had, and ... I have given a strict order, which Obergruppenführer Pohl has carried out, we have delivered these riches to the Reich, to the State. We have taken nothing from them for ourselves. A few, who have offended against this, will be judged in accordance with an order that I gave at the beginning: he who takes even one Mark of this is a dead man. A number of SS men have offended against this order. They are very few, and they will be dead men WITHOUT MERCY! We have the moral right, we had the duty to our people to do it, to kill this people who would kill us. We however do not have the right to enrich ourselves with even one fur, with one Mark, with one cigarette, with one watch, with anything.

That we do not have. Because we don't want, at the end of all this, to get sick and die from the same bacillus that we have exterminated. I will never see it happen that even one ... bit of putrefaction comes in contact with us, or takes root in us. On the contrary, where it might try to take root, we will burn it out together. But altogether we can say: We have carried out this most difficult task for the love of our people. And we have suffered no defect within us, in our soul, or in our character.' (Jewish Virtual Library, and other sources)

Himmler had a complex personal life. In July 1928, he married Margaret Boden, a nurse who shared his interest in homeopathy. They had one daughter, Gudrun, but were also foster parents to the son of an SS officer who had died before the war. Himmler and his wife tried to run a farm but his work and other commitments kept him travelling and ultimately living in the city. They saw each other less and less. He had an adulterous relationship with his mistress Hedwig Potthast from 1939. He and Hedwig had a son and daughter. His wife tolerated the relationship, and both she and Hedwig remained loyal to him.

Towards the end of the war, Himmler pledged his loyalty to Hitler, but then quietly fled Berlin. He was disowned by Hitler, and secretly tried to find ways to negotiate surrender when it was obvious to everyone that the war was lost. Whilst trying to escape, Himmler was apprehended at a road block manned by Soviet POWs on 21st May 1945. He was handed over to the British on 23rd May. When he was undergoing a routine medical examination he bit onto a cyanide capsule, and killed himself.

Joseph Goebbels

Paul Joseph Goebbels was born on 29th October 1897 in Rheydt near the Ruhr. His father, Fritz, was a bookkeeper. His mother, Maria Catharine (née Odenhausen) was a former servant. Joseph was the second of four children. His older brother was Hans; his younger sisters were Elisabeth and Maria.

Goebbels' childhood and adult life was marred by disability. He had a deformed right leg due either to a club foot or osteomyelitis. He wore a metal brace, and had a distinctive limp. Because of his disability he was rejected for military service in World War One. This was a source of anger and frustration to him, and at times he would claim an honourable military record.

He studied literature and philosophy at the universities of Bonn, Wurzburg, Freiburg and Heidelberg. He successfully completed his Doctorate in 1921, following which he worked as a journalist, and attempted to become a published author.

He was somewhat of a philanderer, and had many successes with women. In 1931, he married Magda Quandt. They had six children and stayed together for the remainder of their lives. In the early 1920s, Goebbels encountered the Nazis, and then he joined the party in 1924. In 1926, Hitler made him 'Gauleiter' (or party leader for the local Nazi branch) for Berlin – in effect giving him control of that city. In Berlin, Goebbels worked closely with the 'Sturmabteilung' (storm troopers - SA). He would encourage their involvement in street violence, brawls, and battles in the city. Goebbels became editor of a Nazi newspaper for Berlin called *Der Angriff* (*The Attack*). He also wrote posters and leaflets for distribution around the city.

He assisted with the Nazis' unsuccessful election campaigns, mastering the art of propaganda in the process, including the use of air travel to increase the number of places Hitler could speak at and maximise his appearance of importance. In 1933, the Nazis came to power, and Goebbels was rewarded by being made 'Reich Minister for Enlightenment and Propaganda'. One of his first and most infamous actions in this new role was to organise the burning of thousands of books by Jewish and anti-Nazi authors.

He helped to develop the increased control of the arts and media by the Nazis.

Goebbels shared Hitler's anti-Semitism, and his belief in Jewish responsibility for Germany's ills and the defeat in the First World War. His abilities in the 'art' of propaganda undoubtedly helped to promote the anti- Semitism of the Third Reich. Many view him today as one of the most effective propagandists of the twentieth century. He used the means that were available at the time. Cinema was already immensely popular, and via that medium Goebbels was able to promote the Nazis anti-Semitism. He is renowned for the film *Der Ewige Jude* (*The Eternal Jew*) in which images of Jews were mixed with images of rats. He preferred a more subtle approach, and commissioned *Jud Süß* (*Suss the Jew*) a 1940 film in which an Aryan girl was raped by a Jew. He was one of the first to use audience research to ascertain which approach was most effective. He acted to reinforce the opinions already present in German society. He was aware that changing opinion and attitudes required repetition of the message and moving in the manner of a convoy, always at the speed of the slowest vessel. He avoiding dictating opinion, rather he would provide information in a format that he knew would lead people to believe that they had reached their own conclusions. Goebbels was undoubtedly one of the main promotors of anti-Semitism and the crimes associated with the Nazi regime. He helped promote early violence against Jews, and through his vast propoganda machine he reinforced the already existing but escalating hatred of Germans towards the Jews.

As the Nazi defeat became more certain, Goebbels took what he believed to be his only option. On 1st May 1945 he arranged for a Nazi dentist named Helmut Kunz to kill his six children by giving them morphine, and then putting crushed cyanide capsules in their mouths. In testimony after the war Kunz claimed not to have given the cyanide, but insisted Magda Goebbels' and Hitler's doctor administered the final dose. Soon afterwards Goebbels and Magda committed suicide, but the details have been debated, with varying accounts. The bodies were unsuccessfully burnt, but not to the extent that they were unrecognisable. Many years later during the Soviet occupation of Berlin the bodies were exhumed, burned, crushed, and the ashes scattered in a river.

***

Reinhard Heydrich

Reinhard Heydrich was born on 7th March 1904 in Halle Ander Saale. He was one of three children. His father Richard Heydrich was a composer and opera singer. His mother was Elisabeth (née Krantz). His father was a German nationalist, and founder of the Hallé Conservatory of Music.

After the First World War there was a revolution in Germany leading to the overthrow of the monarchy, and a period of civil unrest. Many of those who had served in the war – Heydrich was too young to have served – joined various 'Freikorps' in which they could put their military experience and comradeship to what they saw as 'good use'. Heydrich joined one of the Freikorps in 1919 when aged only 15 years. In 1922 he joined the 'Reichmarine' (navy). By 1924, he was promoted to midshipman and was sent for officer training. By 1926 he had achieved the rank of ensign, and was assigned as a signals officer on the battleship Schleswig-Holstein. By 1928 he had been promoted to sub- lieutenant.

In 1931, Heydrich married Lina von Osten, with whom he would have four children. He also joined the SS Intelligence Service after being personally interviewed by Himmler. He was promoted to the rank of SS-Sturmbannführer (Major). He began to suffer from gossip and rumours at this time about his perceived Jewish heritage although this was never proven. In 1932 Himmler promoted Heydrich to the head of the 'Sicherheistdienst' (Security Service - SD), and by 1934 he became head of the Gestapo. In 1936 all German police forces were amalgamated, with Himmler as the head and Heydrich as his deputy. In this position of power and influence he was given the task of helping to organise the 1936 Berlin Olympic Games.

Heydrich was one of the organisers of Kristallnacht on 9th November 1938 when Jewish properties, businesses and synagogues were attacked. Jews who could do so were encouraged to leave Germany at that time. Those who remained there found that their civil rights and liberties had all disappeared. They were unable to trade or conduct business with non-Jews. Their travel was restricted. They faced increased hostility and violence. Many found themselves being moved to ghettos and camps for their own protection. In 1940 Heydrich helped to enforce the 'Night and Fog' decree in which those accused of endangering German society were arrested under cover of night time, or fog. In September 1941 Heydrich was appointed Deputy Reich Protector of Bohemia and Moravia.

On 20th January 1942 Heydrich chaired the infamous Berlin-Wannsee Conference at which the 'Final Solution to the Jewish Question' was planned. This will be referred to in more detail elsewhere. On 27th May 1942 Heydrich was seriously injured in an assassination attempt by members of the Czech army in exile. He died as a result of his injuries on 4th June 1942.

***

Adolf Eichmann

Otto Adolf Eichmann was born on 19th March 1906, in Solingen, Germany. He was the eldest of five children from the marriage of Adolf Karl Eichmann - a bookkeeper by trade - and

Maria (née Schefferling), a housewife. His father moved to Linz in Austria in 1913 and the rest of the family followed in 1914. His mother died in 1916 and his father remarried. Young Adolf was not successful at school. On leaving education he went to work with his father at a mining company. From 1925 until 1927 he was employed as a clerk at a radio company. From 1927 until 1933 he worked at an oil company.

Eichmann joined the Nazi Party in April 1932. Seven months later he joined the SS. He returned to Germany after the Nazis were banned in Austria. In 1934 he joined the SD or Security Service and was appointed to Jewish Department at the headquarters in Berlin. He was assigned to read and prepare reports on Zionist and other Jewish movements. In 1935 Eichmann married Veronika (Vera) Liebl. They had four sons.

In 1937 Eichmann was sent to British mandated Palestine to assess the possibility of German Jews being moved there. That plan never came to fruition but it was an early option considered by the Nazis to remove Jews from Germany. In 1938 he was posted to Vienna to help organise Jewish emigration from Austria.

In July 1938, Eichmann was promoted to SS-Obersturmführer (Second Lieutenant) and was appointed to the Central Agency for Jewish Emigration in Vienna. On 1st September 1939 Germany invaded Poland. In October 1939 Eichmann was transferred to Berlin to command the Central Office for Jewish Emigration for the entire Reich.

On 20th January 1942 the now infamous Berlin-Wannsee Conference was convened. It was Eichmann who compiled the list of Jewish populations for all the countries of Europe. He took the minutes for the conference. Following the conference, and under Eichmann's supervision, the deportations of Jews to extermination camps commenced. The specific orders for the deportations of Jews – for slave labour and extermination – came from Himmler. Eichmann's department was responsible for collecting information on Jewish populations in each area, for seizing property, and for arranging and scheduling transportations. Rudolf Hoess, commandant of Auschwitz, took his orders directly from Eichmann even though Himmler had ultimate operational oversight and power.

On 19th March 1944 the Nazis invaded Hungary. Eichmann arrived in Hungary on the same day. The rounding up of Jews began on 16th April. The first transportations started on 14th May with four trains a day, each containing 3,000 Jews, leaving for Auschwitz. Between seventy five percent and ninety percent of Hungarian Jews were selected for immediate death on arrival at Auschwitz. By 6th July 1944 it is estimated that over 437,000 Hungarian Jews had been killed in just 56 days – a killing rate of nearly eight thousand men, women, children, and babies per day.

By December 1944 Soviet forces were close to encircling Budapest. On New Year's Eve, Eichmann fled Hungary. He was subsequently captured by US forces when living under a false name. He escaped US custody when he realised his true identity had become known. In 1950 he arrived in Buenos Aires, Argentina. In 1956 he gave a series of interviews to a former Nazi journalist. This helped bring his existence to the knowledge of Israelis who were seeking a number of missing senior Nazis. Most notable of these Israeli Nazi-hunters was Simon Wiesenthal, who instructed private detectives to locate him. On 11th May 1960 Eichmann was captured by Mossad and Shin Bet agents, under the direct order of Israel's Prime Minister David Ben-Gurion. He was drugged and moved around safe houses in Argentina before being transported to Israel.

Eichmann's trial began on 11th April 1961. The judges adjourned to consider their verdict on 12th December, and delivered their guilty verdict – with a sentence of death – on

15th December. Eichmann appealed, and many pleaded for clemency. He was hanged on 31st May 1962. His final words before death were, 'Long live Germany. Long live Argentina. Long live Austria. These are the three countries with which I have been most connected, and which I will not forget. I greet my wife, my family, and my friends. I am ready. We'll meet again soon, as is the fate of all men. I die believing in God.' Eichmann's body was cremated and the ashes were scattered in the Mediterranean Sea.

Reflecting about Eichmann in his 1988 book *Justice Not Vengeance*, Simon Wiesenthal wrote, 'The world now understands the concept of "desk murderer". We know that one doesn't need to be fanatical, sadistic, or mentally ill to murder millions; that it is enough to be a loyal follower, eager to do one's duty.'

Rudolf Hoess

Rudolf Hoess will be referred to in more detail elsewhere as he was the most significant commandant of Auschwitz, who was tasked with developing Birkenau and enforcing the orders of Himmler regarding the Final Solution. He was responsible for most of the brutality of the regime that existed there. He was reasonably cooperative at the Nuremberg Trial, and his testimony gave the fullest insight into what happened at Auschwitz - the chain of command, the orders that arose from the Final Solution, and the utter brutality of the place. Hoess also wrote a detailed autobiography whilst confined in custody, and awaiting execution.

Rudolf Franz Ferdinand Hoess was born on 25th November 1901 in Baden- Baden. He was the only son and eldest of three children born to Franz and Lina Hoess. He had a strict upbringing, with his father instilling military- type discipline on family life, and establishing in Rudolf an almost fanatical devotion to duty. He describes himself as a lonely child who preferred the company of adults. He claimed – though how true this is cannot be proven – that as a teenager he was abducted by Gypsies. His family expected him to enter the priesthood as they were devout Catholics. However, when in his early teens Rudolf confessed to a priest about a schoolboy misdemeanour. His father found out about this, and Rudolf believed the priest had betrayed the sanctity of the confessional. He soon rejected Catholicism.

At the age of 14, Rudolf joined the 21st Regiment of Dragoons. By the age of 15, he was involved in combat, and saw action in Turkey, Baghdad and Palestine. At the age of 17 he was made Sergeant, and became the youngest non- commissioned officer. Hoess was wounded three times during the war. He described in his autobiography how he had his first sexual experience with a nurse when he was recovering from injury. He was awarded the Gallipoli Star, and the Iron Cross First and Second Class.

After the war, Hoess completed his education. Like many ex-military men he took up arms in the chaos of post- revolutionary Germany. He joined the East Prussian Volunteer Corps, and then one of the many Freikorps. In 1922, after hearing Hitler speak, he joined the Nazi party. In 1923, at the request of Martin Bormann, Hoess was involved in beating to death Walther Kadow, a schoolteacher whom Hoess and others believed to be a traitor. In May 1924, Hoess was sentenced to 10 years' imprisonment. He wrote about his prison experience at length, and implied later on that it equipped him to understand the inmates of camps he ran better. In 1928 – as part of a general amnesty – Hoess was released from prison. He joined the Artaman League, which was a nationalist movement dedicated to promoting the values and lifestyle of rural Germany. Whilst with the Artaman League he met and married Hedwig Hensel with whom he would have two sons and three daughters.

In 1934, Hoess joined the SS. In 1939, he met Himmler whom he admired greatly. In 1939, Hoess was assigned to Dachau concentration camp. Here, under the guidance of Theodor Eicke, he learned the methods and techniques of inmate control, cruelty, uniforms, labour, deprivation, violence, corporal punishment and summary execution. He would develop these techniques further at Auschwitz. As well as Dachau he was also based at Sachsenhausen camp.

On 1st May 1940, Hoess was made Commandant of Auschwitz, a position he held initially for three and a half years. He was tasked with expanding the capacity of Auschwitz and developed it to include Auschwitz I, Auschwitz II (Birkenau) and Auschwitz III (Monowitz). Initially, Auschwitz was similar to other concentration camps, and housed a mixture of prisoners including Germans, Poles, and Russians. In June 1941, Hoess was summoned to Berlin to a meeting with Himmler. He was advised by Himmler of Hitler's plan for the extermination of all European Jews, and that Auschwitz, because of its size, location, and isolation, had been chosen for this purpose. He was advised that all of his operational orders would come directly from Eichmann. The orders were to be treated with the highest level of secrecy, but Hoess did tell his wife in 1942. It is apparent from his affidavit to the Nuremberg Trial and from his autobiography that Hoess did not question these orders.

As part of his new role at Auschwitz, Hoess visited the death camp at Treblinka to study the killing methods there, which he found to be inefficient. Various methods were tried at Auschwitz-Birkenau, but many of these proved distasteful and crude to Hoess. Primo Levi, in the introduction to Hoess' autobiography is scathing: 'Experiments had been conducted at other camps, but mass machine-gunnings and toxic injections were inconvenient; they needed something faster and more reliable. Above all the Germans had to avoid 'bloodbaths', because they had a demoralising effect on the executioners. After the bloodiest actions, several SS-men killed themselves; others got methodically drunk. What they needed was something aseptic, something impersonal, to safeguard the mental health of the soldiers. Collective gassing set off by motors was a step in the right direction, but it had to be perfected.'

In 1941, his deputy Karl Fritzsch tested Zyklon B on some Russian prisoners. Hoess had found his favoured method of mass-killing, and the slaughter increased in volume and speed. As Primo Levi described it, 'Hoess and his assistant got the brilliant idea of resorting to Zyklon B, a poison used on rats and cockroaches, and it was all for the best. After testing it on nine hundred Russian prisoners, Hoess felt 'greatly at ease': the mass-killing had gone well, both quantitatively and qualitatively – no blood, and no trauma. It's one thing machine-gunning a bunch of naked people on the edge of a pit that they themselves have dug, but inserting a container of poison through an air conduit is fundamentally different. Rudolf Hoess' highest aspiration was reached, his professionalism had been demonstrated, and he was the finest technician of mass slaughter. His envious colleagues were clobbered.' (*Commandant of Auschwitz*, Primo Levi introduction, p.24)

Hoess felt comfortable that sufficient numbers could be killed in the gas chambers at Birkenau. The only problem encountered was the rate of disposal of corpses. In November 1943 Hoess was replaced as Commandant, and his roles then included inspecting concentration camps. On 8th May 1944, Hoess returned to Auschwitz as commandant to oversee Aktion Hoess. In this operation, approximately 437,000 Hungarian Jews were killed in a 56 day period between May and July 1944. The numbers killed proved difficult to manage, and thousands were burned in open pits. Some were burned alive.

Hoess fled from Auschwitz on 18th January 1945. He was captured by British forces in March 1946. He was given away by his wife, who feared that one of her sons would be sent into Soviet captivity. Hoess was beaten by his captors as many of them knew what he had been responsible for.

On 15th April 1946, Hoess gave evidence at the Nuremberg Trial. On 25th May 1946, he was handed over to the Polish authorities. His trial on Poland was from 11th to 29th March 1947. He was accused of being responsible for killing three and a half million people, to which he stated, "No, only two and one half million – the rest died from disease and starvation." On 2nd April 1947, he was sentenced to death. He was hanged at Auschwitz I on 16thApril 1947. The gallows were built right next to the gas chamber in that part of the Auschwitz complex. Four days before his execution Hoess sent a message to the State Prosecutor of Poland. The message included: 'My conscience compels me to make the following declaration. In the solitude of my prison cell I have come to the better recognition that I have sinned greatly against humanity. As Commandant of Auschwitz I was responsible for carrying out part of the cruel plans of the Third Reich for human destruction. In so doing, I have inflicted terrible wounds on humanity. I caused unspeakable suffering, to the Polish people in particular. I am to pay for this with my life. May the Lord God forgive one day what I have done.' Was this remorse, regret, or contrition? He is said to have reaffirmed his Catholicism before death. Perhaps these words acknowledging his wrongdoing were part of that process, and a need to accept sin in order to seek forgiveness and absolution. We may never know. He was survived by his wife Hedwig and their children Annegret, Klaus, Hans-Jurgen, Ingebrigitt and Heidetraut.

Hans Frank

Hans Frank was born on 23rd May 1900 in Karlsruhe to Karl and Magdalena. He had an older brother Karl Junior, and a younger sister Elizabeth. He joined the German Army in 1917, and like many former soldiers after the war he enlisted with the Freikorps. In 1919 he joined the German Workers party. In 1925 he married Brigette Herbst, a secretary. They had four sons and one daughter. Their youngest son Niklas (born in 1939) is still alive. He has written about his father and travels widely giving talks about the Holocaust and endeavouring to ensure lessons continue to be learned about the past.

Hans Frank studied law, and passed his exams in 1926. He went on to become Hitler's personal legal advisor and the lawyer for the Nazi Party. He represented many Nazis in high profile trials before the Nazis came to power. In 1930 Frank was elected to the Reichstag. In 1933 he was appointed Minister of Justice for Bavaria. From 1934 he was Minister Without Portfolio.

In September 1939 Frank was assigned Chief of Administration to Gerd von Runstedt in the German Military Administration in occupied Poland. From 26th October 1939, he was assigned Governor General of the occupied Polish territories, tasked to oversee and control those areas of Poland that had not been directly incorporated into Germany. He was given the SS rank of 'Obergruppenführer'. In this capacity, he oversaw the segregation of Jews into ghettos, the most notable and infamous of which was the Warsaw ghetto. It was Frank who also oversaw and authorised the eradication of the Warsaw ghetto in what was one of the bloodiest and brutal sieges of the Polish occupation. As a result of the brutality in that siege Frank became known as 'The Butcher of Warsaw'.

Frank kept detailed diaries which became key pieces of evidence at the Nuremberg Trial. A speech made on 16th December 1941 was to help provide compelling evidence against him. In that speech he stated: "A great Jewish migration will begin in any case. But what should we do with the Jews? Do you think they will be settled in Ostland, in villages? We were told in Berlin, 'Why all this bother? We can do nothing with them either in Ostland or in the Reichkommissariat (English: Realm Commissariat). So liquidate them yourselves.' Gentlemen, I must ask you to rid yourselves of feelings of pity. We must annihilate the Jews wherever we find them and whenever it is possible." (Speech to senior officials as reported in the Office of the Chief Counsel for the Prosecution of Axis Criminality).

Frank was captured by US forces on 3rd May 1945. He attempted to cut his own throat and tried again to take his own life by lacerating his arm. He was one of the defendants at the Nuremberg Trial between 20th November 1945, and 1st October 1946. Evidence at the trial included a film prepared by US forces of conditions at the various concentration camps the allies had liberated. Frank was seen to visibly react on seeing this film. (As cited in *Nuremberg Evil on Trial* pp. 50-51)

Frank was certainly involved in much of the brutal suppression of Jews in Poland, including the crushing of the uprising at the Warsaw ghetto. He claimed at Nuremberg not to have fully known about the exterminations happening in the camps, although he did know about deportations. He was asked if Hitler supported his work as Governor General. Frank gave a lengthy reply:

'All my complaints, everything I reported to him, were unfortunately dropped into the wastepaper basket by him. I did not send in my resignation fourteen times for nothing. It was not for nothing that I tried to join my brave troops as an officer. In his heart (Hitler's) he was always opposed to lawyers, and that was one of the most serious shortcomings of this outstandingly great man. He did not want to admit formal responsibility, and that, unfortunately, applied to his policy too, as I have found out now. Every lawyer to him was a disturbing element working against his power. All I can say, therefore, is that by supporting Himmler's and Bormann's aims to the utmost, he permanently jeopardised any attempt to find a form of government worthy of the German name. In answer to my repeated questions as to what happened to the Jews who were deported, I was always told they were to be sent to the east, to be assembled, and put to work there. But the stench seemed to penetrate the walls, and therefore I persisted in my investigations as to what was going on. Once a report came to me that there was something going on near Belzec. I went to Belzec the next day. Globocznik showed me an enormous ditch which he was having made as a protective wall and which many thousands of workers, apparently Jews, were engaged. I spoke to some of them, asked them where they came from, how long they had been there, and he told me, that is Globocznik, "They are working here now, and when they are through – they come from the Reich, or some from France – they will be sent further east." I did not make any further enquiries in that same area. The rumour, however, that the Jews were being killed in the manner which is now known to the entire world would not be silenced. When I expressed the wish to visit the SS workshop near Lublin, in order to get some idea of the value of the work that was being done, I was told that special permission from Heinrich Himmler was required. I asked Heinrich Himmler for this special permission. He said that he would urge me not to go to the camp. Again some time passed. On 7th February 1944 I succeeded in being received by Adolf Hitler personally – I might add that throughout the war he received me three times only. In the presence of Bormann I put the question to him. "My Fuhrer, rumours about the extermination of the Jews will not be silenced. They are heard everywhere. No one is allowed in anywhere. Once I paid a surprise visit to Auschwitz in order to see the camp, but I was told there was an epidemic in the camp and my car was diverted before I got there. Tell me, my Fuhrer, is there anything in it?" The Fuhrer said, "You can very well imagine that there are executions going on – of insurgents. Apart from that I do not know anything. Why don't you speak to Heinrich Himmler about it?" And I said, "Well, Himmler made a speech to us in Krakow and declared in front of all the people whom I had officially called to the meeting that these rumours about the systematic extermination of the Jews were false; the Jews were merely being brought to the East". Thereupon the Fuhrer said, "Then you must believe that". (As cited in Nuremberg Evil on Trial pp 215-216)

Frank was convicted at Nuremberg: 'As Governor of Occupied Poland Frank administered a policy intended to destroy that country as a nation. There was widespread killing of those likely to resist German domination. The economic demands made were out of all proportion to the country's resources. Millions of native Jews were exterminated. It may be true that Frank was not the originator of the crimes committed by his government, but he was a knowing participant in the terror it practised.' He was sentenced to death by hanging. When he approached the gallows he was asked if he had any last statement he wished to make. He said, 'I am thankful for the kind treatment during my captivity, and I ask God to accept me with mercy.' He was hanged on 16 October 1946. His son Niklas Frank is a campaigner against the Far Right in Germany, and is a prolific speaker to students and others, helping to ensure lessons are learned from the past.

***

Dr Josef Mengele

Dr Josef Mengele is one of the most notorious and reviled people associated with Auschwitz, and the depravity that occurred there. Not only was he an SS officer, he was also a physician involved in acts of bestial cruelty that ran contrary to all standards and principles of the medical profession. He has been remembered since as 'the Angel of Death'.

Mengele was born on 16th March 1911 in Gunzberg, Bavaria, the eldest of three children to Karl and Walburga. His father ran a company producing farm machinery. As a child he did well academically at school, and in 1930 he attended the University of Munich to study medicine and philosophy. In 1931 he joined Stahlhelm, Bund der Frontsoldaten, a paramilitary organisation that eventually became amalgamated with the Sturmabteilung (SA) in 1934. In 1935 Mengele obtained a PhD in anthropology. In January 1937 he obtained work at the Institute for Hereditary Biology and Racial Hygiene in Frankfurt. Here he was employed as assistant to Dr Otmar Freiherr von Verschuer, who specialised in conducting genetic research. Mengele himself focused on researching genetic factors resulting in cleft lip, cleft palate and cleft chin. His thesis on this subject earned him a 'cum laude' Doctorate in Medicine in 1938.

In July 1939 Mengele married Irene Schonbein. They had one son who was born in 1944. Mengele joined the Nazi Party in 1937, and joined the Schutzstaffel (SS) in 1938. He did his basic military training with the mountain infantry, and was called up for active service in June 1940. He volunteered for the medical service with the Waffen-SS and was appointed to the rank of SS- Untersturmführer (Second Lieutenant) in the medical reserve battalion until November 1940. He was subsequently assigned to the SS-Rasse-und- Seidlungshauptampt (SS Race and Resettlement Office) in Posen, where he evaluated candidates regarding their Germanisation.

In June 1941, Mengele was posted to Ukraine. He was awarded the Iron Cross (Second Class). In January 1942 he joined a panzer division as a battalion medical officer. In honour of his service he was awarded an Iron Cross (First Class). He was seriously injured during action in the summer of 1942. He was transferred to the Race and Resettlement Office in Berlin. He worked again with von Verschuer at the Kaiser Wilhelm Institute for Anthropology, Human Genetics and Eugenics. In April 1943 he was promoted to SS-Haupsturmfuhrer (Captain).

Early in 1943 Mengele applied to be transferred to the concentration camp services as he saw this as an opportunity to further his genetic research. He was posted to Auschwitz. His appointment was made by SS-Standortarzt Eduard Wirths, Chief Medical Officer at the camp. Mengele was given the position of Chief Physician to the 'Zigeunerfamilienlager', or Gipsy Camp at Birkenau.

Since 1941 the Nazis had an expressed policy of Jewish extermination. That policy was made more clear and had increased in practice after the Berlin- Wannsee Conference of January 1942. By July 1942 the SS at Birkenau were already conducting assessments and selections in which those fit for work and labour would be separated from those destined to be gassed. Mengele became involved in these selections in part so that he could obtain subjects for his experiments. He had a particular interest in twins due to his fascination with heredity and genetics.

Although medically trained it is apparent that Mengele and other SS Doctors did not treat inmates at Auschwitz. They would supervise Doctors within the inmate population who were tasked with trying to provide medical care. Mengele would make weekly visits to the hospital barracks and sent to the gas chambers any inmates who had not recovered after two weeks in bed. Mengele was also known to have been involved in administering the Zyklon B crystals into the gas chambers.

In 1943 there was an outbreak of 'Noma' (a form of facial gangrene) in the Gypsy camp. He had the patients isolated in separate barracks. Selected children were killed under Mengele's orders so that their preserved heads and organs could be sent to the SS Medical Academy in Graz for research and study. During a typhus epidemic in the women's camp Mengele ordered that 600 women should be sent to the gas chambers – this will be referred to in more detail in the account of Kitty Hart-Moxon's experience of Auschwitz. The building was cleaned and disinfected. The occupants of a neighbouring block were bathed, deloused and given new clothes before being moved into the newly-cleaned block. The process was repeated until all of the blocks had been disinfected. Mengele used a similar process during an epidemic of scarlet fever. As a result of this and other actions he was promoted to the position of First Physician at Birkenau.

Mengele is most notorious for his medical experiments. He had a particular interest in identical twins, dwarfs, those with deformities, or those with different eye colours (Heterochromia Iridium). He was given a grant by Deutsche Forschungsgemeinschaft with which he built a pathology laboratory attached to Crematoria II at Birkenau. Mengele would send regular specimens and reports to his old mentor and colleague von Verschuer. He was keen to research issues that confirmed 'Eugenic' theories, racial supremacy and heredity. For this purpose he found twins to be most useful. The subjects selected for experimentation were treated better than other inmates in Auschwitz. He developed a kindergarten for his child subjects, and for Gypsy children under the age of 6 years. He used to introduce himself to the children as Uncle Mengele. His kindness did not extend much beyond what was deemed to be immediately necessary. He was personally responsible for causing numerous deaths through his experiments, lethal injections, shootings and beatings.

The twin experiments included introducing infections (often into already weak and scared children), blood transfusions, and amputations. Many twins died during these experiments, and the surviving twin would then be killed for a comparative autopsy. He is also reported to have injected chemicals into eyes, glue into fallopian tubes, opened unnecessary wounds to study the progress of infection and numerous other cruel experiments. He is even reported to have stitched two twins together to form a conjoined twin. Those twins died from infection.

On 17th January 1945, as Soviet forces neared, Mengele left Auschwitz with two boxes of specimens. Most of the records at Auschwitz had been destroyed by the SS in anticipation of the inevitable arrival of the Soviets. In June 1945 he was captured by US forces, but was soon released by mistake (possible because he did not have an SS blood group tattoo on his arm). He remained in hiding until fleeing Germany in April 1949, and sailing for Argentina in July of that year. His wife refused to travel with him, and they eventually divorced in 1954. He married his sister-in-law Martha in Uruguay in 1958. They bought a property in Buenos Aires. Mengele died in Brazil on 7th February 1979 after suffering a stroke. The Israelis had spent many years hunting him as one of the most significant Nazis involved with the Holocaust, but he managed to live his life out in freedom and relative comfort.

***

Hermann Göring

Hermann Göring was born on 12th January 1893 in Rosenheim, Bavaria. His father Heinrich Ernst Göring was a former cavalry officer and had been the first Governor General of the German protectorate of South West Africa (modern Namibia). At the time of Göring's birth his father was serving as Consul General in Haiti. Göring had five older half siblings from his father's first marriage, and was the fourth of five children from his father's second marriage to Franziska Tiefenbrunn, a Bavarian peasant. His godfather was Dr Hermann Epenstein, a wealthy and affluent physician and business man. He provided the Göring family with a home in the form of a small castle at Venldenstein, near Nuremberg. It may be pure coincidence that for some fifteen years Göring's mother was Epenstein's mistress.

Goring was sent to boarding school at the age of 11, but found the regime to be too harsh. He sold a violin to purchase a train ticket home. Once he was at home he feigned illness until he was told he did not have to return to the school. He was known as a child, to enjoy physical activity, and he became an accomplished mountain-climber.

At the age of 16 he was sent to the Military Academy at Berlin Lichterfelde, from which he graduated with distinction. His IQ was tested during his later detention at the Nuremberg Trial, and was found to be 138 – very much above average. In 1912 Göring joined the Prince Wilhelm Regiment (112th Infantry) of the Prussian Army. The next year his mother's affair with Epenstein ended, and the family moved to Munich. Soon afterwards his father died.

Göring was married twice. In February 1922 he married Karin von Kantzow. She struggled with ill-health, including epilepsy and tuberculosis. She died in October 1931. In April 1935 Göring married Emmy Sonnemann with whom he had a daughter born in 1938.

Göring saw active service in World War I. In 1914 he was an infantry lieutenant. He transferred to the air force as a combat pilot. In 1918 he was the last Commander of the Richthofen Fighter Squadron. He had a distinguished war record, and was credited with shooting down twenty-two allied aircraft. He was awarded the Pour le Mérite and the Iron Cross (First Class). Following the war he worked for a while as a show flier and pilot in Denmark and Sweden.

He was drawn to the Nazi Party, and shared Hitler's belief in the causes for Germany's defeat in the First World War. He was an attractive asset for the Nazis due to his background and war record. In 1922 Hitler appointed him as head of the SA Brownshirts. In 1923 Göring took part in Hitler's failed Munich Beer-Hall putsch (attempted coup). He was badly wounded and fled Germany for four years. He escaped to live in Austria, Italy and Sweden. His mental health deteriorated, and he was admitted to a psychiatric hospital and also to an asylum for dangerous lunatics. During his time in psychiatric treatment he became addicted to morphine.

Göring returned to Germany in 1927 and rejoined the NSDAP. A year later he was appointed to the position of Deputy to the Reichstag. Over the next five years Göring used his contacts in business, the military, and the upper echelons of German society to help smooth Hitler's rise to power.

In 1933 following Hitler's election Göring was made Prussian Minister of the Interior, Commander-in-Chief of the police and Gestapo, and Commissioner for Aviation. As one of the creators of the Secret Police (with Himmler and Heydrich) he helped to set up the early concentration camps for the detention of political opponents.

Under the apparent pretext of a threatened communist coup Prussia was 'cleansed', and thousands of officers and men were purged. They were replaced by men from the SA and SS who took over policing Berlin. Around about this time there was a major fire at the Reichstag. It is commonly believed that Göring personally organised this. He used the fire to implement an emergency decree which effectively destroyed most civil rights and resulted in the imprisonment of Communists and Social Democrats, and the banning of the Left Wing press.

On 1st March 1935 Göring was appointed to the position of Commander-in- Chief of the Air Force. He was responsible for the rapid build-up of aircraft numbers, and the training of pilots.

In 1936 he was given responsibility for implementing the 'Four Year Plan' to control and direct the rebuilding of the German economy. In this position in 1937 he also created the state owned Herman Göring Works (a vast industry with 700,000 employees) which earned him a huge fortune. From this wealth he purchased a palace in Berlin, and a built a hunting mansion. With his wealth and positions of power Göring's vanity became legendary. He would change clothes and uniforms several times a day, and often dressed in the style of a bygone era. He was also notoriously corrupt, and known for involvement in bribery.

Göring identified closely with Hitler's territorial aspirations. He played a key role in the Anschluss in 1938 and the invasion of Czechoslovakia. In August 1939 he was appointed as Reich Council Chairman for National Defence, and on 1st September he was designated as Hitler's successor. In 1940, after directing the Luftwaffe campaigns against Poland and France, Göring was promoted to Reich Marshall.

Göring was soon to fall out of favour with Hitler. In August 1940 he launched the aerial campaign against Great Britain. Göring anticipated a rapid victory against the RAF that would pave the way for the land invasion of England. When that victory was within sight he decided to redirect attacks against British citics rather than military targets. This gave the RAF time to repair damaged airfields and to replenish its supply of aircraft. The Battle of Britain was lost, and Göring was not forgiven by Hitler. The Luftwaffe under his command suffered further failures over Russia and in defending Germany from allied attacks. By 1945 he became increasingly despised by Hitler who blamed him for Germany's losses. As the end of the war – and Germany's defeat – neared, Hitler declared that he would remain in his bunker in Berlin until the end. Göring, who was in Bavaria at the time, misinterpreted this as an indication that Hitler was abdicating, and requested to take charge of the Third Reich. Hitler reacted to this with fury. Göring was dismissed from all the posts he held, was expelled from the Nazi Party, and was arrested.

On 9th May 1945 Göring was captured by allied forces. Much to his surprise he was put on trial at Nuremberg. He was notable amongst all of the defendants at Nuremberg for his defiance of the court process and willingness to challenge the prosecution robustly. The court found him guilty on two of the four counts he was facing - specifically that, 'As the Plenipotentiary for the Four Year Plan, Göring issued directives forcing prisoners-of-war to work in the armament industry, and directed the despoliation of conquered territory. He persecuted the Jews, principally to confiscate their property and to curtail their economic activities. His own admissions are enough to condemn him.' He was sentenced to death by hanging, but on 15th October 1946, just two hours before his planned execution, he committed suicide in his cell after biting onto a concealed cyanide capsule.

***

Rudolf Hess

Rudolf Hess was born on 26th April 1894 in Alexandria, Egypt to an ethnically German couple. His father, Fritz Hess, was a successful Bavarian merchant. His mother was Clara Hess (née Munch). Hess had a younger brother and sister. Hess studied at a German language school in Alexandria from 1900 to 1908. He was then sent to a boarding school at Bad Godesberg in Germany. His father was keen on Rudolf joining the family business and so in 1911 he was sent to École Supérieure De Commerce in Switzerland. In 1912 he was sent on an apprenticeship at a trading company in Hamburg.

When the First World War started Hess enlisted after a few weeks of the commencement of hostilities. He joined the 7th

Bavarian Field Artillery Regiment as an infantryman. He saw action at the Somme and the first battle of Ypres. At the start of November 1914 he was transferred to the 1st Infantry Regiment stationed near Arras. He was awarded the Iron Cross, Second Class. He was promoted to the rank of Corporal in April 1915. He was subsequently made a Senior Non-Commissioned Officer and received the Bavarian Military Merit Cross. He was injured in battle, and promoted to Platoon Leader while serving in Romania. He was injured twice by shrapnel in 1917. In October 1918 he commenced flying training but did not complete it, or fly combat missions as the war had ended. He was discharged from the military in December 1918. On leaving military service he joined the Thule Society – an anti-Semitic group. He also joined the Freikorps as did many other ex-service personnel, and was involved some of the civil unrest of 1919.

In autumn 1919 Hess enrolled at the University of Munich to study History and Economics. His Geopolitics professor was Karl Haushofer, a proponent of the idea of Lebensraum (living space) for Germans. Hess eventually introduced this idea to Hitler, and it became a key part of Nazi policy, and a justification for the invasion of other territories.

Hess first heard Hitler speak in 1920, and was almost immediately devoted to him. They shared a deeply-held belief that Germany's loss in the war was due to Jews and Bolsheviks. Hess was an early member of the NSDAP. In 1921 he was injured protecting Hitler from a bomb planted by Marxists. In 1922 Hess joined the Sturmabteilung (SA). He was involved in civil unrest, including the attempted Beer Hall Putsch. He was sentenced to 18 months imprisonment which he served in the same prison as Hitler. It was here that Hitler dictated *Mein Kampf* to Hess and another prisoner Emil Maurice. In 1925 Hess became Hitler's private secretary. Hess married Ilse Prohl on 20th December 1927. They had one son.

On 30th January 1933 the Nazis came to power in Germany, and Hitler was appointed Reich Chancellor. In April 1933 he made Hess Deputy Fuhrer and Reich Minister Without Portfolio. Hess was one of the organisers of the annual Nuremberg Rallies. As Nazi anti-Semitism became more blatant, Hess' department was given some of the responsibilities for drafting the Nuremberg Laws of 1935 which forbade relationships between Aryans and Jews, and which greatly limited the freedoms Jews in Germany had hitherto enjoyed.

After the German invasion of Poland in September 1939 Hess was appointed by Hitler as second-in-line after Goring. Hess was a renowned hypochondriac who was obsessed with the possibility of food being poisoned. He was in all probability mentally ill. In 1941 Hess flew to the UK in a lone mission to secure a peace deal. He was captured after being injured, landing in a parachute jump. He remained in custody until the trials at Nuremberg, where he was sentenced to life imprisonment. He died in Spandau Prison aged 93 on 20th December 1987, after apparently hanging himself.

Julius Streicher

Julius Streicher became known at the Nuremberg Trial as the epitome of Nazi anti-Semitism and racial hatred. He is an example of how a consistent message, delivered through the popular media of the day, can convey government policy to a wide audience. Indeed, he went beyond government policy, and became one of the chief promoters of intolerance. Although not a senior Nazi, and never one of the direct inner-circle of the Nazi leadership, Streicher was an immense influence on the promotion of the message Hitler and others wanted the German people to accept. He was best known as the editor of *Der Stürmer*, a weekly publication that was rabidly anti-Semitic, and contributed greatly to the hatred the Nazis felt and promoted. Streicher was born on 12 February 1885 in Fleinhausen, Bavaria. He was one of nine children born to Freidrich and Anna. His father was a schoolteacher. Julius Streicher initially worked in schools. In 1909 he joined the German Democratic Party. In 1913 he married Kungunde Ruth, and they had two children. Their marriage lasted until his wife's death in 1943. In 1945 he married Adele Tappe, his secretary.

He joined the German Army in 1914, reaching the rank of Lieutenant, and was awarded the Iron Cross. Streicher developed a reputation as a compelling and effective public speaker. In 1921 he joined the fledgling Nazi Party and helped to double its membership. He took part in the Munich Putsch. As a reward for his successes, in 1925, he was made Gauleiter of Franconia.

In 1924, he began to edit *Der Stürmer*, an anti-Semitic weekly that was full of warnings about the lechery and predatory tendencies of Jewish men towards German schoolgirls. At its peak *Der Stürmer* had a circulation of half a million. It was never particularly popular with adults, but it was popular with schoolchildren who were more easily convinced, and less likely to challenge its messages of hate: they were more likely to enjoy its lewd and pornographic style. Streicher tried to justify his attitudes as being based on race rather than religion. He urged segregation and discrimination against Jews. He stood as a defendant at the Nuremberg Trial, and was asked, amongst other things, about a speech he made in April 1933 in which he said, 'For fourteen years we have been crying to the German nation, "German people, learn to recognise your true enemy," and fourteen years ago the German Philistines listened, and then declared that we preached religious hatred. Today German people have awakened; even over all the world there is talk of the eternal Jews. Never since the beginnings of man has there been a nation which dared to fight against the nation of blood-suckers and extortioners who, for a thousand years, have spread all over the world.' (As cited in *Nuremberg Evil on Trial* p. 217)

Streicher was popular with Hitler, and indeed Hitler continued to read *Der Stürmer*, but his behaviour and corruption led to his being made subject to house arrest in 1941, and that situation continued until the end of the war.

At the Nuremberg Trial, Streicher was convicted of crimes against humanity. The sentence of the court stated: 'For his 25 years of speaking, writing and preaching hatred of the Jews, Streicher was widely known as 'Jew-Baiter Number One'. In his speeches and articles, week after week, month after month, he infected the German mind with the virus of anti-Semitism, and incited the German people to active persecution.' The judgement continued: '... Streicher's incitement to murder and extermination at the time when Jews in the East were being killed under the most horrible conditions clearly constitutes persecution on political and racial grounds in connection with war crimes, as defined by the Charter, and constitutes a crime against humanity.'

Streicher was hanged on 16th October 1946. Even at his execution he continued to defy and challenge the authority of those who were about to take his life. At the steps below the gallows, when asked to identify himself, he screamed 'Heil Hitler!' When asked to confirm his name he stated, 'You know my name well,' before eventually yelling, 'Julius Streicher!' As the rope was about to be placed around his neck he screamed, 'Purim Fest 1946' – 'Purim' is a Jewish holiday commemorating the execution of an ancient persecutor of the Jews. When asked if he had any last words he shouted, 'The Bolsheviks will hang you one day!' (As cited in *Nuremberg Evil on Trial* pp. 341 – 342)

***

AUSCHWITZ-BIRKENAU

Main entrance Auschwitz I. "Work Brings Freedom"

Guard Post Auschwitz I. Prisoners would be forced to march past this position or stand for hours as punishment in all weathers despite exhaustion and disease

AUSCHWITZ-BIRKENAU

Cattle truck, Birkenau. Similar to the carriages prisoners were transported to Auschwitz in from across Europe

Torture and punishment posts. Auschwitz I. Prisoners would be tied to these posts and other inmates would be ordered to parade past them.

AUSCHWITZ-BIRKENAU

Electrified fencing. Auschwitz I

Execution wall against which prisoners were shot. Auschwitz I

AUSCHWITZ-BIRKENAU

Gas chamber and crematoria. Auschwitz 1

Gallows from which Rudolf Hoess was hanged next to gas chamber at Auschwitz I. The original gallows no longer exist but this replacement is a replica at the same site. To the left of the picture is the gas chamber. Approximately 200 metres to the right of here is the Hoess Villa

Crematoria Auschwitz I. This is a replica. In the room next door is the original gas chamber.

SIMON BELL

Main Entrance at Birkenau looking into the camp

AUSCHWITZ-BIRKENAU

Selection ramp. Birkenau

SIMON BELL

Remains of gas chamber and crematoria. Birkenau

AUSCHWITZ-BIRKENAU

Remains of gas chamber and crematoria. Birkenau

The vastness of Birkenau. This site stretches beyond the range of vision.

AUSCHWITZ-BIRKENAU

Remains of gas chamber and crematoria. Birkenau

A pit of human ash at Birkenau. These pits were where ash from the crematoria was stored in piles before being sent to make fertilizer, or to be thrown into the river or ponds, or to be used on the roads within the camp.

AUSCHWITZ-BIRKENAU

Inside a barrack hut. Birkenau

International Holocaust Memorial. Birkenau

AUSCHWITZ-BIRKENAU

Memorial next to a pit of human ash at Birkenau. Other storage pits can be seen in the background as well as the ruins of one of the crematoria and gas chambers.

SIMON BELL

Drainage ditch dug by prisoners at Birkenau

Ruins of gas chamber and crematoria. Birkenau

International Holocaust Memorial. Birkenau

AUSCHWITZ-BIRKENAU

The bleak grimness of Birkenau

CHAPTER FIVE
A HISTORY OF AUSCHWITZ AND ITS BRUTALITY

'One image stuck in my mind from the moment I heard it described. It was of a 'procession' of empty baby carriages – property looted from the dead Jews – pushed out of Auschwitz in rows of five towards the railway station. The prisoner who witnessed the sight said they took an hour to pass by.'
   Laurence Rees, Auschwitz, The Nazis and The Final Solution.

Auschwitz I and Auschwitz II (or 'Birkenau') are what most of us think of when we consider this place of depravity, cruelty, destruction and industrial slaughter. Some may also know of Auschwitz III or 'Monowitz'. In reality there were some forty camps within the broader location of Auschwitz. The camps were built by the Nazis in the town of Oświęcim in Upper Silesia in southern Poland and called by the Germans 'Auschwitz'. Auschwitz was the largest extermination and labour camp built by the Nazis. It was built at Oświęcim due to the established rail, road and river links, and because of the industrial complexes of IG Farben.
(Interessen **G**emeinschaft **Farben**industrie AktienGesellschaft)

AUSCHWITZ-BIRKENAU

The camp inmates were used to provide slave labour for that company. The area also offered isolation, which allowed many of the horrors that took place to occur with less outside awareness. In total the Nazis built over 300 main concentration camps (including sub-camps) across Europe; although some estimate there were as many as 15,000 labour, death, and concentration camps or sites (*Jewish Virtual Library*). Some housed political and other prisoners. Some were used to contain a workforce in the harshest of conditions. Some – Auschwitz-Birkenau, Treblinka, Sobibor, Chelmo, Majdanek and Belzec – were established purely as extermination camps. At these places there was little but the façade of labour and imprisonment. The sole purpose was to kill, at an industrial rate. For many years the Nazis maintained that they were controlling, relocating, employing, and dispersing the Jewish populations of Germany and the occupied territories. That all changed in January 1942 with the Berlin-Wannsee Conference at which the Final Solution was first discussed and accepted as policy. Auschwitz-Birkenau and the other extermination camps were given a very specific role, and most Jews who entered these places died soon after arrival.

Auschwitz I was built using established pre-war military barracks. Auschwitz II, or Birkenau, was built nearby, mainly using the forced labour of Soviet prisoners, thousands of whom died in the process. All of the Auschwitz camps provided slave labour for the industrial works of I G Farben.

Prior to the Berlin-Wannsee Conference and Operation Reinhard, Auschwitz did not greatly differ from other Nazi concentration camps. Following Berlin- Wannsee the role of Auschwitz, and particularly Birkenau, changed drastically. Birkenau was built primarily as a place of extermination. Although many inmates lived there, most died soon after arrival, particularly the elderly, the very young, or those perceived to be infirm. The selection process at the ramp of Birkenau, as trains arrived, is synonymous with the callous cruelty of that camp.

No book or scholarly work about Auschwitz can be true to the history without addressing the reality of what happened there. For those who are new to the subject some of this reality may be difficult or distressing to comprehend, but it is a reality that needs to be addressed. We who live today – who were not there – merely read or hear words. The brutality of those words may be upsetting, but they can never truly convey the graphic and painful actuality of events as they occurred and were experienced.

The Germans were meticulous record-keepers. The Nazi records suggest that at least 1,100,000 Jews were sent to Auschwitz, plus nearly 150,000 Poles, 23,000 Roma, 15,000 Soviet prisoners of war, and 25,000 prisoners of other nationalities, including Czech, French, Yugoslavian, Russian, Byelorussian and Ukrainian (*Auschwitz The Residence of Death. Auschwitz - Birkenau State Museum Publication*). Those records do not include those sent straight to their death. By the time of the transportations from Hungary in 1944 the numbers arriving were so vast that fewer efforts were made to record details. The total numbers to die at Auschwitz are open to some debate, but little is gained by arguing over the obscenity of precise figures. The official estimate is that about 1.1 to 1.3 million people died there, of whom the majority were Jews from across Europe. Rudolf Hoess, the Camp Commandant responsible for much of the building and developing the killing processes used at Auschwitz, claimed at the Nuremberg Trial in 1946 that 3 million people died. His affidavit stated at The Nuremberg Trial:

'I commanded Auschwitz until December 1943, and estimate that at least 2,500,000 victims were executed and exterminated there by gassing and burning, and at least another half million succumbed

AUSCHWITZ-BIRKENAU

to starvation and disease making a total dead of about 3 million. This figure represents about 70 to 80 percent of all persons sent to Auschwitz as prisoners, the remainder having been selected and used for slave labour in the concentration camp industries. Included among the executed and burned were approximately 20,000 Russian prisoners-of-war (previously screened out of prisoner-of- war cages by the Gestapo) who were delivered to Auschwitz in Wehrmacht transports operated by regular Wehrmacht officers and men. The remainder of the total number of victims included about 100,000 German Jews, and great numbers of citizens, mostly Jewish, from Holland, France, Belgium, Poland, Hungary, Czechoslovakia, Greece, or other countries. We executed about 400,000 Hungarian Jews alone at Auschwitz in the summer of 1944.' (As cited in Nuremberg Evil on Trial pp. 204)

Some survivors suggest that 2 million is a more accurate figure. Some who lived through Auschwitz refer to witnessing many thousands of men, women, and children being thrown into pits and being burned alive because the gas chambers and crematoria could not cope with the demand placed upon them. In the circumstances, it is accepted that people were killed, or died due to starvation and disease, and as such the exact numbers become almost irrelevant: Auschwitz-Birkenau was a killing factory. It was a place where the Nazis developed and mastered mass slaughter on an industrial scale that humanity had never seen before. The other extermination camps were brutal places of slaughter too, and are worthy of study and research in their own right.

Rudolf Hoess was Commandant of Auschwitz from 1940 until 1943. He later became part of the concentration camp inspectorate, before returning to Auschwitz. The accounts Hoess gave at Nuremberg, and in his autobiography, give a powerful insight into him as a man, as a Nazi, as a military officer, and as a major instigator of the Holocaust. During cross-examination at The Nuremberg Trial on 15th April 1946 Hoess confirmed that Adolf Eichmann had stated that over two million Jews had been 'destroyed' at Auschwitz. He stated:

'In the summer of 1941 I was summoned to Berlin to Reichführer SS Himmler to receive personal orders. He told me something to the effect – I do not recall his exact words – that the Führer had given the order for a final solution to the Jewish question. We, the SS, must carry out that order. If it is not carried out now then the Jews will later on destroy the German people. He had chosen Auschwitz on account of its easy access by rail, and also because the extensive site offered space for measures ensuring isolation.'

This order was what was referred to as a 'secret Reich matter', but Hoess confirmed at the trial that he had admitted to his wife what was happening at the camp when she asked him in 1942. Many might find it hard to believe that his wife did not already know, as the family lived in a villa on the edge of Auschwitz main camp site, where the smells of smoke, death, disease, and filth must have been overwhelming, and all-pervading.

Hoess confirmed that Adolf Eichmann came to the camp about four weeks after he had received the order from Himmler, in order to discuss the details of how that order would be carried out. Eichmann was tasked by Himmler to give Hoess his instructions. Hoess was asked at the Nuremberg Trial to confirm further details from his sworn affidavit in which he stated:

'Mass executions by gassing commenced during the summer of 1941 and continued until fall 1944. I personally supervised executions at Auschwitz until 1st December 1943 and know by reason of my continued duties at the Inspectorate of Concentration Camps, 'WVHA', that these

executions continued as stated above.' (As cited in *Nuremberg Evil on Trial* pp 204)

('WVHA' was SS-WVHA, or SS-Wirtschafts-Verwaltungshauptampt, the Economic and Administrative Main Office of the Nazi SS.)

Hoess gave details about the physical isolation of Auschwitz. He stated:

'The Auschwitz camp as such was about three kilometres from the town. About 20,000 acres of the surrounding country had been cleared of all former inhabitants, and the entire area could be entered only by SS men or civilian employees who had special passes. The actual compound called 'Birkenau', where later on the extermination camp was constructed, was situated two kilometres from the Auschwitz camp. The camp installations themselves, that is to say, the provisional installations used at first were deep in the woods and could from nowhere be detected by the eye. In addition to that, this area had been declared a prohibited area and even members of the SS who did not have a special pass could not enter it. Thus, as far as one could judge, it was impossible for anyone except authorized persons to enter that area.'

(As cited in *Nuremberg Evil on Trial* pp. 201 & 202)

Hoess went on to describe the selection and killing process. All works regarding Auschwitz and other camps describe various forms of selection. The selection process for many began long before arrival at the camps. Selection was a feature of existence in Germany under the Nazis as the anti-Semitic policies took hold, and became more apparent in occupied lands and in the ghettos that Jews were forced to live in. Daily life became a struggle to avoid or survive that random or cruel decision that dictated who would work and who would not, who would eat or go hungry, who would remain or who would be transported, and who would live or die. In his Nuremberg Trial evidence Hoess described the selection at Auschwitz, or more specifically Birkenau. He gave comparisons with other camps, and the way the killing process was developed. It is a shocking piece of evidence in a court case strewn with material that horrified the world:

'The 'final solution' of the Jewish question meant the complete extermination of all Jews in Europe. I was ordered to establish extermination facilities at Auschwitz in June 1941. At that time, there were already in the General Government (of Poland) three other extermination camps: Belzec, Treblinka, and Wolzek. These camps were under the Einsatzkommando of the Security Police and SD. I visited Treblinka to find out how they carried out their exterminations. The camp commandant at Treblinka told me he had liquidated 80,000 in the course of one half year. He was principally concerned with liquidating all Jews from the Warsaw Ghetto. He used monoxide gas, and I did not think his methods were very efficient. So when I set up the extermination building at Auschwitz, I used Zyklon B which was a crystallized prussic acid which we dropped into the death chamber from a small opening. It took from three to fifteen minutes to kill the people in the death chamber, depending upon climatic conditions. We knew when the people were dead because the screaming stopped. We usually waited about one half hour before we opened the doors and removed the bodies.
After the bodies were removed, our special Kommandos took off the rings and extracted the gold from the teeth of the corpses (Hoess confirmed that the gold was melted down and sent to Berlin)" ... "Another improvement we made over Treblinka was that we built our gas chamber to accommodate 2,000 people at one time whereas at Treblinka their ten gas chambers only accommodated 200 people each. The way we selected our victims was as follows: We had two SS Doctors on duty at Auschwitz to examine the incoming transports of prisoners. The prisoners would be marched by one of the Doctors who would make spot decisions as

they walked by. Those who were fit for work were sent into the camp. Others were sent immediately to the extermination plants. Children of tender years were invariably exterminated since by reason of their youth they were unable to work." (As cited in *Nuremberg Evil on Trial* pp. 205 & 206).

There is a callous and brutal indifference to suffering and death in the whole passage of evidence, but particularly in the last sentence, that sums up the total disregard for human life that was held by Hoess, the Nazis, and others involved in the cruelty of Auschwitz.

The testimony Rudolf Hoess gave to Nuremberg has been an essential element in understanding Auschwitz and what happened there. Of equal or even more assistance has been the autobiography Hoess wrote in prison in Poland after being convicted at Nuremberg. (He was handed over to authorities in Poland for trial and subsequently execution there).

'*Commandant of Auschwitz*' was first published in a Polish translation in 1951. A German version was published in 1958, and an English translation was made from that version. Some may argue that this is a piece of work written under duress – and to a degree that is true - but it is a work written by an avowedly military man, with a need to be, or appear to be, truthful. There are aspects of his account that can be seen as a personal interpretation of himself, of his acquaintances, of events, and of specific acts. He has a somewhat idealistic view of his life, his family, his experiences, his friendships and of those he worked with and for. It may well be that as recalled and written by Hoess, this is how he genuinely perceived these aspects; or that he has embellished or glossed over faults, flaws, and failings.

But there are also elements when the militarily 'correct' Hoess appears to feel it is his duty to be as truthful and precise as possible.

This particularly applies to his role in the creation of Auschwitz, and the events that occurred there. This is of immeasurable use to historians and scholars. It is also of immense use to survivors and those who lost loved ones. It is of use in challenging those who seek to deny the reality of what happened at Auschwitz. Hoess was tasked with creating Auschwitz, and importantly, without his enthusiastic and active involvement, Auschwitz II or Birkenau, the most notorious site of industrial slaughter in history, could never have existed.

The words of Hoess – even if they seem casual, cold, brutal, and indifferent to the human suffering that they relate to – are crucial to our understanding of the camps and those who controlled life and death within them. His autobiography gives some understanding of Hoess as a man, but that is based largely on his own recollections and perceptions of himself. It is of particular use here with regard to his memories and interpretations of Auschwitz, and the activities that occurred there. Those recollections of Hoess will be drawn upon to add an understanding for the benefit of any who have not previously accessed his account.

There are some who feel that this is a book that should be banned. To do so would merely drive copies underground, and with the power of the Internet it will always be available. It is much better that students, scholars, political activists, or those who simply desire to understand the Holocaust should be able to access the first-hand account of a man who held responsibility for the most significant killing factory in human history.

Hoess does not sanitise or deny the brutality of Auschwitz. His attitude to some of the cruelty is casual, and may be interpreted as callous. He implies no hatred for many of those who died. He describes following orders and performing the duties expected of him in a cold, almost matter-of-fact manner. Summary executions are necessary. Punishment killings, and forcing inmates to watch them or march past bodies are essential for the smooth running of camp life. The presence of disease, malnutrition and suffering are dismissed as unfortunate consequences. And the mass killing of millions of innocent people is reflected and discussed in a way that lacks emotion or concern. He lacks any obvious sense of expressed remorse, and does not seem to grasp the magnitude of the events he was involved in, or why these would cause the rest of the world such horror.

A brief reference to Hoess in his own words conveys so much about the deeds he facilitated, and his attitude to those who were sent to the camps. Hoess maintained that he was not anti-Semitic, but that he understood that Jews were enemies of the state, and that his role was to imprison them, force them into work if they were capable, or to kill them if they were incapable of work. He states:

'I must emphasise here that I have never personally hated the Jews. It is true that I looked upon them as the enemies of our people. But just because of this I saw no difference between them and the other prisoners, and I treated them all the same way. I never drew any distinctions. In any event the emotion of hatred is foreign to my nature. But I know what hate is, and what it looks like. I have seen it and I have suffered it myself.' (Commandant of Auschwitz p.132).

Is Hoess being disingenuous here, or does he genuinely believe that he never hated the Jews, that he was not anti-Semitic, or that he did not treat them differently to other prisoners? It is certainly true that many groups were forced into slave labour, selected for immediate death, or were killed later on if they broke rules, attempted escape, displeased a guard, or were 'no longer of use'. Perhaps Hoess genuinely believed he was balanced and consistent in his actions, and that the only difference with Jews was the number brought to Auschwitz, and the very specific orders regarding their extermination.

Hoess describes the summary executions of prisoners at Auschwitz. He shows no compassion for them as individuals (apart from when a German officer was executed), but rather he divides the prisoners into his perception of those who died with or without dignity. He shows callous disregard, too, in how he describes the reaction of other prisoners to the executions and the display of bodies. With reference to escape attempts he states:

> 'But these projects of escape always involved the prospect of reprisals, the arrest of family and relations, and the liquidation of ten or more fellow-sufferers. Many of those who tried to escape cared little about reprisals, and were prepared to try their luck. Once beyond the ring of sentry posts the local civilian population would help them on their way (if they were Poles – author's note). The rest was no problem. If they had bad luck, then it was all up with them. One way or another it was the solution to their problems. The other prisoners had to parade past the corpses of those who had been shot while trying to escape, so they would see how such an attempt might end. Many were frightened by this spectacle, and abandoned their plans as a result.' (Commandant of Auschwitz pp.118-119)

Those who survived Auschwitz describe such executions as cruel and incredibly distressing events that had an immense impact on them. Many survivors describe being forced to watch the executions (murders), the random selection of other inmates to die, or being made to march past recently killed people. For prisoners already terrorised such events must have been incredibly distressing. Hoess does not reflect this in his account, and merely seems to suggest the actions were necessary. Although he recognises some of the impact on prisoners it is not referred to with any compassion or acknowledgement that these were fellow human beings.

Hoess describes the extermination process in Auschwitz. It is a brutal explanation of the killing operation. It does not make for easy reading, but neither should it be sanitised to conceal the reality of what was involved:

'Jews selected for gassing were taken as quietly as possible to the crematoria, the men being separated from the women. In the undressing room, prisoners of the special detachment, detailed for this purpose, would tell them in their own language that they were going to be bathed and deloused, that they must leave their clothes neatly together and above all remember where they had put them, so that they would be able to find them again quickly after delousing. The prisoners of the special detachment had the greatest interest in seeing that the operation proceeded smoothly and quickly. After undressing, the Jews went into the gas chambers, which were furnished with showers and water pipes and gave a realistic impression of a bath house.

The women went in first with their children, followed by the men who were always fewer in number. This part of the operation nearly always went smoothly, for the prisoners of the special detachment would calm those who betrayed any anxiety or who perhaps had some inkling of their fate. As an additional precaution these prisoners of the special detachment and an SS man always remained in the chamber until the last moment.

The door would now be quickly screwed up and the gas immediately discharged by the waiting disinfectors through vents in the ceilings of the gas chambers, down a shaft that led to the floor. This ensured the rapid distribution of the gas. It could be observed through the peep-hole in the door that those who were standing nearest to the induction vents were killed at once. It can be said that one third died straight away. The remainder staggered about and began to scream and struggle for air. The screaming, however, soon changed to the death rattle and in a few minutes all lay still. After twenty minutes at the latest no movement could be discerned. The time required for the gas to have an effect varied according to the weather, and depended on whether it was damp or dry, cold or warm. It also depended on the quality of the gas, which was never exactly the same, and on the composition of the transports which might contain a high proportion of healthy Jews, or old and sick, or children. The victims became unconscious after a few minutes, according to their distance from the intake shaft. Those who screamed and those who were sick or weak, or the small children, died quicker than those who were healthy or young.

The door was opened half an hour after the induction of the gas, and the ventilation switched on. Work was immediately begun on removing the corpses. There was no noticeable change in the bodies and no signs of convulsions or discolouration. Only after the bodies had been left lying for some time, that is to say for several hours, did the usual death stains appear in the places where they had lain. Soiling through opening of the bowels was also rare. There were no signs of wounding of any kind. The faces showed no distortion. The special detachment now set about removing the gold teeth and cutting the hair from the women.

After this, the bodies were taken up by lift and laid in front of the ovens, which had meanwhile been stoked up. Depending on the size of the bodies, up to three corpses could be put into one oven retort at the same time. The time required for cremation also depended on this, but on an average it took twenty minutes. As previously stated, crematoria I and II could cremate about 2000 bodies in twenty-four hours, but a higher number was not possible without causing damage to the installations. Numbers III and IV should have been able to cremate 1,500 bodies in twenty-four hours, but, as far as I know, these figures were never attained.' (Commandant of Auschwitz pp. 197-199)

Primo Levi provided an introduction to the autobiography of Rudolf Hoess. In his own works Levi largely maintained a lack of obvious anger, despite the horrors he had witnessed and experienced in Auschwitz. Of Hoess' book he stated:

> 'This book is filled with evil ... it has no literary quality, and reading it is agony.'

It is a difficult book to read. These few passages give an indication as to the utter disregard for human life that Hoess demonstrated. Some who deny elements of the Holocaust may have difficulty explaining the detail (however unpleasant it is) of his autobiography. He had no personal axe to grind. When he wrote this (at the time only 114 pages) he had been convicted at Nuremberg, and was in custody in Poland. He knew with certainty that he was going to die. As heartless as his words may seem, they are the words of the man who created Auschwitz-Birkenau, and who most determinedly endeavoured to enforce the Final Solution to the Jewish Question.

It is difficult to convey in the words of a book such as this the true horror of Auschwitz. Many, if not most of the records kept by the Nazis were destroyed before the camp was liberated by Soviet forces. But some records remained at the site and elsewhere. The Auschwitz-Birkenau State Museum has a vast archive and is dedicated to ensuring the preservation of this part of history. Many survivors, their relatives, scholars, and others, are immensely helped by the dedication and expertise of the Auschwitz staff. Some of the archive has been recorded in other published works. One such resource is Auschwitz Chronicle 1939 – 1945, From The Archives of The Auschwitz Memorial and The German Federal Archives. Published in 1989, this work by Danuta Czech is an essential read for scholars and historians. Danuta Czech is the former head of research at the museum and commenced work on this most comprehensive of studies in 1955. Based on over 3,500 eyewitness accounts by former prisoners, with original camp documents that details transport and admission lists, orders from the Commandant, orders for experiments, secret messages, and other information it is a weighty volume of over 800 pages. It details day by day the activities of the camp from its creation to its liberation. The information is at times quite matter of fact in how it is described. It can appear to be casual and almost dismissive in the specifics of activities, that issuing of prisoner numbers, and the sending to death of innocents in their hundreds of thousands. It may be of use to the reader to get some idea of the camp through a few excerpts from different periods in the history of the camp. The author would recommend Auschwitz Chronicle as an essential study aid for those who seek to learn about this subject in more detail.

On 22 August 1939, a matter of days before the German's invaded Poland, Hitler addressed the commanding general of the Wehrmacht: "Our strength is our speed and our brutality. Genghis Khan drove many women and children to death, deliberately and joyously. History sees him as a great founder of a state. What weak western European civilisation says about me doesn't matter. I have given the order – and I will have anyone shot who expresses even one word of criticism – that the aim of the war is not to reach definite lines but rather the physical destruction of the enemy. So I have assembled my Death's Head Formations, for the time being only in the East, with the command to send man, woman and child of Polish origin and language to death, ruthlessly and mercilessly. This is the only way we can win the living space we need … Poland will be depopulated and settled with Germans." (Auschwitz Chronicle page 1)

The origins of the Holocaust are detailed elsewhere. Auschwitz gradually expanded and developed into a place providing slave labour for various industries and as a place dedicated to extermination, particularly after the Berlin-Wannsee Conference. On 1 March 1941 Himmler visited the camp on an inspection. He issued orders to the commandant to expand Auschwitz to hold

30,000 prisoners, to build a camp for 100,000 prisoners of war on the site of the village of Birkenau, to make 10,000 prisoners available to IG Farben for the construction of an industrial site, to cultivate the whole area agriculturally, and to expand the camp workshops.

In August 1941 Zyklon B was first used to kill Russian POWs in a test experiment conducted by Camp Commander Karl Fritzsch. Further executions by shooting and gassing take place on a daily basis. The shootings often occurred at the death wall in the courtyard of Block 11.

To give an idea of how the rate of death increased, the figures recorded for May 1942 are as follows day by day: 89, 73, 103, 90, 87, 144, 92, 138, 63, 55, 62, 110, 89, 67, 65, 96, 78, 104, 85, 115, 114, 107, 100, 94, 113, 279, 92, 89, 63, and 51. Between 5th and 11th May 5200 Polish Jewish prisoners were gassed in Chamber 1.

On 24 January 1943 the following is detailed: "Approximately 2,000 Jewish men, women, and children arrive from the Grodno ghetto in an RSHA transport. Following selection 175 men and 112 women are admitted to the camp as prisoners. The other approximately 1,713 people are killed in the gas chambers."

On 2 April 1943 the tattooed numbers 39853-39963 were issued to 123 female prisoners sent in a group transport. The number 39934 was issued to Kitty Felix (Kitty Hart-Moxon), and 39933 to her mother. Kitty is referred to later. She had her tattoo surgically removed many years ago and had her mother's tattoo removed after she died. Kitty has these numbers preserved.

On 10 September 1942 the records state: "1,000 Jews arrive from Malines Camp with the eighth RSHA transport from Belgium. In the transport are 376 men and 124 boys and 386 women and 114 girls. A first selection was carried out in Cosel, where about 200 men were chosen for the Schmelt Organisation. After the selection in Auschwitz, 21 men and 64 women are admitted to the camp and receive Nos. 63223-63243 and 19295-19358. The other 715 people are killed in the gas chambers. SS Camp Doctor Kremer takes part in the selection and the gassing."

Throughout 1943 the death rate through murder in the gas chambers and by other means increased and remained steadily high. The death rate through illness, disease and starvation was also getting higher.

By February 1944 the occupancy of the three main camps was:

Auschwitz I	17,177 male prisoners
Auschwitz II	18,378 male prisoners
	24,637 female prisoners
Auschwitz III	13,477 male prisoners

By May 1944 the transportation of Hungarian Jews is in full flow. A report from a resistance movement in the camp states that over 100,000 Hungarian Jews have already been killed, with the SS men involved in the extermination working 48 hours uninterrupted followed by an eight hour break.

By August 1944 the occupancy of the three main camps was:

Auschwitz I	15,971 male prisoners
Auschwitz II	19,424 male prisoners
Auschwitz II	39,234 female prisoners
	30,000 unregistered Hungarian Jews in the transit camp
Auschwitz III	30,539 male prisoners
Total	135,168 prisoners

23 October 1944 the record states: SS Camp Doctor Mengele conducts a two hour selection among the female Jews sent from the Plazow concentration camp. He sends 1,765 women to Transit Camp B-IIc. The remaining women are killed in the gas chambers."

AUSCHWITZ-BIRKENAU

By January 1945 the death marches were in full flow. The Soviet forces were near and the Nazis were keen to remove prisoners who could travel and to destroy evidence of the activities.

Auschwitz Chronicle is an incredibly detailed and lengthy work. It took many years of research through thousands of documents and other archive material. These few excerpts give an idea of the detail it contains as it cites records from every day of the camp's operational existence.

The bestial brutality of Auschwitz peaked during that 56- day period from May to July in 1944, when approximately 437,000 Hungarian Jews were deported to Auschwitz, most of whom were killed. Soon after this time the Nazis, and most notably Himmler, knew that the war was inevitably going to end in defeat. The German forces were being attacked and beaten on two significant fronts in Europe, and had lost control in the Mediterranean, Italy and North Africa. On 7th October 1944 men of the Sonderkommando staged a moderately successful revolt (for which they were all executed). Himmler was pragmatic. In November he ordered Eichmann to cease deportations of Jews from Budapest, telling him, 'If until now you have exterminated Jews, from now on, if I order you, you must be a fosterer of Jews.'(As cited in *Auschwitz. The Nazis and The Final Solution*, Laurence Rees p. 325)

On 26th November 1944 Himmler ordered the destruction of the gas chambers and crematoria. After the buildings had been dismantled they were blown up in January 1945, just before the Soviet forces liberated the camp. The Nazis attempted to erase all evidence of what had happened there. The Kanada camp, with its huge stocks of personal effects, was destroyed. Other stores such as those containing human hair were cleared (unsuccessfully it transpired). Records were burnt and removed. The Nazis wanted to remove all incriminating documents and material. Part of this included removing prisoners. When the Soviets arrived on 27th January they found around 600 prisoners alive at Monowitz, just less than 6,000 at Birkenau and just over 1,000 at Auschwitz I. Most of the other prisoners had been moved in the weeks and months before, and had been forced on what became known as 'Death Marches'. Prisoners were made to walk in appalling conditions for hundreds of miles to move away from the Soviet armies. Occasionally they were transported for part of the journey by train or in trucks. Many thousands died on these journeys. Prisoners were starving, and not dressed in any way appropriately for the bitter cold of winter. They were denied basic provisions, and often had to steal from passing farm vehicles, or forage in fields. Those who could not walk or keep up the pace would be shot. They were moved to other camps in Poland and elsewhere in occupied Eastern Europe. They were also taken to camps in Germany such as Bergen-Belsen. It is possible that the Germans had little idea where they were taking them.

British, US and other forces advancing from the west found scenes of utter horror at camp after camp. The US forces filmed many of these camps, and that footage was used in evidence at the Nuremberg Trials. The US films, and footage taken by Soviet forces that liberated Auschwitz, remain in the public domain, and in the Internet age are easily accessible. Although recorded in black and white cine-film they convey graphically the visual horror of what the allies found. It is recommended that students of this period of history should access these films. The material is distressing, but that of course, is the reality of genocidal horror.

CHAPTER SIX
THE GERMANS, RACISM, ANTI-SEMITISM, AND COMPLICITY

There is a straight line from, "You have no right to live among us as Jews," to, "You have no right to live among us," to "You have no right to live."

Raul Hilberg

The prevailing attitudes of anti-Semitism in Europe in the first half of the twentieth century had developed over a 2,000-year period. The views of the Nazis reflected the views of many people, not just Germans, and the popularity of the Nazi proposals, attitudes, and actions were willingly accepted. The far right, the far left, and even religious fundamentalists, share a certainty, an absolutism, an assuredness, a belief, that their credo, their ethos, their explanations of the world, their solutions, their perceived causes, are the only truth. To contradict such intensely held beliefs makes one at best a fool, at worst an enemy.

In considering the development of the barbaric activities of Auschwitz one has to consider the most significant camp commandant, Rudolf Hoess. He and others, such as Goebbels,

Göring, Frank, Eichmann, Mengele, and Heydrich were not mere puppets and disciples of Hitler. They did not just jump to his command and believe his hatred on the basis of powerful public oratory or the ramblings of Mein Kampf. They already shared his anti-Semitic inclinations, as did many in Germany and elsewhere. It is easy to allow the argument of 'just following orders' because that absolves wrongdoers of responsibility.

It is easy to blame the complicity of conquered nations on fear of an occupying power, but when one looks at the actions across Europe there was tacit and enthusiastic cooperation and active involvement. Even British police cooperated in the occupied Channel Islands, and allowed the small Jewish population to be deported to camps. And elements of the British popular press in the 1930s and 1940s were enthusiastic supporters of Hitler and Nazism. Many of those who lived in the occupied lands were not just quietly complicit, they were actively involved in the policies we now know as the Holocaust, but which some prefer to call the Shoah. And many stood by and did nothing when they knew full well that friends, neighbours, colleagues, compatriots and more importantly fellow human beings, were being oppressed and killed. As Pastor Martin Niemöller wrote:

First they came for the Communists ...
and I did not speak out
Because I was not a Communist

Then they came for the Socialists ...
and I did not speak out
because I was not a Socialist

Then they came for the trade unionists ...
and I did not speak out
because I was not a trade unionist

Then they came for the Jews ...
and I did not speak out
because I was not a Jew

Then they came for me ...
and there was not one left
to speak out for me

The Germans could not have done what they did without the active and enthusiastic participation of other nations. In conquered lands the police, military, law enforcement, councils, government officials, and society in general helped to isolate Jews into ghettos, assisted with identifying Jews, and participated in the act of selection and transportation. Many within these lands volunteered to serve with German forces and many – French, Dutch, Ukrainian, Lithuanian, etc. and other citizens volunteered for roles in places like Auschwitz – including joining the SS - and were active and enthusiastic participants in the killing process.

For hundreds of years prior to the Second World War Germany (or Prussia) had been a land of education and culture. We must wonder why these people – and fellow- Europeans – so readily accepted the Nazi perspective on race and Jews, and so enthusiastically bought into it. Anti-Semitism was rife in Europe long before the Nazis came to power. Indeed, even in British culture it was acceptable. Shylock in the *Merchant of Venice* and Fagin in *Oliver Twist* are two obvious caricatures that spring to mind. The hatred of Jews was present long before World War I. They were already demonised across the continent, and had been subject to massacres and pogroms for throughout the previous 2,000 years. They were limited in the employment that society felt was acceptable for Jews. Many worked as merchants, bankers, doctors, dentists and even money- lenders. Of course a lot of Jews did menial jobs too. The defeat in the First World War coincided with the development of Marxist Communism. The Russian Revolution had only recently occurred in 1917 (and was followed by years of unrest), and in Germany the Communists were one of many factions seeking to fill the power void after the First World War. For the anti-Semites it was an easy leap to blame the Russian Revolution on Jews, and to use that as fuel to an already burning fire. Add to that the belief that Jews had contributed to Germany's defeat, the crippling financial punishments imposed on Germany, the loss of territory, and the hyper-inflation all Germans suffered, it was easy to cite the Jews as being responsible. For the Nazis it was not a case of imposing anti-Semitic ideas on the people: they merely worked on established views and reinforced them. The cause of the Nazis was undoubtedly helped by anger at the defeat in the war, and by the signing of the Armistice in November 1918 by those they viewed as the 'November Criminals'. Although it was clear to politicians that surrender was in Germany's best interests, to the former soldiers it was a betrayal. Many of these former soldiers returned to Germany and joined the various 'Freikorps' that had been established. A major aim of these units was the defence of Germany from the threat of international Communism, and by default the Jews.

Hitler and the Nazis saw Jews as lesser human beings. They hijacked and distorted Darwinian theories. They saw Jews as being unworthy of sharing the same land as Germans. Later on, when Goebbels became the chief agent of propaganda, he would use film to support Nazi opinion. There was a famous film in which scientists conducted an experiment observing stag beetles fighting. One of the assistants expressed sadness about the fight to the death. She is told by a supposedly wise professor 'There is no such thing as a quiet life anywhere in nature … They all live in constant struggle, in the course of which the weak perish. We regard this struggle as completely natural, but we would think it unnatural if a cat lived peacefully with a mouse or a fox with a hare.' (Laurence Rees, *The Nazis - a Warning From History* p. 35)

Hitler and the Nazi élite had a simple outlook: rather than blaming the many ills Germany was suffering on the multiple factors involved (including German aggression in 1914, and a worldwide Depression) they sought to apportion the blame elsewhere. And the intelligentsia in France and the U.S. who had helped decide the rules of surrender were clearly Jewish too.

The simplicity of Nazism appealed to the masses. It was not something that could be argued with. When they were sold the idea of Aryan purity, greater Germany, the need to gain land for homes and food, the wrongs of the war, the guilt of the Jews, and the irrelevance of other races, the Germans bought it hook, line, and sinker. They even quietly accepted Aktion T4 with the active and enthusiastic participation of doctors and other health professionals. (AktionT4 included sterilising mentally and physically disabled Germans, and ultimately euthanasia for those deemed to be impure or of little use to the perfect Aryan state). It was not a difficult task to convince professionals, never mind ordinary members of the public, that some people, German people at that, were not worthy of life, and that their existence caused an impurity to the German race.

If such attitudes already existed it was no great leap to seeing Jews (and later Roma, Communists, Slavs, homosexuals, etc) as being unworthy of life. They dehumanised them. Jews ceased to be viewed as people. They were 'sub- human', and in some respects had no more right to life than vermin. Dehumanising an enemy is part of the process of making cruelty and killing easier. The Jews had already lost most of their rights of citizenship in Germany long before the War. By the mid-1930s, and certainly by Kristallnacht on 9th November

1938, they were entirely unwelcome in Germany, and the writing, unfortunately, was on the wall. During Kristallnacht, Nazi stormtroopers destroyed Jewish property and businesses, and set fire to synagogues. Thousands of German Jews were rounded up, four hundred were killed, and up to thirty thousand male Jews were sent to concentration camps. While the mayhem and killing were taking place, ordinary German citizens stood by and watched.

    Hitler, ably assisted by others, but particularly by Goebbels, gradually introduced and promoted anti-Semitic policies. Although Hitler did not disguise his hatred of Jews, he was aware that a more subtle approach was required. The Nazis stood on an election platform seeking to right the wrongs of defeat in war and the injustice of Treaty of Versailles. They sought to create full employment and restore national pride. Jews were identified as being responsible for many of Germany's ills, and although the Nazi stormtroopers were actively and openly violent, a less aggressive approach was encouraged among the general population. Boycotts of Jewish businesses were deemed to be more acceptable with the electorate, and did not raise alarms abroad. The anti-Semitic policies were gradually introduced, and for many German Jews the dangers were not always obvious. Some clearly saw what was developing and chose to leave, which suited the Nazis. There was even a Nazi proposal to relocate Jews in Africa (Palestine was also considered). Himmler wrote, 'I hope to see the term "Jews" completely eliminated through the possibility of large- scale emigration of all Jews to Africa or some other colony.' (*Auschwitz, The Nazis and The Final Solution* p.45)

    As German forces moved across continental Europe during the war the Nazis began to seek out 'Lebensraum', or living space for German people. This necessitated displacing established populations and relocating them further to the east. Included among the large groups being relocated were Jews, who found they were being confined to ghettos with no citizen rights. For the Nazis this vast population became less manageable.

Hitler had made clear his thoughts about exterminating the Jews in a speech to the Reichstag in 1939. He was less open in public with this as a plan or clear policy, but it was discussed at high level with the Nazi leadership.

The Berlin-Wannsee Conference

The Protocol of the 20th January 1942 conference at Berlin-Wannsee, at which the chief of the Sicherheitpolizei, Reinhard Heydrich, and Adolf Eichmann of the Reichssicherheitshauptampt led the formal process of discussing and planning what would become known as 'The Final Solution of The Jewish Question'. This of course referred to the mass extermination of the Jews in Germany, the occupied lands, and other countries of Europe. Page 6 of that document contained a breakdown of the estimated populations of Jews in each country of Europe. The total estimated was 11 million, most of whom (80%) lived in Eastern Europe. This is an English translation of that page:

'Another possible solution of the problem has now taken the place of emigration, i.e. the evacuation of the Jews to the East, provided that the Führer gives the appropriate approval in advance. These actions are, however, only to be considered provisional, but practical experience is already being collected which is of the greatest importance in relation to the future final solution of the Jewish question. Approximately 11 million Jews will be involved in the final solution of the European Jewish question, distributed as follows among the individual countries:

COUNTRY	NUMBER
A. Germany proper	131,800
Austria	43,700
Eastern territories	420,000
German General Government	2,284,000
Bialystok	400,000
Protectorate Bohemia and Moravia	74,200
Estonia – free of Jews	
Latvia	3,500
Lithuania	34,000
Belgium	43,000
Denmark	5,600
France/ German occupied territory	165,000
France/unoccupied territory	700,000
Greece	69,600
Netherlands	160,800
Norway	1,300
B.	
Bulgaria	48,000
England	330,000
Finland	2,300
Ireland	4,000
Italy, including Sardinia	58,000
Albania	200
Croatia	40,000
Portugal	3,000
Romania including Bessarabia	342,000
Sweden	8,000
Switzerland	18,000
Serbia	10,000
Slovakia	88,000
Spain	6,000

Turkey (European portion)	55,500
Hungary	742,800
USSR	5,000,000
Ukraine	2,994,684
White Russia, excluding Bialystok	446,484

Total: over 11,000,000

The number of Jews given here for foreign countries includes, however, only those Jews who still adhere to the Jewish faith, since some countries still do not have a definition of the term 'Jew' according to racial principles.

The handling of the problem in the individual countries will meet with difficulties due to the attitude and outlook of the people there, especially in Hungary and Rumania. Thus, for example, even today the Jew can buy documents in Rumania that will officially prove his foreign citizenship.

The influence of Jews in all walks of life in the USSR is well known. Approximately five million Jews live in the European part of the USSR, in the Asian part scarcely ¼ million.'
(Translation source http://prorev.com/wannsee.htm)

***

There is an alarmingly clinical simplicity to the estimations offered. The Jews of Europe had become mere numbers – a population to be eradicated – rather than fellow human beings. They were a problem of a practical and an industrial nature, and the numbers in each country were of relevance purely because of the efforts and resources that would be required to eliminate them. For Hoess and others involved in the Final Solution it is highly probable that they had dehumanised Jews so much (after all they came from an anti-Semitic culture, and were governed by a class who enthusiastically sold this) that they almost certainly did not perceive that they were killing people or fellow human beings who were worthy of compassion, or life. That obviously does not excuse their actions (they are inexcusable) but may go some way to explain them. Of course the German anger at the defeat in 1918 and all that followed does not explain the complicity of conquered countries in anti-Semitism, or even the active participation of supposedly civilised British police and officials in the Channel Islands.

The horror and brutality of The Final Solution started off from humble beginnings of hatred, distrust, intolerance and scapegoating. Its beginnings were in established anti-Semitism in Germany and across Europe. The Nazis regime in Germany and the occupied territories did not create anti-Semitism. They had an intense hatred of Jews, but they did not initiate such views in others. Anti-Semitism was already rife. The Nazis took the hatred to an extreme level, but without the active cooperation, engagement, collusion and willing participation of others it could never have resulted in the nearly complete extermination of a whole population from across many countries.

When the world reflects on the Holocaust and subsequent genocides it is worth noting that soldiers are armed, and they fight, and they invade, and they conquer; but always at the behest of politicians and political leaders. Armies and politicians do not bear sole responsibility. The politicians are elected (except in totalitarian states) by the people, and the people are best positioned to replace or depose their leaders. They are also able to challenge wrongful deeds. Armies too, operate within rules, and must take responsibility for crimes committed during times of war or occupation. Germany, the German people, the German armed forces, and the Nazis all have responsibility for the crimes of the Holocaust, but so do those in the occupied lands who allowed the horror to take place, who did nothing, who were complicit by deed, or who enabled it by inaction.

***

CHAPTER SEVEN
JEWISH
RESISTANCE — LESSONS
IN COURAGE

It is an intriguing question (and for some Holocaust deniers a source of doubt) that Jews did not resist more; after all they often outnumbered their oppressors and guards. In truth there was a great deal of heroic overt and covert resistance. But we need to consider a number of factors that may have limited the potential to resist more effectively. Jews in Germany had ceased to enjoy the rights of citizenship long before the war. They were already a downtrodden and often an impoverished people. As Nazi power increased and expanded they were able to take away Jewish individuality more and more. The enforced rules and pass books, the wearing of a yellow Star of David, the closure of businesses, restrictions on movement, and loss of property, all contributed to turning people into a collective group rather than individuals. By the time the regime expanded into Poland and elsewhere they created ghettos, and had for a number of years been using concentration camps to contain political and other prisoners. The ghettos enforced containment, poverty, starvation and lack of freedom on a people already broken. Summary arrests and executions were commonplace which reinforced fear of resistance. When resistance did occur it was dealt with swiftly and violently. There was resistance – Warsaw is the best known example of a ghetto uprising - but it was often futile. One has to be aware that usually men and boys were the first to be selected for transportation. This left women, young children, the elderly, and the infirm, to fight to just survive. How could they resist with violence too? They were in ghettos and isolated from the outside world. They had little or no financial means beyond bartering personal belongings for essential food and clothing. To fight, they needed arms, ammunition and outside help. In Poland and elsewhere these could only be obtained from the local population who were often hostile to Jews, and would readily betray them to the Nazis if they showed any signs of resistance. By the time of the first transportations they knew the futility of fighting. Many of course also believed they were merely being relocated or being sent to work for the war effort and so arriving at a camp was thought of as just being part of that process.

Once at the camps (often after several days of travel in dreadful conditions) they were already broken further. They would emerge from a carriage to barking dogs, screamed orders, violence and mayhem. When told to do something, they did it. They were immediately divested of all remnants of personal identity. They were separated from loved ones. Those not sent immediately to their death were stripped, showered amongst hundreds of strangers, shaved, clothed in ill-fitting garb, and tattooed. Their identity had gone. They had become a number. They were ordered to roll calls at all hours and in all conditions. They slept in barracks they were sent to. They ate when permitted; they toileted when they were allowed. They spoke with permission. They worked until they dropped. They starved. They caught diseases, they died of illness, they were beaten, and some were killed in front of others, including public executions. Those without fight, who had given up, became 'Musselmanner' (German for Muslim-man based on the appearance of a Muslim at prayer) and were watched helplessly as they weakened, faded and died. Those who could do so 'organised', stole, and bartered, sometimes with items taken from the dead. And all the time there was the constant threat of selection and death. Any that lasted more than a few weeks would have known what fate awaited them. And in such poor physical and psychological health they would also have known that resistance was futile. Of course some did resist, and some opted for suicide by going to the electrified fences. Despite the dangers in the camps there was resistance. There was a notable uprising and escape from Sobibor that resulted in that camp having to be closed and destroyed by the Nazis. There were uprisings in Auschwitz-Birkenau by the Sonderkommando (including most famously the blowing up of crematoria) but they were publicly executed as a result. The Germans would also execute people who had not been involved in uprisings or resistance activities to send clear messages to other inmates of the fatal consequences of resistance. Former Auschwitz Camp Commandant Rudolf Hoess referred to the resistance in his evidence at the Nuremberg Trial in 1946 stating, "Still another improvement we made over Treblinka was that at Treblinka the victims almost always knew they were going to be exterminated, and at Auschwitz we endeavoured to fool the victims into thinking they were to go through a delousing process. Of course, frequently they realized our true intentions, and we sometimes had riots and difficulties due to that fact. Very frequently women would hide their children under the clothes, but of course when we found them we would send the children to be exterminated." He then added – as if this was needed – "We were required to carry out these exterminations in secrecy, but of course the foul and nauseating stench from the continuous burning of bodies permeated the entire area and all the people living in the surrounding communities knew the exterminations were going on at Auschwitz."

(Nuremberg Evil on Trial pp. 206)

But there was subtle and essential resistance too. The mere determination of many to live was resistance. Bartering, organising, and stealing all helped with survival. Deceit against the guards, covert contacts with other inmates, bending and breaking rules – all helped to sustain the human spirit

That the inmates actively resisted at all was a feat. They were in extremely poor mental and physical health. Added to the brutal conditions and fear of death there was the daily struggle just to survive. In psychology there is an old theory known as Maslow's Hierarchy of Needs. This is a theory proposed by Abraham Maslow in his 1943 paper '*A theory of Human Motivation*'. It is a simple but effective way of understanding our basic requirements for existence and success in life. When considered with the circumstances camp inmates faced it is clear how the lack of these essentials would have impacted upon them so greatly.

Physiological needs
The physical requirements for survival – air, water, food, clothing, warmth, shelter, sex, procreation.

Safety needs
This includes – personal security, financial security, health and well being, safety against accidents and illness etc.

Love and belonging
This includes – interpersonal needs, friendship, intimacy and family. People need a sense of belonging and acceptance among social groups whether they are large or small groups. People need to love and to be loved.

Esteem

This includes the premise that – all people need to have self-esteem and self-respect. They also need to feel accepted, respected and valued by others. Maslow suggested 'lower' esteem is respect from or by others, while 'higher' esteem is self-respect. Being deprived of these needs can lead to a sense of inferiority, weakness and helplessness.

Self-actualization

This states - "What a man can be, he must be". The need to recognise one's potential and to be able to aim to achieve it. Examples might include becoming a good parent or succeeding in work, sport or some other area.

Many of those who survived the camps had what would now be recognised as Post-Traumatic Stress Disorder. Sadly at the time this was not acknowledged. Most people are now familiar with the Post-Traumatic Stress Disorder or PTSD. It is commonly associated with soldiers returning from combat, or those who have been involved in major disasters. It actually afflicts many people, but in the 1940s it was not recognised. It would certainly not have been considered in camps like Auschwitz-Birkenau at the time of the Holocaust, and may well have been a factor in the apparent compliance of inmates. They were in effect broken as people. In very simple terms the symptoms of PTSD actually spell the word **TRAUMA**.

Traumatic events have occurred

Re-experience of traumatic events as intrusive thoughts, memories, nightmares or flashbacks

Avoidance of anything associated with the trauma and emotional numbing

Unable to function – significant social, occupational, and interpersonal impairment

Month – symptoms lasting for more than a month

Arousal – high arousal, startle reaction, poor concentration, irritability, insomnia, and hyper-vigilance.
(Taken from Dept. of Health and National Institute for Mental Health in England, *Understanding Childhood Sexual Abuse*)

For a more formal definition of PTSD, reference can be drawn from the *World Health Organisation's ICD-10 Classification of Mental and Behavioural Disorders*. It defines it as follows:

'This arises as a delayed and/or protracted response to a stressful event or situation (either short-or long-lasting) of an exceptionally threatening or catastrophic nature, which is likely to cause pervasive distress in almost anyone (e.g. natural or man-made disaster, combat, serious accident, witnessing the violent death of others, or being victim of torture, terrorism, rape, or other crime).' The first part of the clinical definition clearly applies to those who were victims of the camp brutality, whether or not they survived the war. The definition goes on to state:

'Typical symptoms include episodes of repeated reliving of the trauma in intrusive memories ('flashbacks') or dreams, occurring against the persisting background of a sense of 'numbness' and emotional blunting, detachment from other people, unresponsiveness to surroundings, 'anhedonia', or *inability to experience pleasure or interest in activities that would normally be pleasurable* (author's italics and explanation), and avoidance of activities and situations reminiscent of the trauma. Commonly there is fear and avoidance of cues that remind the sufferer of the original trauma. Rarely there may be dramatic, acute bursts of fear, panic or aggression, triggered by stimuli arousing a sudden recollection and/or re-enactment of the trauma or of the original reaction to it. There is usually a state of autonomic hyperarousal with hypervigilance, an enhanced startle reaction, and insomnia. Anxiety and depression are commonly associated with the above symptoms and signs, and suicidal ideation is not infrequent'.

The definition is clarified further with, 'The onset follows the trauma with a latency period which may range from a few weeks to months (but rarely exceeds 6 months). The course is fluctuating, but recovery can be expected in the majority of cases. In a small proportion of patients the condition may show a chronic course over many years and a transition to an enduring personality change.'
(World Health Organisation ICD-10 Classification of Mental and Behavioural Disorders)

This definition of PTSD, as understood by most, would seem to apply after, rather than during, the event. Certainly survivors of the Holocaust will have experienced various forms and severity of PTSD. Those in the camp who survived initial selection would undoubtedly have been traumatised. They had experienced a range of traumatic and violent events from the initial transport, to selections and separation from loved ones, to witnessing brutality and death, through to the brutal cruelty of daily life.

For those to whom the PTSD diagnosis does not fit there are other diagnostic possibilities. One to be considered would be 'Adjustment Disorder' which is defined as 'States of subjective distress and emotional disturbance, usually interfering with social functioning and performance, and arising in the period of adaptation to a significant life change or to the consequences of a stressful life event (including the presence or possibility of serious physical illness). The stressor may have affected the integrity of an individual's social network (through bereavement or separation experiences) or the wider system of social supports and values (migration or refugee status). The stressor may involve only the individual or also his or her group or community.' *(World Health Organisation ICD-10 Classification of Mental and Behavioural Disorders).* There were certainly significant adjustment difficulties for camp inmates of a severity that the normal healthy mind, unaccustomed to such trauma and changes, would find difficult to cope with. It is highly likely that many inmates would have had needs that fulfil the criteria for Adjustment Disorder.

Yet another of the many diagnostic possibilities associated with camp life would be depression. In the *ICD-10* there are sub-categories of depression which for simplicity will be limited here to mild, moderate, and severe where it is stated in general terms that 'the individual usually suffers from depressed mood, loss of interest and enjoyment, and reduced energy leading to increased fatigability and diminished activity. Marked tiredness after only slight effort is common. Other common symptoms are:
(a) Reduced concentration and attention;
(b) Reduced self-esteem and self-confidence;
(c) Ideas of guilt and unworthiness (even in a mild type of episode);
(d) Bleak and pessimistic views of the future;
(e) Ideas or acts of self-harm or suicide;
(f) Disturbed sleep;
(g) Diminished appetite.
During a severe episode it is very unlikely that the sufferer will be able to continue with social, work, or domestic activities, except to a very limited extent'. (*World Health Organisation ICD-10 Classification of Mental and Behavioural Disorders*).

One does not need to be a mental health specialist to see how one, some, or all of these three diagnostic possibilities could apply to those living as inmates in the camps and to those who survived. There are multiple other possible diagnoses throughout the *ICD-10*. When one considers the presentation and demeanour of the inmates referred to as 'Musselmanner' it is clear how it can be concluded that they may have been mentally ill as well as physically ill, and suffering from starvation.

Levels of malnutrition in the camps were severe. What diet inmates received was barely enough to sustain life. Watery 'soup', small pieces of black bread, and a beverage called coffee but lacking in caffeine, was all that was on offer. The normal resting adult uses seventy five percent of their calories merely in keeping alive – breathing, digestion, heart activity, thought, urine production, cell replacement etc. So the poor diet was not enough to allow even those essentials to occur without the body having to eat into fat reserves, muscle tissue, and bone marrow. The inmates were also expected to work. They did this in freezing temperatures in winter, and searing heat in summer. To cope with the weather extremes their bodies would try to generate heat by shivering, or to cool down by perspiration. Those automatic responses would in turn use up valuable energy. Malnourishment slows down the metabolism. If insufficient nutrition is ingested the body effectively cannibalises itself by eating away at reserves. Muscles on limbs waste away, and the muscle of the heart similarly shrinks. All bodily functions slow down as a means of survival. Some functions cease – women stop menstruating to lessen the chance of pregnancy. A starving body cannot sustain itself, let alone another life. Generalised weakness and lethargy follow. Cognitive or thinking processes become impaired. Simple decision-making becomes difficult. Depression and pervasively low mood occur, which can result in suicidal thoughts and acts, or simply overwhelming and unshakeable feelings of hopelessness, worthlessness and despondency.

In extreme cases, delirium is manifested, and the malnourished person can lose some awareness of the reality that others perceive. Resistance to disease decreases and infections set in. Some infections that would be dealt with easily when in good health become fatally dangerous. Common colds, chest infections, and diarrhoea all became killers. Many of the diseases found in Auschwitz such as typhus and dysentery, were known killers even without weakened hosts waiting to be infected. The bodies of camp inmates were so frail that when allied forces arrived many of those who had survived were killed due to eating more nutrition than their bodies could cope with. This is now recognised as 'Re-Feeding Syndrome'. Sadly it was not something known of at the time. That so many died when being given normal amounts of food and drink is evidence of how desperately malnourished the camp inmates were. These levels of starvation, weakness and disease only go to emphasise the incredible and phenomenal reality that many could and did resist the cruelty of camp life and Nazi brutality.

The impact of life in the camps is sometimes referred to as 'KZ Syndrome' (after the German Konzentrationslager) or 'Concentration Camp Syndrome'. This describes a range of physical and psychological impacts associated with incarceration in circumstances of extreme cruelty and brutality. It is used in reference to other survivor groups and even individuals. More properly it is now more appropriately known as 'PTSD', but it is interesting to refer to in its own right. Extensive details of research into the mental health of Auschwitz survivors can be found in *Auschwitz Survivors, Clinical-Psychiatric Studies*, which has contributions and research from a number of eminent Polish psychiatrists. Dr Antoni Kepinski (1918 – 1972), was a Professor of Psychiatry and Chair of Psychiatry at the Academy of Medicine in Krakow. He was also a former concentration camp prisoner. He wrote a paper entitled *The So-Called 'KZ-Syndrome' – An Attempt at Synthesis*. In that paper he stated, 'There are limits to human experience, which cannot be gone beyond without impunity. If the border is crossed, there is no way back to the previous life. Something in the basic structure is changed: one is not the same as before. This otherness is usually referred to as 'personality

change' and in the case of schizophrenia the technical term 'defect' is used, not very appropriate for man. Personality changes observed in former prisoners refer to three areas:
1. 'General life dynamic', that is, subjectively perceived as a frame of mind,
2. Attitude towards people and
3. Ability to restrain oneself'.

    He adds further that, 'Every man has his 'small islands' of recollections, which are present even against his will. The island may be various, greater and smaller, nice and ugly. They appear to accompany a given mood and situation and sometimes they come back without any reason. For former prisoners, their camp experiences are a great island, too great to allow them to see the rest of the world, so great that the small islands look unimportant. The island has become their main point of reference in their post-camp life. It has changed their attitude to life, their hierarchy of values, relationships with people, and influenced their life purposes; it comes back in dreams with an agonising regularity. It is impossible to leave this island.'
(As cited in *Auschwitz Survivors, Clinical-Psychiatric Studies,* Przeglad Lekarski 2013 pp. 165 -166)

    Of course, this describes PTSD but it encompasses a range of other mental disorders that are apparent with some of those who lived through and survived the hardships of camp life.
    As a modern point of reference, in the television age, we can see images on news channels most weeks of war- ravaged refugees in Third World transit camps or in war-torn, far-off lands - large groups of bewildered people resigned to whatever fate has destined for them. Or we can take our minds back but a few years to the famine in Ethiopia that resulted in *Live Aid*. We

saw thousands of starving and diseased individuals who were too weak to do anything apart from await death. In Auschwitz and other camps such starvation was enforced, and the inmates – in that dreadfully broken state of health – were expected to work and respond to the harshest of regime orders.

One has to wonder how those who survived managed when the accepted ideals for life were removed. Kitty Hart-Moxon is a well-known survivor who has provided detailed accounts of her experiences as an inmate of Auschwitz and on the Death March. She is an incredibly impressive woman, and has dedicated much of her life to educating and informing about the Holocaust, based on her own personal experiences. It is recommended that those wanting to fully appreciate the nature of survival against the odds should read Kitty's book *Return to Auschwitz*, or better still, attend one of her lectures. As Kitty says, 'to survive, the essentials are as of all animals – firstly one must get away from the predator, and then as long as one has food, water, air, clothes, shoes and a lavatory; one can survive.' Kitty and other survivors have a modesty that prevents them stating the obvious about the other key essential which was, and is, strength of mind and spirit. To meet a Holocaust survivor is a humbling experience.

The greatest factor by far in controlling inmates was the dehumanization, the loss of their individuality, and the loss of their mental and physical ability to resist. Former Auschwitz inmate Primo Levy wrote eloquently in his poem 'If This is a Man':

> *You who live safe*
> *In your warm houses,*
> *You who find, returning in the evening,*
> *Hot food and friendly faces:*
> *Consider if this is a man*
> *Who works in the mud*

Who does not know peace
Who fights for a scrap of bread
Who dies because of a yes or a no.
Consider if this is a woman,
Without hair and without name
With no more strength to remember,
Her eyes empty and her womb cold
Like a frog in winter.
Meditate that this came about:
I commend these words to you,
Carve them in your hearts
At home, in the street,
Going to bed, rising;
Repeat them to your children,
Or may your house fall apart,
May illness impede you,
May your children turn their faces from you.

In the more detailed book also entitled '*If This is a Man*' Primo Levi describes the very basics of survival through determination and resistance of resolve and ingenuity. 'One learns quickly enough to wipe out the past and the future when one is forced to. A fortnight after my arrival I already had the prescribed hunger, that chronic hunger unknown to free men, which makes one dream at night, and settles in all the limbs of one's body. I have already learnt not to let myself be robbed, and in fact, if I find a spoon lying around, a piece of string, a button which I can acquire without danger of punishment, I pocket them and consider them mine by full right.' He elaborates further on the physical discomfort: 'On the back of my feet I have those numb sores that will not heal. I push wagons, I work with a shovel, I turn rotten in the rain, I shiver in the wind; already my own body is no longer mine; my belly is swollen, my limbs emaciated, my face is thick in the morning, hollow in the evening, some of us have yellow skin, others grey. When we don't meet for a few days we hardly recognize each other.' (Primo Levi *If This is a Man* p. 43).

Levi describes the methodical practices of control used in his book *The Drowned And The Saved*, and how such methods helped to break resistance from the moment of arrival at the camps, or 'lager' as he refers to them. 'Various aspects can be identified in this aggression. It is necessary to remember that the 'concentrationary' system even from the origins (which coincide with the rise to power of Nazism in Germany) had the primary purpose of shattering the adversaries' capacity to resist: for the camp management, the new arrival was an adversary by definition, whatever the label attached to him might be, and must immediately be demolished to make sure that he did not become an example or a germ of organised resistance. On this point the SS had very clear ideas, and it is from this viewpoint that the entire sinister ritual there must be interpreted – varying from lager to lager, but basically similar – which accompanied the arrival: kicks and punches right away, often in the face, an orgy of orders screamed with true or simulated rage; complete nakedness after being stripped; the shaving off of all one's hair; the fitting out in rags. It is difficult to say whether all of these details were devised by some expert or methodically perfected on the basis of experience, but they certainly were willed and not casual: it was all staged, and this was quite obvious.' (Primo Levi *The Drowned and the Saved* p.24)

Amongst the inmate ranks were prisoners involved in control and in the running of the various activities. The 'Kapos' (fellow inmates, who were often prisoners in the camps for crimes of violence), sometimes Jews, or others who merely wanted to stay alive, were involved in policing, sharing and gathering intelligence, dispensing food, and running barracks and work groups. The Sonderkommando had a short life expectancy, particularly those working at the gas chambers and crematoria. The camps contained a weakened population, policed by complicit fellow inmates, and with enthusiastic participation in acts of brutal cruelty by people other than Germans. It's no great surprise that a few hundred armed guards could contain and control a camp like Auschwitz-Birkenau even when it contained many thousands of inmates. One has to remember the inmates had the will and desire to resist, and would have resisted more, but how could they, in all circumstances, resist guards with machine guns who were more than willing to kill them, when they had only resolve and empty hands with which to fight?

Some inmates survived by doing what they needed to do. The Sonderkommando followed orders they found repugnant and instinctively wrong. They would assist in the killing process and the disposal of bodies. They would search the corpses of the dead – including the bodies of people that they knew - looking for concealed contraband. They did this knowing that to refuse would result in instant death, and knowing that very shortly they too would be entering the gas chambers to be killed. When the Sonderkommando resisted, sometimes violently by armed rebellion and blowing up crematoria, they were dealt with summarily and brutally. The Sonderkommando at Auschwitz did stage an infamous revolt on 7th October 1944. Some of them had been planning a revolt since June with the help of an underground resistance movement led by Yaakov Kaminski. Planning any organised rebellion was difficult due to the phenomenally high mortality rate, the layout of the camp, the security, and the risks of Kapos revealing the plot to the guards. Unfortunately, the SS learned about the plans. Kaminski was informed upon and killed. Some of the conspirators survived and continued to 'organise' weapons. The breaking-point for many of the Sonderkommando came the day before the actual revolt. A request went out for volunteers to join Otto Moll, a notorious SS overseer of crematoria, who had become commandant of the sub- camp at Gwilice. They knew this was not what it seemed to be. The last group of Sonderkommando selected to work in another camp were killed by the SS, and their bodies were burnt in Crematorium II. The next day some of the Sonderkommando recognised the half burnt bodies of their former colleagues. They knew they were also likely to be executed, so at 1.30 p.m. on 7th October the rebellion began. Armed with rudimentary weapons the Sonderkommando at Crematorium IV mutinied. They attacked the SS and set fire to the crematorium. Some of the Sonderkommando escaped and fled to nearby woodland before reaching the village of Rajsko. Unfortunately, this was still well within the secure area of Auschwitz. At about the same time the Sonderkommando at Crematorium II also fought against the SS and shoved one of the guards alive into one of the ovens. Approximately 250 Sonderkommando were killed during the revolt. Three members of the SS died. All of those who escaped were captured and shot. Any who were believed to have been involved in the plot were also killed. In total this was another 200 inmates slain (as described in *Auschwitz, The Nazis, & The Final Solution* pp. 322-324).

Inmates learned to steal and barter. They learned subterfuge. They learned to be deceitful. They learned to cheat death by any means possible. They learned quickly that their fate rested largely in their own hands, but that ultimately they could be selected for death on a whim, or that they could be placed on a work force with a poor survival rate. The heavier the work, the quicker people died. Outdoor work would kill more quickly than indoor work, particularly in winter. Jobs that seemed dangerous such as emptying latrines filled with human faeces and urine, were actually good jobs because they were inside and protected from the elements; and the Nazis - fearing the risks from infected faeces – left them alone.

Inmates learned to use the dead for their own survival. A dead person had no need for clothes, or shoes, or a bowl and spoon, or for hidden food. These were all things that the living could use to improve their own chances. The skills and resources to survive had to be learned quickly. If an inmate had no bowl with which to wash, or to use as a toilet, or from which to eat food, they would die. Others could not help because they too wanted to live. The fortunate few had family and friends to support them, and act as allies in the quest for life. Most inmates were isolated and on their own. Those who were alone, who had no obvious allegiances, camaraderie, or support, were likely to die sooner.

When considering the volume of odds stacked against inmates it is quite incredible that any survived. There was hostility from the environment, the guards, the system, and the elements. There was the constant threat of physical violence and summary execution. There was the ever- present risk of selection. There was poor mental health, poor physical health, malnutrition, diseases, infestations with lice, robbery, and theft from other inmates. There was the inhumane workload, long hours, poor work conditions, and hostility from those who ran the work Kommandos. And of course there was a system – a barbaric system beyond comprehension today – that had as its primary objective the wholesale murder of millions.

CHAPTER EIGHT
SURVIVOR ACCOUNTS

Oxford English Dictionary: 'Survivor: noun. A person who survives, especially a person remaining alive after an event in which others have died.'

How limited a noun is 'survivor' when used with reference to those who lived through so much! Those who emerged alive at the end of the Second World War from the camps in Europe did so much more than merely survive. But for now 'survivor' is probably the best the English language has to offer. This book has already addressed some of the hardships experienced and each of those individual events would be a major trauma for most people. The isolation, poverty, and loss of basic citizen rights, physical and verbal assaults, transportations, being sent to ghettos, living through the ghettos, more violence, the threat of death at the hands of another, or through disease and starvation; the loss of loved ones, constant fear, selections, more transportations, arriving at camps, more selections, seeing loved ones taken away, being housed in unfamiliar surroundings; slave labour, famine, more disease, roll calls, violence, summary executions, selections, seeing death daily … the list is inexhaustible and – were it not for the proof of history – it would be unbelievable. No scholarly account, or history book, or film, or other work, can properly address survival in a way that compares to personal accounts. There is also a power in the personal reflections and observations of those who were there that cannot be conveyed or matched by any amount of reading, study, and research. It is therefore only right that some of those accounts are referred to here, as to do otherwise would deny the voices to those who are the witnesses of history.

It would be easy to just cherry-pick general points from various recorded accounts, but that would be a disservice to survivors. Only a few thousand survivors were found in Auschwitz at the time of liberation in January 1945. Many thousands more had been moved earlier, and had either been sent to other camps, or forced on the many death marches.

The greatest tribute to the survivors is their very existence. That so many – despite phenomenal odds – emerged at the end of the war, having survived the brutalities of camp life, is astonishing. It is a credit to their fortitude and resolve. It is also in no small part due to pure good luck – although 'luck' as a word can unintentionally appear to cheapen their experiences. Thousands survived the many camps. A number of Auschwitz inmates survived because they had been relocated weeks, months, or years before the liberation. Some survived the death marches that preceded the arrival of Soviet forces. Some of course were liberated at Auschwitz or at other camps. That any survived, given the poor health and pitiful state they were found in, is somewhat miraculous. But they did survive. The journey after liberation varied from individual to individual, and depended in part on where they were liberated from, and by which of the allied forces they were assisted. All survivors were devastated by their experiences. Many had lost the majority, if not all of their family members and loved ones. For many, returning to their original homes was not an option. Those homes had been occupied by others, and were in places that remained hostile. As we have already stated, anti-Semitism was not exclusively the preserve of Germans and the Nazis. It was a phenomenon across Europe. Were survivors to return to their home hamlets, villages, towns, and cities, they would have found themselves unwelcome, and at risk of harm. Past lives for many were something to leave behind and move on from. And so the survivors spread far and wide, to Palestine, America, Australasia, South Africa, Great Britain and elsewhere. A new Diaspora was created from the horror of war that bore no comparison to the Jewish population that had lived, traded, thrived, and at times suffered for two thousand years in Europe.

Modern Jews have their own established state. There continue to be disputes about Israel, and it is a territory marred by conflict with neighbours and ongoing criticism about how some of the non-Jews within and near to its borders are treated. Issues about Israel will not be debated here. It is suffice to observe that whatever some people may feel about Israel there is little debate that it is a strong, confident, and powerful country that Jews identify as their own land. Those Jews who survived and remained in Europe, or who migrated to other lands, bore the scars of the Holocaust, and had a determination to ensure that anti-Semitism could never again rise to the levels of social acceptability and terror that can lead to the death of millions. They also sought – quite understandably – to ensure that as a people, as a faith, and as survivors, their community and their descendants were secure. The United Nations (UN) and North Atlantic Treaty Organization (NATO) in a great part are founded as a consequence of what happened in Europe. The Universal Declaration of Human Rights, the European Convention of Human Rights and The Human Rights Act all owe their existence to a determination that 'genocide-never again' should be a pledge stated in law. The unity between European nations through trade and politics is linked to the shared shame and fear of war, and the need to ensure cooperation between states rather than conflict. When the far right gain political successes or broad public support the voices of opposition are loud and powerful. The United States is pledged to support Israel, and many other countries have a similar determination to protect that state. Whether countries are for or against Israel they still recognise why it was established, and share a common purpose to act and prevent further genocides. The descendants of Holocaust survivors, and of those who fought in the Second World War, all recognise the need to act now rather than to wait until it is too late. Sadly, other genocides have happened since, but at least the international community is generally inclined to act positively rather than to simply ignore the wholesale slaughter and suffering of innocents.

All those who survived the Holocaust carried an emotional baggage of huge trauma, and experiences beyond the comprehension of others. Many found that in the new lands they moved to, where they often stayed with distant relatives, or within established Jewish communities, they were actually forbidden to talk about the camps, the ghettos, the slaughter, and the Holocaust. The memories became locked away secrets held only in the mind of the survivor and a select few confidantes. Some, as this author can testify, became mentally ill. But they merely joined a community of other mentally ill people, and the uniqueness of their experiences became insignificant in the care that they received. They were just other patients among many in the large asylums that housed lunatics in the post-war years. Some, through choice, decided not to tell anyone, and even their spouses, children, and grandchildren, knew nothing of what they had lived through.

Thankfully, for us who live today, and for generations in the future, some chose to talk and to record their experiences for posterity. There are now many hundreds of survivor accounts in books and articles. The world is willing and keen to listen. Centres, museums, and organizations around the globe are dedicated to recording and documenting survivor stories. Many survivors, despite (or because of) advancing years, are determined to inform others through writings, lectures, television documentaries, and films. Their accounts, even seventy years after the liberation of Auschwitz, are of immense historical importance.

There are many well-written personal survivor accounts. Some have made films, and have contributed in other ways to the recorded history of the Holocaust. Each account is powerful, and relays to us today the enormity of what happened within living memory. Every account is unique, but there are abundant similarities in how the hardship, cruelty, deprivation, brutality, callousness, and casual disregard for human life have been documented. Each account also tells of resilience, determination, resistance, resolve, fortitude, and hope. No one – no matter how well- read, well-researched, well-meaning, or well-informed – can convey these accounts with the same clarity and power as those who lived through them can. It is therefore only right and proper that this section is given over to parts of selected personal accounts that are available in the public domain. The original writers of these selected accounts will be cited out of respect for their words, and out of an even greater respect for those survivors not named. No one account is more worthy than another. And the accounts referred to herein are chosen because they are examples this writer has found useful or because of personal meetings and correspondence with the survivors. It is strongly recommended that efforts are made by readers of this book to obtain and read the full accounts referred to. Those accounts are of immense historical importance, and it is any scholar's privilege to read them. It can also not be recommended or stressed enough that all who are able to should seek out survivor accounts, and if at all possible attend any centre or event at which a survivor is talking. At the very least we owe survivors our attention, and willingness to listen. If we fail to do that, we fail to honour history.

Primo Levi

For many people the first accounts they read in the years following the war was the work of Primo Levi in his books *If This is a Man*, *The Truce*, and *The Drowned* and *The Saved*. Levi, an Italian Jew, was born in Turin in 1919, and trained as a chemist. Tragically, he took his own life in 1987. He was arrested during the war due to his involvement with partisan anti-Fascist activity, and was transported to Auschwitz. Following his death *The Guardian* newspaper said: 'The death of Primo Levi robs Italy of one of its finest writers … one of the few survivors of the Holocaust to speak of his experiences with a gentle voice.' It is that gentle voice that grabs the reader. He speaks not of anger, or the need for revenge. He does not seek to forgive his former oppressors. He seeks to understand those who imprisoned him, who inflicted unspeakable cruelty, and who took the lives of so many innocents. His lack of obvious anger or bitter condemnation is a source of surprise to some. His works are articulate in quality, and present a humanity and observation that at times belies the brutality of camp life and the bestial cruelty it involved. He writes of the inmates:

'There comes to light the existence of two particularly well- differentiated categories among men – the saved and the drowned. Other pairs of opposites (the good and the bad, the wise and the foolish, the cowards and the courageous, the unlucky and the fortunate) are considerably less distinct, they seem less essential, and above all they allow for more numerous and complex intermediary gradations.' (If This is a Man pp. 93 & 94)

Of life in the lager he states:

'Here the struggle to survive is without respite, because everyone is desperately and ferociously alone. If some 'Null Achtzehn' (meaning 'Zero Eighteen', or, he doesn't exist any more) vacillates, he will find no one to extend a helping hand; on the contrary, someone will knock him aside, because it is in no one's interest that there will be one more 'musselman'* dragging himself to work every day; and if someone, by a miracle of savage patience and cunning, finds a new method of avoiding the hardest work, a new art which yields him an ounce of bread, he will try to keep this method secret, and he will be esteemed and respected for this, and will derive from it an exclusive, personal benefit; he will become stronger and so will be feared, and who is feared is, ipso facto, a candidate for survival.' (If This is a Man p. 94)

*Musselman, or Musselmanner was used in the camps to describe those who had become so ill, so weak, so discased, so mentally spent, that they had given up all hope, and all resistance. It is a word derived from the German for Muslim man, and is believed to describe the look of a Muslim at prayer. Those deemed to be Musselman were usually beyond all hope of survival. Most accounts by survivors refer to the phenomenon of Musselman.

Levi describes the attitude of civilians towards him and his fellow inmates: 'In fact, we are the *untouchables* to the civilians. They think, more or less explicitly – with all the nuances lying between contempt and commiseration – that as we have been condemned to this life of ours, reduced by our condition, we must be tainted by some mysterious, grave sin. They hear us speak in many languages, which they do not understand and which sound to them as grotesque as animal noises; they see us reduced to ignoble slavery, without hair, without honour and without names, beaten every day, more abject every day, and they never see in our eyes a light of rebellion, or of peace, or of faith. They know us as thieves and untrustworthy, muddy, ragged and starving, and mistaking the effect for the cause, they judge us worthy of our abasement. Who could tell one of our faces from the other? For them we are 'Kazett', a singular neuter word.' (*If This is a Man* pp. 126 &127)

Levi's account of 26th January 1945 (the day before Auschwitz was liberated) is incredibly moving. He and his fellow inmates had all but given up on life. He writes:

'We lay in a world of death and phantoms. The last trace of civilization had vanished around and inside us. The work of bestial degradation, begun by the victorious Germans, had been carried to its conclusion by the Germans in defeat. It is man who kills, man who creates or suffers injustice; it is no longer man who, having lost all restraint, shares his bed with a corpse. Whoever waits for his neighbour to die in order to take his piece of bread is, albeit guiltless, further from the model of thinking man than the most primitive pygmy or the most vicious sadist.' (*If This is a Man* pp. 177 & 178)

In *The Drowned and The Saved* Levi addresses the lies and excuses of his former oppressors, the denial of wrongdoing, and their minimization and attempts to absolve themselves of responsibility. He quite properly indulges his right to be critical:

'No one will ever be able to establish with precision how many, in the Nazi apparatus, could not **not** know (Levi's emphasis) about the frightful *atrocities that were being committed; how many knew something but were in a position to pretend they did not know; and, further, how many had the possibility of knowing everything, but chose the more prudent path of keeping their eyes and their ears (and more importantly their mouths) well shut. Whatever the case, since one cannot suppose that the majority of Germans light-heartedly accepted the slaughter, it is certain that the failure to divulge the truth about the lagers represents one of the major collective crimes of the German people, and the most obvious demonstration of the cowardice to which Hitlerian terror had reduced them: a cowardice which became an integral part of the mores, and so profound as to prevent husbands from telling their wives, parents their children. Without this cowardice the greatest excesses would not have been carried out, and Europe and the world would be different today.'* (*The Drowned and the Saved* p.4)

Levi observes with controlled anger some thoughts on the complicit and active involvement of German industry in the slave labour and cruelty of the camps. *I G Farben* was of course the main industry to benefit directly from the ready supply of labour from Auschwitz. But as Levi states (and other survivors and historical accounts can verify):

'Willed ignorance and fear also led many potential 'civilian' witnesses of the infamies of the Lagers to remain silent. Especially during the last few years of the war, the lagers constituted an extensive and complex system, which profoundly penetrated the daily life of the country; one has with good reason spoken of the *univers concentrationnaire* (his italics), but it was not a closed universe. Small and large industrial companies, agricultural combines, agencies and arms factories drew profits from the practically free labour supplied by the camps. Some exploited the prisoners pitilessly, accepting the inhuman (and also stupid) principle of the SS, according to which one prisoner was worth another, and if the work killed him, he could be immediately replaced; others, a few, cautiously tried to alleviate their sufferings. Still other industries – or perhaps the same ones – made money out of supplying the lagers themselves: lumber, building materials, the cloth for the prisoners' striped uniforms, the dehydrated vegetables for the soup, etc. The crematoria ovens themselves were designed, built, assembled and tested by a German company, *Topf* of Wiesbaden. (It was still in operation in 1975, building crematoria for civilian use, and had not considered the advisability of changing its name.) It is hard to believe that the personnel of these companies did not realize the significance of the quality and quantity of the merchandise and installations that were commissioned by the SS command units. The same can be said, and has been said, with regard to the poison employed in the gas chambers at Auschwitz: the product, substantially hydrocyanic acid, had already been used for many years for pest control in the holds of boats, but the abrupt increase in orders beginning with 1942 could scarcely go unnoticed. It must have aroused doubts, and certainly did arouse them, but they were stifled by fear, the desire for profit, the blindness and will stupidity that we have mentioned, and in some cases (probably few) by fanatical Nazi obedience.' (*The Drowned and the Saved* p.5)

It is doubtful if any survivor, before or since, has written with such poetic and articulate passion as Primo Levi. Sadly he remained a tormented man who took his own life 42 years after being liberated from Auschwitz.

Sam Pivnik

Sam Pivnik was born in 1926 in Bedzin in south western Poland. In 1943 Sam and his family were sent to Birkenau. There his parents, two sisters, and three brothers were murdered. He was eventually liberated from Neustadt in May 1945 by British forces. He moved to the UK and at the time of writing still lives in London. In 2012 his book '*Survivor - Auschwitz, The Death March and My Fight for Freedom*' was published. He was assisted in writing it by M J Trow. It is a powerful and moving account of the German invasion of Poland, the cruelty and control inflicted on the residents of his home town, of capture and transport to Auschwitz, and of his experiences of cruelty and suffering in the camp, and on the Death March.

Sam describes how his life changed forever on his thirteenth birthday when the Nazis invaded Poland. For those who fail to understand the power and control exercised by an occupying army he writes, using vivid imagery.

'*I remember very clearly Friday 8th September. That was the day the Einsatzgruppen (German for 'task forces', 'deployment groups') arrived. We had no name for them and no idea what the precise mission was that they were undertaking. Most of them looked like policemen in a sort of combat uniform. Others had Wehrmacht uniforms but they somehow looked different, with black epaulettes and collar flashes. They wore eagle badges on their sleeves and they turned up in the usual motley crew of motorcycles, trucks and jeeps. These were the execution squads, the men tasked by the Nazi high command with systematic attacks on my people. This particular unit I now know was commanded by SS-Obergruppenfuhrer Udo von Woyrsch, a Silesian nobleman who had been a member of the Nazi party for years. The gruppe was about two thousand strong, made up of that peculiar combination which characterised these units. They were all members of the Sicherheitsdienst, the various police departments called Gestapo, Kripo and Ordo. They were ordered by Heinrich Himmler, head of the SS, to spread fear and terror throughout the Katowice area. They were the beginning of what the world has come to know as the Holocaust.*'

Sam describes how throughout the afternoon and evening there were the sounds of gunfire and the smell of burning. Eventually a few days later the Pivnik family ventured out from the safety of their home.

'The sight we saw was almost unimaginable. All weekend the Einsatzgruppen had been carrying out their mission, and the results were everywhere. There were bodies lying in the streets, sprawled in the agony of death, rivulets of their blood a rusty brown in the gutters. I had never seen a dead body before and these were people I knew – neighbours and family friends who days ago had been carrying out their work and going about their business without, I now realises, a real care in the world. Most of them were elderly Jews, easily identifiable by their devout traditional clothes and hats – the easiest targets for the rifle butts and bullets of the Einsatzgruppen. It would be a comfort to think that these men died quickly, but I don't think it was like that. They would have been taunted, humiliated and slapped around first, kicked to the ground, and shot where they lay – the bruises on their blackening faces were testimony to that.'

In these few sentences Sam describes the onset of Nazi terror. He adds:

'The most ghastly sight I remember was that of Jews hanging from the trees that grew in the square, black coated men who looked like some ghastly parody of Christmas tree decorations. I remember how still they looked, their hands and feet dangling, their bodies at the mercy of the weather ... Only God knows how many people died in Bedzin that weekend, and it was not only Jews who died.'

Sam discusses the deportations, and his first experience of transports. He is aware in hindsight that Nazi policy towards 'The Jewish Question' often changed. At one point they had considered relocating Jews to Madagascar. Then the policy was to move them to the East, but obviously for Poles, as far as the Nazis were concerned, they were already in the East until the Soviet Union could be conquered and provide more space. Deportations became a part of daily life.

'By May or June 1942, we noticed another change. It wasn't just the young, active men who were appearing on the lists of the Judenrat (councils of Jewish elders), it was the old and the crippled, the people who needed all the help society could give them. Except that society wasn't giving them any help at all. Old ladies with their 'sheitels', their traditional black wigs; old men with no teeth and people with an artificial arm or leg; those confined to wheelchairs; the blind. They were expendable, all of them surplus to requirements in the brave new world Hitler and Himmler were cooking up between them.'

Sam describes how by 1942, at the age of fifteen, he and others were beginning to understand the purpose of the frequent selections and transportations, and they had already heard of Belsen, Treblinka and Sobibor. 'More and more in the summer of 1942 there was talk of the camp at Oswiecim which the Germans called Auschwitz. It wasn't far away, and people knew people who knew people. There was talk of a little white house where Jews were sent to be killed. But that was nonsense, surely. This was the 1940s, the twentieth century; things like that had happened in the dark ages under madmen like Genghis Khan and Timer I Leng. People who whispered those things must be idiots.'

Sam talks about a major '*Aktion*' (term used for any non-military campaign to further Nazi ideals of race, but most often referred to the assembly and deportation of Jews to concentration or death camps) when all Jews of the area were rounded up and moved to a football field. He estimated that there were 20,000 there. This was his first

159

experience of an SS selection. 'Shortly before midday, an SS officer made an announcement over the tannoy system and the muttered hubbub fell into silence. We were told a selection was to be made – the first time I had come across the idea. We were all to be divided into three groups. Essential workers, Group A, would stay here in Bedzin, Group B would be sent to the labour camps. Group C – and in German it sounded even more sinister, would be *'umgeseidelt im Osten'* – resettled in the East.' Those who stayed in Bedzin were moved to a ghetto area. The Jews in the Bedzin ghetto stole and resisted as best they could. They were aware of uprising in the Warsaw ghetto in April 1942 which gave them hope. The Nazis had learned from that experience and in all probability already had plans for Bedzin. In late July the Nazis started the clearance. The Pivnik family hid in their home but from their confined space they could see the street outside and the brutality of the SS action. They hid for days in the sweltering summer heat. Eventually they ran out of water. To go and find water would have been fatal. Sam recalls his mother sprinkling some sugar into a cup containing liquid, and then the cup was passed around. The liquid was urine. It took the Nazis just four days to liquidate the Bedzin ghetto. The Pivniks joined a column of Jews leaving the town. He remembered some local Gentiles jeering and mocking, while others were in tears. They were marched to the train station where SS guards screamed orders and insults. They all stood in silence. Anyone who spoke was hit. Eventually the train arrived, and they were forced aboard with accompanying kicks, hits, and insults from the SS. After a journey of about an hour they reached their destination:

'*I could see rows of upright concrete posts, curving inwards at the top, and rows of barbed wire strung between them. Beyond that were more rows, this time of low, single- storey huts. This was a camp, probably, we all* told ourselves, one of the labour camps they'd been sending Bedziners to for months. There was a screech of brakes and the carriage doors were thrown open. 'Raus! Raus!' I hadn't appreciated how guttural and heartless the German language sounded until I heard it on that platform. We scrabbled together our few belongings and stumbled onto the concrete, blinking in the sunlight. There was a wall of noise – a voice snarling orders over a loudspeaker system, guards in the uniform of the Waffen-SS pushing and prodding with their guns, big dogs on chain leashes growling and barking, their teeth bared, their hair standing on end.

It was difficult to tell who was more rabid – the dogs or their handlers. But it was the other men who fascinated me. I'd seen the SS and their outfits before, but these people wore prison clothing, with vertical stripes of blue and dirty white that looked like pyjamas, and they were yelling at us too. They told us to leave our luggage, to put it there on the Rampe. We'd get it later, they said, and they told us to line up. We were all numb with shock. What kind of camp was this? My father stood with his mouth open, frowning, trying to make some sort of sense of what was happening.'

He describes how one of his neighbours tried to get some answers, and spoke to one of the men in striped trousers. From nowhere he brought a wooden club down on his head, and shouted at him to shut up and do as he was told … '*And then, as if to emphasise that might is right, he gave him a thump with the stick, calling him between blows, a filthy fucking Jew.*' The man who had asked the question was now lying on the floor bleeding and gasping in shock. Sam had a slightly different encounter when a man in striped pyjamas whispered to him, "Tell them you're eighteen."

They began to be lined up in columns, and suffered further blows from sticks and screamed orders from the SS men. Gradually the groups were separated into different columns. Sam's column was full of families, the elderly and children, all of whom were scared and panic-stricken. The other column was full of men from their teens to their fifties. The column of men moved off, and Sam heard his mother say in Yiddish, "Szlamek - save yourself!" before giving him a shove in the direction of the men's column. For Sam this would be the last time he saw his family.

Sam tells how they were marched past a smartly- dressed SS officer carrying doeskin gloves, who looked each one of them up and down. He would flick his gloves to the left or right. SS men would haul people out of the column and direct them as he had instructed. Those to the left were being sent back along the platform to join the women, children, families and the old. They were moved to one side to watch as the family column went through the same selection procedure. Some were directed back towards the trucks.

Sam and his column were marched at a running pace by the SS men and those who were in striped pyjamas. Any who fell behind would be pummelled and kicked. They reached a bleak barrack hut where they were ordered to strip and leave their clothes in neat piles. Anyone who did not move quickly enough would be clubbed. Sam realised that the men in pyjamas were not from the SS but were in some way chosen. Many seemed to be enjoying themselves. The newly arrived prisoners were ordered to hand over gold and money. Recently removed clothing was searched. The now naked prisoners were given soap and taken to a shower area. After showering they were forcibly shaved of all bodily hair. Sam realised straight away that the whole process was to remove their identities and dehumanise them. It had taken just two hours. They were led to an area for formal registration – Nazi efficiency – when he became aware that he was having a number tattooed onto his left forearm. Afterwards he looked at this mark. '*It read 135913. I was an animal, stamped with an indelible number like sheep on their way to slaughter.*'

From here he was moved to another room where he was issued with clothing that *'served to continue the essential anonymity of the camp. A trusty threw me a bundle of clothes and told me to put them on. Everything was striped – a shirt, a jacket, a pair of trousers, a cap. There was no underwear and the pair of wooden clogs was several sizes too big. In fact, nothing fitted at all and the cloth was rough and coarse, smelling disgusting. It was the ultimate in hand- me-downs. I didn't know it at the time but I was wearing a dead man's clothes.'*

It was dark after the induction was over, and Sam and the other new inmates were force-marched to the quarantine block that was to be the initial accommodation. The march involved further beatings with clubs and more screamed orders. Arriving at the block a fellow-inmate awaited them but this man had an armband with the letters KAPO stencilled on it. They were ordered to sleep five to a bunk. A final bit of advice at the end of that day was 'Cause any trouble and you're as good as dead.' The day had been traumatic enough for Sam who was, it must be remembered, only a teenager, who had been separated from his family, and although he did not know it, he was alone:

'My stomach growled and hurt – I hadn't eaten for three days and the only drink I'd had was my own sugared piss. The bunks were dusty and rickety, every slight movement causing the timber to creak and groan on the uneven earth floor. Instead I lay in the darkness, listening to the breathing and snoring of others, shaking uncontrollably. Nothing could have prepared me for what happened during that long, dreadful night. I felt a rhythmic rubbing from behind and half turned to see a face leering in the darkness. He was a man in his forties who I remembered from the Kamionka. I didn't know his name and had never spoken to him and here he

was, taking advantage of this bizarre night to bugger me. I couldn't believe that anyone could think of this after all we'd been through, but he clearly had other ideas and I felt my arse suddenly wet. I daren't cry out, for fear of the Kapo's club or a bullet from the SS.'

He describes lying in bed all night and remembering the words of a trusty: '*Your family ... they're already in heaven.*'

Sam Pivnik eloquently explains the onset of war, the immediate targeting of Polish Jews, the move to the ghetto, arrival at Auschwitz, selection, the loss of relatives, and the horror and trauma that was experienced in those first few hours in the camp. His book goes into more detail, including the Death March and a number of occasions when he managed to evade death. His book, as are those written by others mentioned here, is recommended reading.

Kitty Hart-Moxon

The author of this book has been fortunate to hear Kitty speak, to spend quality time in her company, to have exchanged correspondence and to have spoken to her often in valued friendship. Most conversations with Kitty will remain private, and will not be referred to here. She is a singularly impressive woman: robust, full of vitality, clear of thought, and absolutely certain about the facts of what she and others experienced. Following her arrival in the UK after the war she had a lengthy career in health care. After retirement she could have opted for an easy life of leisure. She chose instead to dedicate her time to writing, speaking, making a powerful documentary and other filmed memoires, advising Steven Spielberg and Meryl Streep on the film *Sophie's Choice*, and ensuring that the truth of the Holocaust remains alive in the minds of those who were not there. She is an acknowledged authority on the Holocaust, and in 1978 she was one of the first survivors to return to Auschwitz. That visit, with one of her sons, was recorded for a television documentary, and then became a book entitled *Return To Auschwitz*.

Kitty was born in 1926 in Bielsko in south-west Poland at the foot of the Beskidy Mountains that divide Poland and what was then Czechoslovakia. At the outbreak of the war she and her family fled their home and moved to the Lublin ghetto. As the SS conducted round-ups in the ghetto the family were forced to flee again. Kitty and her mother were separated from the rest of the family, and, using fake documents, they travelled to Germany where they worked in forced labour. In March 1943 they were identified as Jews, imprisoned, and sentenced to death. The execution did not take place, and they were sent instead to Auschwitz. Kitty and her mother remained in Auschwitz from April 1943 until November 1944. The full details of their time in Auschwitz are testament to their resilience, fortitude, and determination. In November 1944 they were transported from Auschwitz to work as forced labourers. They were subsequently driven from camp to camp on foot in often atrocious conditions, compounded by their state of health after all that time in Auschwitz. Thousands died on these death marches. They eventually made it to a camp outside Salzwedel, and were liberated by US forces in April 1945. Kitty spent 18 months in Displaced Persons camps where she worked for the British Military Government, and the Quaker Relief Team. In 1946 she recorded her experiences of Auschwitz, and later referred to that material in her book. Kitty and her mother eventually obtained entry permits to England. They struggled on arrival in the UK and Kitty has referred in discussions and correspondence to the problems they faced from the community that was meant to welcome them. She was almost forbidden from talking about the experiences in Europe and the Holocaust.

All of Kitty's recorded material will not be referred to, but there are some specifics of her time in the ghetto, in the Auschwitz Women's Camp and working in the area known as 'Kanada Camp' that are worthy of mention here.

Kitty and her family arrived in the Lublin Ghetto to a world of hardship and deprivation. She has expressed frustration that people today show little appreciation of how life was in the ghetto. Often the question is asked about the supposed lack of resistance, even in the face of overwhelming military force, and a hostile local population. As Kitty has written:

'One question above all is repeatedly put to survivors of the Holocaust. Why, when the number of Jews threatened was so enormous was there so little open resistance? Even in the face of bayonets and machine-guns would it not have been worth attempting a concerted rush at the enemy?'

In a talk Kitty gave that the author attended, she described how, on one occasion, a friend of hers had failed to step off the pavement when a German soldier approached. Without an obvious second thought the soldier pulled out his hand-gun and shot her friend in the head, killing her instantly. An awareness of this casual brutality was a salutary lesson that Kitty and others had to quickly learn.

Returning to the question she has been asked so often about resistance Kitty states:

'People who ask this have no idea of the circumstances prevailing at the time. In the first place, nobody in their wildest fantasies guessed the extent of the massacre which the Nazis had in mind. If today a Jewish, Chinese, Muslim or Jehovah's Witness community in Liverpool, Wolverhampton or London was warned that its members

were to be rounded up and put in preventive detention, would any of them believe or guess that they were destined to be converted into fertilizer? Even towards the end of the Second World War, in spite of detailed reports, photographs and incontrovertible evidence smuggled out to the allies, a large number of well-informed people still refused to believe in the existence of this remorseless genocide; and, to their shame, a number of those who knew it must be true still did not want the facts publicized or have anything done about the problem. For those of us on the spot, there was a confusion which the Germans deliberately encouraged. In Lublin, most local Jews were swiftly deported from the ghetto to make way for dazed newcomers, so that few remained who really knew their way around the district. As the war spread, Jews who had been brought in on transports from Holland, France and elsewhere were dumped in the ghetto and left to find their own feet. The few Polish Jews who had managed to remain found difficulty communicating through language barriers. All money brought in was invalid. Newcomers received no immediate issue of local currency with which to buy food, so in exchange for bread they had to part with what valuables they still possessed. Even as they struggled to get their bearings they were shipped out so that another batch could be moved in. There was no time to coordinate any mass movement against the oppressors. Lublin, like several other ghettoes, was basically a giant transit camp with a constantly shifting population. Moreover effective resistance would have required help from non-Jewish Poles in the rest of the city. This was rarely forthcoming. You paid dearly for every contribution from outside. Throughout history there has often been strongly anti-Semitic feeling in Poland among certain elements, and now they not only allowed the Germans to do what they liked with Polish Jews, but actively collaborated with the invader. A few showed genuine compassion and courage, but others were only too glad to find Jews hiding and hand them over to the Nazis.'

Kitty, and others, did resist in the ghetto. She would leave the confines of that part of the city to go on foraging and bartering expeditions, but always with the risk of capture by the Germans, or by hostile Poles. Some Jews in the ghetto fought, but as Kitty says:

'Nevertheless a few, alarmed or angered by being treated like cattle, did strike back, turning on their oppressors and fighting with their bare hands. It was as swift a way as any of committing suicide.'

On 2nd April 1943, after surviving all that the war had already thrown at them, Kitty and her mother were forced into caged train carriages, and travelled with hundreds of others. What awaited them was beyond their wildest comprehension:

'I was drowsing, propped up against the wire mesh, when the train slowed and finally clanked and grated to a halt. The familiar screaming and bellowing started up right away. 'Everybody out. Off the train. Get a move on!' We scrambled down awkwardly in near darkness. It was still night, but in the distance was a hint of dawn. There were hundreds of people stumbling about, trying to find their footing on the lumpy ground. We were dazed, unable to get our bearings. Guards moved in, screaming and shoving us into columns. We marched along the railway line, tripping and lurching as we went. Mother and I stayed side by side. We came to a gate with a motto above it in iron lettering, silhouetted against the sky: ARBEIT MACHT FREI – 'Work Brings Freedom'. Men who must have been in a different part of the train were taken in through the gate, along with some of the women. It was impossible to make out which women were chosen or why. The rest of us were formed into fives and went staggering on, picking our way with the help of the erratic glare from three layers of illuminated, electrified fencing. Above them stood a rank of high watchtowers. The railway line petered out. We kept going until we were halted at another gate and a guardhouse. This was in fact the entrance to Auschwitz II or Birkenau, though at the time we knew nothing of the names or the significance of any part of this place. A dank chill caught at us. The whole area was shrouded in a clinging grey mist. But dawn was breaking. Or was it really dawn? A reddish glow through the mist was flickering in the weirdest way, and there was a sickly, fatty, cloying smell. Mother and I glanced at each other, baffled. Who would be roasting meat, great quantities of it, at this hour of the morning?'

Within the first few hours Kitty got to understand the concept of 'organising' - stealing, bartering and trading in order to survive. They went through the process of showering, shaving, tattooing and being issued with clothing. They encountered the brutality of kapos who would whip and beat them almost on a whim. On the first night Kitty's immediate neighbour on her bunk was a gypsy woman who told her that she had arrived at the camp two weeks earlier:

'She sounded very strained and feeble, but in the gloom she brought her face close to mine and said: 'I see great strength in your eyes, child. Let me have your palm and I'll see what it has to say'. She bent closely over it. 'Yes, I can see you will come out of here. How, I don't know, but you will be one of the few to see freedom again. Remember, you must never lose your will to live. Fight for your life, or you'll be finished very quickly'.

Early the following morning they were all woken up by screaming and whistles. Kitty tried to wake the gypsy but she was cold and dead. Kitty became aware that the small amount of bread that was hidden in her own clothes when she went to sleep was missing, possibly stolen.

'But the dead gypsy still lay there, so I searched her and found several rations of bread hidden away. I hesitated for a moment, then helped myself to the bread and to her shirt, which was less rough than my ex-army garment, and could be worn underneath without showing. This was the first time I had ever taken from the dead. It wouldn't be the last.'

Kitty describes in detail her months in Auschwitz: the disease, starvation, hopelessness, hardship, death and executions; and how every day was an achievement to survive, and how 'organising' helped to ensure adequate food and clothing.

She witnessed the callous indifference to human life of Dr Mengele and his 'medical' colleagues. Kitty, like many other inmates suffered with poor physical health. If possible they would mask their true condition to prolong the possibility of survival, but occasionally sores, injuries, weakness, frailty, and lesions would give the secret away. At a time when she had multiple sores the order went out confining them to the barrack for a selection.

'I can still conjure up a picture of the three men striding down the Lagerstrausse, (main street of the camp) accompanied by an armed guard. Those of us who had been inmates long enough recognized all three: Mengele, the SS doctor; Rapportfuhrer* Taube, whom amongst ourselves we derided as the Abortfuhrer, Lavatory Leader; and Lagerfuhrer Hoessler, the SS officer in charge of camp discipline. They turned and made their way towards Block 22. Not ours today thank goodness. Every one of the women had to strip and parade naked in front of Mengele. In his immaculate white gloves he stood there pointing sometimes to the right, sometimes to the left. Anyone with spots on her body, or anyone whose slumping and shuffling denoted a Musselmann, was directed to the right. That meant death. On the left *you were allowed to rot a little longer. Of the 400 girls parading before him that day, Mengele chose 320 to die.'*

*****Rapportführer** (Report Leader) was a paramilitary title of the SS, specific to the Totenkopfverbande (Concentration Camp Service). An SS-Rapportführer was usually a mid- level SS-non-commissioned officer (often an Oberscharführer or Hauptscharführer) who served as the commander of a group of Blockführer who themselves were assigned to oversee barracks within a Concentration Camp.

Kitty obtained work in the part of the camp known somewhat ironically as 'Kanada', as it was seen as being like a land of riches. This was a place where the personal belongings of new arrivals and those sent to death would be searched and sorted. The work was deemed essential and as such, as long as it was completed, it held some possibility of continued life. But all of the items searched and sorted had belonged to someone condemned to death. Those working in Kanada might even find themselves searching the property of a loved one. Kanada was also near to the gas chambers and crematoria. She tells how a friend of hers bade her to see what was happening.

'I did not want to look. I was too afraid of what I might see. But I had to go and stand beside her. Not fifty yards away was an incredible sight. A column of people had been shuffling from the railway line into a long, low hall. When the place was full, there was a delay; but I went on watching, hypnotised. What I was witnessing was murder, not of one person, but of hundreds of innocent people at a time. Of course we had known, had whispered about it, and had been terrified of it from a distance; but now I was seeing it, right there in front of me.

On the outside of the low building a ladder had been placed. A figure in SS uniform climbed briskly up. At the top he pulled on a gas mask and gloves, tipped what looked from there like a white powder into the opening in the roof, and then hurried back down the ladder and ran off. Screams began to come out of the building. We could hear them echoing across to our hut, the desperate cries of suffocating people. I held my breath and pressed my hands over my ears but the screams were so loud you'd have thought the whole world must be able to hear them. 'It's over.' Someone was shaking me. It's all right, it's gone quiet. They're all dead now.' It could not have taken more than ten minutes.'

This was followed soon after by men of the Sonderkommando, fellow prisoners, removing the bodies from the gas chamber and loading them into the ovens of the crematoria. Men of the Sonderkommando could find themselves burning friends, neighbours, or relatives. Some of the Sonderkommando committed suicide by throwing themselves onto the electrified wire, or by walking into the gas chamber, or by throwing themselves into the crematoria. Most Sonderkommando would be killed within a short period of this work to stop them telling others what they were doing.

In early to mid-1944 the Germans transported hundreds of thousands of Jews from Hungary to Auschwitz. The Nazi need to slaughter these people became more urgent due to the advance of the Red Army. The gas chambers and crematoria struggled to cope with the volume of work. Kitty and the other women in Kanada noticed large pits and trenches being dug near to the crematoria. Logs and brushwood were brought near in huge volumes. The Nazi plan was to exterminate over four hundred thousand Hungarian Jews. This caused practical problems. The women in Kanada saw the long columns of newly arrived prisoners - men, women and children. Smoke gushed from the crematoria and also from the pits and trenches in the ground.

'Inside our block the air became so black and foul that we opened the window, which only made it worse. And the sound was far worse than the screams to which we had hardened ourselves. This time it was the screaming of thousands in agony, quite different from the muffled retching and howling of those hit by gas. No selections on the ramp. Just a continuous, insane, conveyor belt of human beings. One of our girls was shrieking along with the victims. 'Don't you see? You know why they're making that noise ... it's different ... they're being roasted alive'. It was true. There was no time even for the mercies of Zyklon B before burning. Hundreds were being thrown alive into the specially dug, blazing pits.'

Few people who survived Auschwitz have been able to so vividly convey the brutality of life and death there as well as Kitty has. The images she gives are incredibly cruel and distressing. But they are only words that we read or hear. Kitty was there. For her the memories live on and she maintains a determination to ensure that the truth is known to others.

Freda Wineman

The author has been privileged to hear one of Freda's talks at the National Holocaust Centre, to chat to her in person, and to exchange email correspondence. She is an impressively dignified and refined lady, who has a genteel air that belies the enormity of what she has experienced. Her account can be heard in person at one of the talks she gives willing audiences, or it can be read in *Survival. Holocaust Survivors Tell Their Story* which is produced by, and available at The Holocaust Centre, Beth Shalom, near Newark in Nottinghamshire.

Freda was born in 1923 in Mertz, Lorraine in north-eastern France. In 1931 her family moved to Sarreguemines, on France's eastern border with Germany. They were Orthodox Jews. In August 1939, as war seemed imminent the town was evacuated to south-west France. War was declared on Freda's sixteenth birthday. When Germany invaded France Freda's family moved further south to St Etienne. Although this was technically in 'Free France' the Vichy government in that area passed new anti-Jewish laws. By 1942 the whole of France was occupied by German forces, and the family were at constant risk of arrest. In May 1944 luck ran out. Freda's mother was arrested after being found in possession of the family's ration books which identified them as Jewish. Freda was on her way home from work when she found out about her mother's arrest. Her first thought was to try and protect her younger brothers, but they were captured and taken to Gestapo headquarters where Freda was beaten and interrogated in an attempt to get her to divulge the whereabouts of other family members. She was moved to a barracks in St Etienne where she was held with hundreds of other Jews. Some days later Freda's entire family had been arrested and they were all put on a train to Drancy, near Paris. They were forced into a cattle truck – 120 in the truck with just a bucket for a toilet. There was no room to move, no food, and no water. After three days and nights they arrived at their destination.

> *'It was dawn. The doors to the cattle truck were unlocked, and all we could hear was dogs barking and guards shouting at us. This was Auschwitz. We had to leave our luggage. I remember the smell of the ashes, and we saw flakes in the air, but could not understand what they were. Men in striped clothing whispered to us to give the babies to older women. My mother took a baby from a young Dutchwoman. Everything happened so quickly. My father and my brothers, David and Armand, were separated from us. I never saw my father again. My mother, my youngest brother Marcel and I were standing in lines. A German officer, whom I now know to have been the infamous Dr Mengele, was holding a stick and was moving people to the left and the right. I went with my mother and Marcel, but was called back … The officer told me to go with*

the young people as my mother would be looking after the small children. I was heartbroken to be separated from my mother and Marcel, but had no choice but to join a group of about 80 people. It was the last time I saw my mother who went with that little Dutch baby in her arms.'

Freda and her family had just gone through one of the selections. Her parents and her brother Marcel would all be murdered at Auschwitz.

Freda tells of – as others have – the dehumanising processes that the Nazis employed. She and the other women were sent to a room where they were ordered to take all of their clothes off and hand over any jewellery they possessed. They were then tattooed before being forced into showers. While waiting in an adjoining room a woman who spoke a number of languages came in. They questioned her about the fate of their loved ones. They were told the harsh reality. In another room their heads were shaved and they were issued with camp clothes. All personal identity had been removed.

Freda realised that her main priority at Auschwitz, beyond survival, was to keep clean. Despite her best efforts she joined the other inmates who succumbed to the many infections that were rife in the camp, and to the problems of malnutrition.

She describes how at that time in 1944 up to ten thousand people a day arrived at Auschwitz. Most were directed straight to the gas chambers. She describes how, 'We became deeply depressed as the dark smoke, the smell and the visible night fires made it obvious what was happening. We were helpless, lost and forgotten. Keeping going from day to day became the hardest thing of all.'

On 17th August 1944 Freda was selected to work in Kanada camp to sort through clothes and property. She tells how, 'It was a tearful, heart-rending task as we recognised some of the clothes and names on the suitcases.' Returning from work they were permitted to shower before going back into the camp. The showers were in the open air. German guards would mock and throw buckets of cold water which was further humiliation for relatively young girls. They would try and sneak shoes and underwear in for friends who were working in other areas. One day they were stopped and three of their group were told to strip in front of the camp commandant. When they were found to have extra clothes on them they were hanged in front of all of their friends.

Freda recalls how in the middle of the huge influx of Hungarians, she and her friends were noticed by three sisters who could see that they were suffering. They gave Freda and her friends a ration of bread to share. Those three sisters survived, and Freda met one of them at the first reunion of survivors in Israel.

Freda remembers some men of the Sonderkommando trying to escape in October 1944. She and her friends witnessed the cruel execution of these men.

At the end of October 1944 Freda and others were transferred to Bergen-Belsen. She remained there until 3rd February 1945, when she and 750 others were taken to Raguhn, a satellite camp of Ravensbruck. Freda was forced into factory work. As the allies advanced they were loaded onto cattle trucks en route to another destination. The train was bombed. Freda tried to escape, but was threatened with being shot by a guard.

Eventually, on 20th April 1945 they arrived at Theresienstadt. By the time they disembarked 250 of the 720 who had started the journey had died. They were liberated by Soviet forces on 9th May. Despite typhus among the prisoners, many of whom were in a pitiful state, the Russians tried very hard to save them.

After the war Freda settled and married in England. It took her over 50 years to confront what had happened to her, and share it with others. As she says of her willingness to talk, "I do so now, because if people like me do not proclaim their experiences for others to hear and reflect upon, then future generations will not learn the lessons of these, perhaps the darkest, moments of our history."

Shlomo Venezia

Shlomo Venezia has provided the world with a rare account. In 2007, his book: '*Inside the Gas Chambers. Eight Months in the Sonderkommando of Auschwitz*' (written with Beatrice Prasquier, following a series of interviews, and published in association with the United States Holocaust Memorial Museum) was published. Few of the Sonderkommando, particularly those linked to the gas chambers, survived to tell their tale. Indeed it was Nazi policy at Auschwitz to send these people into those same places of murder in order to remove the likelihood of them talking.

Shlomo was born in Salonika in Greece in December 1923. It is somewhat of an irony that his ancestral family had been forced to leave Spain in 1492 when Jews were expelled from that country. Prior to settling in Greece they had lived in Italy. They did not have family names, but in the case of his family they chose a name that corresponded to the city they lived in, Venice, hence Venezia.

Shlomo's account does not refer to many dates as it follows the format of questions and answers. It is referred to here as it details an aspect of life, and death, in Auschwitz that few have been able to share. Shlomo arrived in Auschwitz-Birkenau on 11th April 1944. Before this time the Germans had invaded Greece, and as was their policy across Europe, they targeted the Jewish population. Shlomo describes his arrival at Auschwitz in a similar manner to other survivors, but despite the familiar words, his experience was unique to him:

'The train hadn't blown its whistle when the transport had stopped en route. So when I heard that peculiar whistle and felt the train suddenly braking I immediately realised that the convoy had finally reached its destination. The doors opened onto the Judenrampe, just opposite the potato sheds. My first feeling was a sense of relief. I didn't know how much longer it would have been possible to survive in this train, without anything left to eat, without any space, air, or toilet facilities. As soon as the train stopped, the SS opened the doors of the carriage and started yelling, "Alle runter! Alle runter!" "Everyone out! Everyone out!"

We saw men in uniform pointing their sub-machine guns, and Alsatians barking at us. Everyone was in a stupor, numb after the journey – and all of a sudden, fierce yells and a whole infernal din to throw us off our guard, and prevent us knowing what was going on. I happened to be near the door, so I was among the first to climb out. I wanted to stay near the door to help my mother get out. We had to jump for it, as the carriage was high and the terrain was sloping. My mother wasn't that old, but I knew the journey would have worn her out and I wanted to help her. While I was waiting for her, a German came up behind me and struck me two heavy blows on the back of my neck with his stick. He lashed out with such force I thought he's split my skull. I instinctively placed both my hands on my head to protect myself. Seeing that he was going to start hitting me again, I ran off to join the others in the queue.

Our captors started hitting people as soon as we arrived, to vent their hatred, out of cruelty, and also so that we'd lose our bearings and obey out of fear, without making problems for them. So that's what I did, and when I turned around to try to find my mother, she wasn't there anymore. I never saw her again. She wasn't there, and neither were my two little sisters, Marica and Marta.'

He describes a typical selection process with the separation of male and female, adult and child, the cruel and arbitrary breaking up of families, many of whom would be sent straight to their death.

After three weeks in quarantine Shlomo was selected for a work duty. The Germans chose eighty men including Shlomo, his brother and his cousins. They were led through the men's sector in Birkenau. 'The first impression I had when I entered *Lager D* was intensely unpleasant. Our group went first through the SS barrack, which was situated at the entrance to every sector to keep note of who entered and left the camp. After the barrack, on the right, I immediately spotted the pool filled with water. Then my eyes rose to the gallows that had been erected at one corner of the pool. This vision had a profound effect on me; I said to myself, 'What a fine welcome they're giving us!'

Soon afterwards Shlomo was told that he had been allocated to a work group. 'Then he asked me if I knew the name of the Kommando to which I had been assigned. Since I didn't have the slightest idea, he told me we were in the "Sonderkommando." "What does Sonderkommando mean?" "Special detachment." "Special? Why?" "Because you have to work in the Crematorium ... where the people are burned.'

Shlomo gives details of his fairly rapid introduction into the work of the Sonderkommando before he found himself involved in work he could never have comprehended. On the first day they were sent to what he referred to as 'Crematorium I' because he did not know of the existence of the first Crematorium at Auschwitz I.

'There were three steps leading inside the building but, instead of going in the Kapo took us all round it. One of the Sonderkommando men came to tell us what to do: remove the weeds and tidy up the ground a bit. What we did wasn't particularly useful, but I suppose that the Germans wanted to keep us busy before making us work at the Crematorium. The *next day we came back to do the same thing. My natural curiosity impelled me to go up to the building to try to see through the window what was going on inside. We had been strictly forbidden to do so, but step by step, I edged up to the window.*

When I got close enough to catch a glimpse, I was left completely paralysed by what I saw. Bodies heaped up, thrown on top of one another, were just lying there. There were bodies of people who were still young. I came back to my companions and told them what I'd seen. They in turn slipped over to see, without the Kapo noticing. They came back ashen faced, disbelieving ... I realised that the corpses were the 'leftovers' from an earlier convoy. There hadn't been time to burn them before the new convoy arrived, and these bodies were piled up to leave room in the gas chamber.'

Few people who survived Auschwitz were able to give first-hand accounts of the gas chambers. Sholmo was one who did:

'I wasn't one of those who had to take corpses out of the gas chamber, but later on I frequently had to do it. Those given this task started by pulling the corpses out with their hands, but in a few minutes the hands were dirty and slippery. In order to avoid touching the bodies directly, they tried using a bit of cloth, but, of course, the cloth in turn became dirty and damp in a few moments. So people had to make do. Some tried to drag bodies along with a belt, but this actually made the work harder, since they had to keep tying and untying the belt. Finally, the simplest thing was to use a walking stick under the nape of the neck and pull the bodies along.'

The Germans saw gassing as efficient, and less messy as a means of mass extermination. It was still an unbelievably cruel death.

'I've never told anyone about this until now: it's such a weight, it's so heartrending, that I find it difficult to speak of those visions of the gas

chamber. You could find people whose eyes hung out of the sockets because of the struggles the organism had undergone. Others were bleeding everywhere, or were soiled by their own excrement, or that of other people. Because of the effect that their fear and the gas had on them, the victims often evacuated everything they had in their bodies. Some bodies were all red, others very pale, as everyone reacted differently. But they had all suffered in death.

People often imagine that the gas was thrown in, and there you were, the victims died. But what a death it was! ... You found them gripping each other – everyone had desperately sought a little air. The gas was thrown onto the floor and gave off acid from underneath, so everyone tried to find some air, even if each needed to climb on top of another until the last one died. I personally think – I can't be sure but I think – that several people died even before the gas was thrown in. They were crammed in so tightly against one another that the smallest and weakest were inevitably suffocated. At a certain moment, under that pressure, that anguish, you became selfish, and there's only one thing you can think of: how to save yourself. That was the effect the gas had. The sight that lay before us when we opened the door was terrible: nobody can ever imagine what it was like.'

Eva Mozes Kor

The author has exchanged emails with Eva who has asked that she be credited regarding her desire to seek forgiveness of former Nazis. Eva is one of the few survivors of Dr Mengele's twin experiments to tell her story. Her book *Surviving The Angel of Death* is a powerful account of life as a child in Auschwitz. She is one of the few who have chosen to seek forgiveness and reconciliation with those who caused so much harm to her and her family. This stance is not accepted by many survivors, but it is a personal approach that Eva has chosen as a path in later life. She now lives in Terra Haute in Indiana in the US. In 1995 she opened a small Holocaust museum which has developed into the CANDLES Holocaust Museum and Education Centre. She gives talks and lectures to a range of audiences at her museum and travels and speaks at numerous international events. She was subject of a powerful documentary entitled *Forgiving Dr. Mengele*. The website for her museum and education centre is www.candlesholocaustmuseum.org.

Eva and her twin sister Miriam were born in the small village of Portz in Romanian Transylvania on 31st January 1934. They were the youngest of four daughters. Their father was 'a religious Jew', and at times could be quite strict. Eva and Miriam were favoured by their mother, and popular with other families because they were twins. In the way of families the world over they would be dressed alike and people would struggle to guess who was who. Eva was the youngest child but felt that she was a stronger personality than Miriam. Their father had wanted a son, in part because only a son could participate in public worship or say the 'Kaddish', the mourner's prayer, when someone died. Eva did not always get positive attention from her father, but she felt that this toughened her up and made her stronger.

They were the only Jewish family in their village. Anti-Semitism existed, but the children were largely oblivious to it. Their father told them of an incident in 1935 when she and Miriam were aged just one year. A violent anti-Semitic party called the 'Iron Guard' controlled the village offices, the police, and the newspapers. They would stir up hatred of Jews by publishing false stories about how evil Jews were, and how they wanted to take over the world. Eva's father and uncle were thrown into jail on trumped up charges; in truth they were arrested solely because they were Jews. On getting out of prison her father and uncle went to Palestine to see if it would be possible to make a living there. They stayed in Palestine for a few months before returning to Romania. Her father tried to persuade her mother to leave and go to live in Palestine, but she refused. It is clear that Eva's father was fearful of the news he was hearing from elsewhere in Romania and from across Europe about the persecution of Jews. Her mother did not want to go. She had four young children and her own family living nearby. She thought that they lived in a nice area, with a good farm and a reasonable lifestyle. She also believed that the family would be safe, as the rumours about Hitler and Jewish persecution were just rumours.

In the summer of 1940 things began to change. Although the village they lived in was largely Romanian the surrounding area was half Hungarian and half Romanian. The Hungarian government had entered into allegiance with Hitler's Germany. The northern part of Transylvania was given to the Hungarians. Rumours spread that the Hungarian army would kill Jews and Romanians. Eva recalls the day Hungarian forces marched into the village, and how her parents allowed them to camp on their property and gave them food.

On returning to school in the autumn of 1940 Eva and Miriam were the only Jewish children there. Two new Hungarian teachers had started. They brought with them books that portrayed Jews in mocking caricatures. Eva also saw her first moving picture which was a short film called *'How to Catch and Kill a Jew.'* The books and films changed the attitude of the other children, and former friends would refer to Eva and Miriam as 'dirty, smelly Jews'. They would be spat at, and beaten at every opportunity. Eva even recalls a maths book in school that posed the question:

'If you had five Jews, and you killed three Jews, how many would you have left?'

Eva and Miriam were wrongly accused of misbehaviour in school. The teacher threw corn kernels onto the floor, and made Eva and Miriam kneel on them. Their classmates mocked and sneered at them. They went home distressed and told their mother, who merely said, *"Children, I am sorry. We are Jews, and we just have to take it. There is nothing we can do."*

The torment for the girls and their family continued as anti-Semitism gained legitimacy in the village and surrounding area. On 31st January 1944 Eva and Miriam had their tenth birthday but they never got to celebrate it. In March 1944 the family had a visit from two Hungarian policemen. The family were ordered:

"Get your belongings! Gather them up. You are going to a transportation centre. You have two hours to pack."

They were transferred to a ghetto in the town of Simleul Silvaniei along with about seven thousand other Jews. She recalls her father being taken away and tortured in an attempt to get him to hand over the family gold and silver.

In May 1944 German guards told them they were being moved to a labour camp which they said was in Hungary. They were advised:

'This is for your own protection. If you work you will live. Your families will stay together.'

They had already heard rumours from the adults that Jews sent to Germany were killed, so they believed that if that if they were being sent to Hungary they would be safe. They were marched to the train tracks and bundled onto cattle trucks, carrying just a few personal possessions. Eva recalls seeing the sense of powerlessness her parents had. The journey lasted several days. They had no food or water, no toilet facilities, and nowhere to lie down or rest. On the third day they realised that they had crossed the border into German occupied Poland. They were instantly terrified as they all understood that Germany and Germans meant death to Jews. On the fourth day the train stopped and they realised that they had reached their destination. It was night time. They could hear

German voices yelling orders but the cattle truck doors stayed shut. As dawn broke their father began to pray. He gathered the family together and said 'Promise me that if any of you survives this terrible war, you will go to Palestine where your uncle Aaron lives and where Jews can live in peace.'

Eva describes how she could hear German voices outside, yelling orders. Dogs barked. The doors of the cattle car were pulled open, and SS guards ordered everyone out:

'I saw tall barbed-wire fences, cement guard-towers everywhere. Soldiers were hanging out of them with the barrels of their guns pointed at us. I have no idea how we got from the cattle car to the selection platform. Miriam and I may have jumped or stepped down a wooden ramp. But pretty soon we were standing on the platform in utter terror, two ten-year-olds in matching burgundy dresses.'

In the subsequent confusion Eva and Miriam were separated from their father and older sisters. An SS guard demanded of their mother confirmation that they were twins. As soon as their mother said they were the guard grabbed them and dragged them away. The terrified girls begged to stay with their mother, but he ignored them. They turned in time to see their mother being forced into another direction. Soon afterwards Eva and Miriam were taken to a building. Their hair was cut short. They were forced to shower. They had their arms tattooed. Eva fought this process by biting a guard's arm, and demanding to see her mother. She was told she would see her the next day, but she knew he was lying. Eventually they were moved to the girls' camp at Birkenau, where they were placed in a barrack hut with other twins aged from two to sixteen years. They were quickly advised to eat everything offered and not to be fussy with food. They were also told for the first time about the gas chambers and crematoria. Some of the other twins took them to the back of the barracks:

> 'We looked up at the sky. Flames rose from chimneys that towered over Birkenau. Smoke covered the whole camp and fine ash filled the air, making it as dusky as the sky after an explosion of a volcano – it was that thick. Again we were hit by that terrible smell. Even though I was afraid to ask, I heard myself saying, "What are they burning so late in the evening?" "People" said a girl. "You don't burn people!" I said. "Don't be ridiculous." "The Nazis do. They want to burn all the Jews."
> Somebody else said, "Did you see how the Nazis divided the people arriving on the trains into two groups this morning? They are probably burning one group right now. If the Nazis think you are young and strong enough to work, you are allowed to live. The rest are taken to the gas chambers and gassed to death." I thought of Mama who was so weak after her long illness. I thought of Papa, clutching his prayer book. I thought of our two older sisters.'

Eva knew that as children they could not work, and wondered why they were being kept alive. They were told then about Dr Mengele and his experiments, but did not know what this could mean.

Eva describes the process of her and Miriam being documented, measured and evaluated by staff on behalf of Mengele. There were some benefits (for want of a better word) to being a Mengele twin. He had a need to maintain some semblance of well being for these children as long as they were of use to him. This meant food and showers in quantities and at intervals denied most other inmates. That, though, was as far as the benefits went:

> 'On Tuesdays, Thursdays and Saturdays, we went to the 'blood lab'. Miriam and I sat on a bench with another set of twin sisters. Someone

tied our upper left arms and right arms with thin, flexible, rubber hoses. Two people worked on me at the same time. A doctor jabbed a needle into my left arm to take blood. He withdrew a vial's worth and then stuck me again. I could see hands taking away bright red vials of my blood. I remember wondering, "How much blood can I lose and still live?" Meanwhile a different doctor gave me an injection of something in my right arm. He stuck five needles in without removing the first one. What was he shooting into my remaining blood?

In those days we didn't know what the experiments were for or what we were injected with. Later we found out that Dr Mengele purposely gave some twins dangerous, life-threatening diseases such as scarlet fever, then followed them with shots of something else to see if it cured the disease. Some shots were attempts to change the colour of eyes.'

Eva and Miriam continued to be experimented on by Mengele and his staff. Many twins died, and it is reported that when one twin died the other would immediately be killed so that Mengele could conduct comparative post mortem examinations.

When the Soviet forces arrived at Auschwitz on 27th January 1945, Eva and Miriam were liberated, along with the few who still remained at the camp who had not been sent on death marches. The Soviets saw a propaganda opportunity, and dressed the twins in striped pyjamas before making them pose for pictures. The line of twins walking between the wire fencing, with Eva and Miriam at the front, has become an iconic image.

For five years after being liberated, Eva and Miriam lived back in Romania where they stayed with an aunt. Romania was by then a Communist country, with a strict regime and an all-seeing and all-powerful secret police force. In 1950 they moved to Israel, and were met on arrival by their long-lost Uncle Aaron. In 1960, Eva met an American tourist called Alex Kor, whom she would marry and settle with in the US. In 1984 she set up an organisation called *CANDLES* (Children of Auschwitz Nazi Deadly Lab Experiments Survivors), which was dedicated to locating Mengele twins. *CANDLES* proved to be a useful support group for survivors it located. In 1995 – two years after Miriam's death – Eva established the *CANDLES* Holocaust Museum and Education Centre in Terre Haute, Indiana.

Eva's story has a twist. In 1993 she travelled to Germany and met Dr Munch, who had been a Nazi doctor at Auschwitz. She was surprised to find that he was not only kind to her, but that she actually liked him. She asked if he knew anything about the gas chambers and he confirmed that what he knew had fuelled his nightmares every day. He then detailed how:

'People would be told they were taking a shower and to remember their clothes hanger number, and to tie their shoes together. When the gas chamber was fully packed, the doors closed hermetically and sealed. A vent-like orifice opened in the ceiling, dropping pellets like gravel to the floor. Somehow the pellets operated like dry ice and turned to gas. The gas began rising from the floor. People tried to get away from the rising gas, climbing on top or one another. The strongest people ended atop a pile of intermingled bodies. When the people on top of the pile stopped moving, that was when I knew, from looking through a peephole and watching it all, that everybody was dead.'

It was Dr Munch's role to sign the mass death certificates. Dr Munch agreed to go with Eva to Auschwitz in 1995 to commemorate the fiftieth anniversary of the liberation. He also agreed to sign an affidavit about what he knew of the operation of the gas chambers. Eva pondered long and hard about how to thank Dr Munch. The power of a former Nazi doctor admitting his involvement added so much weight to the many survivor accounts. She decided to write him a letter of forgiveness. On 27th January 1995 Dr Munch arrived at Auschwitz with his son, his daughter and his granddaughter. Eva arrived with her son and daughter. Dr Munch signed his document, and Eva read and signed her statement, in which she not only forgave Dr Munch, but also forgave Dr Mengele. For Eva, a burden of pain had been lifted. As Eva says: *'Anger and hate are seeds that germinate war. Forgiveness is a seed for peace. It is the ultimate act of self-healing.'*

Eva's Declaration of Amnesty that she read at the fiftieth anniversary of the liberation of Auschwitz states:

'I hope in some small way, to send a message to the world
a message of forgiveness; a message of peace,
a message of hope, a message of healing.
Let there be no more wars, no more experiments
without informed consent, no more gas chambers,
no more bombs, no more hatred, no more killing,
no more Auschwitzes.'

Not all survivors agree with Eva's desire to forgive. Some argue that no one can forgive on behalf of someone else. Others feel that the crimes committed during the Holocaust and by the Nazi regime and its sympathisers can never be forgiven. There is validity to such views, but Eva has undoubtedly found comfort in her approach, and has gained a personal sense of power over those who caused her and her family so much harm.

Those who deny the Holocaust and deny the accounts of survivors, often cite doubt about figures, supposed inconsistencies in accounts, or an apparent lack of proof. What proof they require is often unclear. Obviously it is unlikely that most survivors will have convenient photographs of their time at the camp or a record documenting arrival there. Why should survivors need to provide such proof? Some visitors to Auschwitz even have pictures taken to prove that they were there, as if this is needed over and above personal testimony. In health care we know that illnesses can be identified by signs and symptoms. A rash, an inflammation, a wound, a blood test, an X-ray, a CT scan, an ECG or similar tests will provide obvious signs of physical problems. The symptoms are what are described by the patient: soreness, itching, irritation, pain etc. In mental health it is not always so obvious. The symptoms can be well described: low mood, anxiety, distress, fear, paranoia, hallucinations, flashbacks etc; but the signs often require a more observant use of sight, hearing, perceptiveness and other skills by the person assessing.

If all mental health problems are put under a general label of 'distress', the issue for professionals and patients is how to qualify or quantify that distress in a way that ensures the best help is provided. In mental health services labels or diagnoses are given to groups of symptoms, or specific types of distress in order to categorise and ensure the most appropriate treatment and care. Distress based on trauma is a difficult one for health professionals (and society in general) to fully appreciate. No matter how graphic the description of events experienced the professional is only hearing or reading words. Those words may be immensely powerful, but they can never fully convey the personal enormity of what they mean to the person expressing them. And the way trauma manifests or how it is described varies from person to person. Two people can describe a very similar experience such as an assault, or bereavement. One may be overtly distressed; one may be quiet and reserved. The emotional pain may not be greatly different. It does not mean that one or the other is more or less in need of help.

AUSCHWITZ-BIRKENAU

In the criminal justice system the burden of proof is on the crime investigators and prosecuting authorities to prove to a standard 'beyond all reasonable doubt'. Sometimes the only evidence is the word of one person against another. If there is physical evidence such as DNA, fingerprints, CCTV or similar it may make achieving the standard of proof easier. If there is a lack of such physical evidence it may merely be the quality of the account given by the victim is seen as being detailed and believable enough to charge someone and put them before a court. If there are multiple victims who give similar accounts then the chances of convicting an offender are greater.

It is known by health professionals that certain signs and symptoms are consistent with various diagnostic possibilities – even in mental health, when there are no obvious injuries, rashes, wounds or inflammations. That is how appropriate treatment and support is planned and offered. And in the criminal justice system if enough people give similar evidence there is a greater chance of successful prosecution.

With the Holocaust there are enough survivors who have given similar accounts quite independently of each other. Their accounts are backed up by abundant physical evidence and also by the accounts given of those who were involved in perpetrating that immense crime against humanity. Somewhat conveniently and helpfully, the Nazis kept detailed records (although many were destroyed), and some senior Nazis, such as Auschwitz Camp Commandant Rudolf Hoess, wrote memoirs, confessions, or autobiographies to explain fully what they had been involved in. The few accounts referred to in this book are consistent and similar enough, and can be backed up by multiple other sources, to ensure that history, and historians, accept that what is said is true. Their words – though painful to read – can never properly convey to those who were not there, just how horrific and incomprehensible those experiences were.

We are privileged to have Holocaust survivors among us, but unfortunately fewer are around now to relay to us their stories in person. We have been able to hear first-hand their accounts of Auschwitz and other death camps. We are fortunate that so many are willing to give talks, to write of their experiences, to contribute to historical documentaries, and to ensure that as far as possible, their memories are recorded as a permanent testimony to what befell Europe in the 1930s and 1940s. Many Holocaust survivors recognise that genocides can happen again, and have happened since that brutal time in history. They are dedicated to the use of education and information as a means of trying to prevent harm in the future. The testimony of the survivors will remain long after they have gone. That testimony should be cherished and honoured by all who desire and seek a greater good for humanity.

Surprisingly there are still Holocaust deniers. How convinced such people are in their denial may be open to debate, but they exist, they have supporters, and they can cause offence. They will ask simplistic questions without really requiring or wanting to hear answers that challenge their viewpoint. *Why didn't the Jews resist more? Why are so many alive and able to tell their story? How come so many met Mengele? How could so many have been killed in such a short period of time?* The questions can be challenged with an alternative slant. *How did so many manage to resist in the ways that they did? How did so many survive despite the odds against them? How did Mengele betray the medical profession so absolutely by his role in selections, murder and barbaric experiments? How come more were not killed considering the concerted efforts at exterminating the Jews of Europe?*

'Why' is the most important question for those who seek to understand, and to acquire knowledge. Why would so many choose to lie about, or exaggerate their experiences? Why would the physical premises of Auschwitz-Birkenau exist in the format it does if it wasn't for its role in the Final Solution, and why is it preserved for its ongoing importance as historical evidence? Why would so many detailed Nazi records exist confirming the planning and implementation of the Final Solution, and the activities of extermination? Why would senior Nazis such as Rudolf Hoess confirm in detail the activities of Auschwitz when they had nothing to be gained by doing so? Why do so many accounts – independently of each other – provide consistency in their descriptions of events, activities, environments, and the naming of people involved? Those who deny or doubt the Holocaust do not have the answers to these questions and do not want the answers. In the style of all conspiracy theorists they seek only information and opinions that they agree with. They do not seek to investigate, question, enquire and find wider views to contemplate because that would complicate their thinking.

'Why?' is a necessary question for today when considering the experiences of those who died, who suffered, and who survived the Holocaust. Why did it happen? Why did so few see the warning signs? Why did so few stand up and challenge the hate before it took hold? Why was it not stopped? Why is hate and intolerance still permitted and acceptable in modern sophisticated societies? Why do we not truly honour those who suffered and died in the Holocaust and other genocides by pledging to ensure we will strive to prevent it happening again, and to ensure lessons from history are learned?

***

The main gate of Auschwitz main camp January 2015, seventy years after the liberation

AUSCHWITZ-BIRKENAU

Auschwitz main camp January 2015

Auschwitz I, seventy years after liberation, January 2015. Inmates did not walk between the electrified fencing but famously the liberating Soviet forces staged photographs of prisoners, including twins, being paraded in these areas

AUSCHWITZ-BIRKENAU

Auschwitz I at night. Hauntingly silent and serene

The gallows where Hoess was hanged, January 2015. In the bitter cold of winter, all of Auschwitz, including the gallows, appears different

AUSCHWITZ-BIRKENAU

Auschwitz I at dusk, January 2015

SIMON BELL

Auschwitz 1, January 2015

AUSCHWITZ-BIRKENAU

Auschwitz 1, January 2015

SIMON BELL

Hanging posts, Auschwitz I, January 2015

AUSCHWITZ-BIRKENAU

Gas chamber entrance, Auschwitz I. This was within sight of the Hoess villa, where the commandant would enjoy family time and entertain guests.

Hole for Zyklon B to be poured into the gas chamber at Auschwitz I. This is the only intact gas chamber at the camp

AUSCHWITZ-BIRKENAU

Auschwitz I, January 2015

SIMON BELL

Block 10, scene of unbelievable medical horror

AUSCHWITZ-BIRKENAU

The Hoess Villa, within sight of the gas chamber of Auschwitz I

The world's press listen at last to the voices of survivors

AUSCHWITZ-BIRKENAU

The Footsteps Team. L-R Jessica Clark, Rainer Hoess, Debbie Callahan-Sepper, Simon Bell, at the liberation anniversary

SIMON BELL

Birkenau, 27 January 2015. Bleak, silent, and bitterly cold

AUSCHWITZ-BIRKENAU

Birkenau, 27 January 2015

SIMON BELL

Birkenau, 27 January 2015

AUSCHWITZ-BIRKENAU

Small groups moving toward the public area for the liberation anniversary. In the distant trees are the international memorial, pits of ash, and the ponds where ash was dumped

SIMON BELL

Birkenau, 27 January 2015

AUSCHWITZ-BIRKENAU

Birkenau, 27 January 2015

SIMON BELL

The screen for the public to view the liberation anniversary, Birkenau, 27 January 2015

CHAPTER NINE
COULD IT HAPPEN AGAIN?

"The only thing necessary for the triumph of evil is for good men to do nothing."

Edmund Burke

The lessons of the Holocaust seem to have been unheeded when we look at subsequent genocides. Holocaust Memorial Day specifically includes the genocides in Cambodia, Rwanda, Bosnia, and Darfur, although in reality other genocides have occurred and are still taking place.

Between 1975 and 1979 the Khmer Rouge, led by Pol Pot, killed between one and three million Cambodians. The Khmer Rouge sought to enforce an extreme form of communism, with a return to what they called 'Year Zero.' Cities and towns were emptied, and the population was forced into the countryside. Those who could not travel were killed. Others perceived to be of the educated, middle, or upper classes were murdered. Religion was banned, and those who practised Christianity, Buddhism, Islam or other faiths were massacred. Many bodies were strewn across rural Cambodia in what became known as 'The Killing Fields'.

In former Yugoslavia the Bosnian Muslims were slaughtered in their thousands by Bosnian Serbs. The break-up of Yugoslavia led to unexpected brutality. In 1992 Bosnia declared its independence, but this was resisted by the Bosnian Serb population who wanted to be part of Greater Serbia. In 1995 Bosnian Serb troops and paramilitaries, led by Ratko Mladic, descended on the town of Srebrenica, and began shelling it. Srebrenica had actually been declared a safe zone by the United Nations. Women and children were forced onto buses and trucks before being removed from the area. The men and boys remained in the town. Up to 8,000 men and boys over the age of thirteen were murdered. Another 3,000 were killed trying to escape – some were shot and some were decapitated. Mladic issued an order to 'block, crush and destroy the straggling parts of the Muslim group'. The order was carried out with brutal efficiency. Approximately 1,500 people were locked into a warehouse, and sprayed with machine gun fire and grenades. Others were murdered in their thousands on farms, football fields and school playgrounds. And many will remember the shock at seeing once more in Europe the images of emaciated people in concentration camps.

In Rwanda in 1994 a million Tutsis and moderate Hutus were massacred over a one hundred day period. Ethnically the Tutsis were no different to the Hutus, but they had been given a privileged position in society during Belgian colonial rule, and the animosity towards them continued long after the Belgians left. They became known as 'the Tall Trees' prior to the genocide. The key phrase on national radio was, 'It's time to chop down the Tall Trees'. This followed the death of the country's President, after his plane was shot down in what was seen as an assassination. The world watched with horror, as secretly-filmed footage showed people being hacked down with machetes, and slain in the streets and public places.

In Darfur, a region in west Sudan, a civil war broke out in 2003. The region of Darfur had been home to about 6 million

Black Africans and Arabs. Conflict developed between the local farmers and the nomadic population, with the nomads being supported by the Sudanese government. An Arab militia – the 'Janjaweed' – has enjoyed continuing government support. They have erased villages and murdered thousands. It is estimated that between 200,000 and 400,000 civilians have died in the conflict and approximately 2.5 million are still displaced. (References taken from the Holocaust Memorial Day Trust http://hmd.org.uk/page/holocaust-genocides)

The United Nations Convention on the Prevention and Punishment of the Crime of Genocide was signed in Paris on 9th December 1948, and came into force on 12th January 1951. It defines genocide as:

In the present Convention, genocide means any of the following acts committed with intent to destroy, in whole or in part, a national, ethnical, racial or religious group, as such:

(a) Killing members of the group;

(b) Causing serious bodily or mental harm to members of the group;

(c) Deliberately inflicting on the group conditions of life calculated to bring about its physical destruction in whole or in part;

(d) Imposing measures intended to prevent births within the group;

(e) Forcibly transferring children of the group to another group

With this legislation, genocide became defined as a crime. It does not matter what the motive is, as long as the intention can be shown to be any of the acts described above. It is useful to consider the simplicity of the UN definition, to remember in what context the Convention arose, to think about subsequent genocides, and then to contemplate carefully about how easy the line between hate, intolerance, and horror can be crossed.

Gregory H. Stanton, President of Genocide Watch, identified eight stages of genocide. They are familiar and recognisable when considering the Holocaust and other genocides. They are also uncomfortably similar to many attitudes found around the world today, including in those countries and regions that are considered to be safe and civilised. The stages are:

Stage 1 - Classification
The differences between people are not respected. There's a division of 'us' and 'them.' This can be carried out through the use of stereotypes, or excluding people who are perceived as different.

Stage 2 - Symbolisation
This is a visual manifestation of hatred. Jews in Nazi occupied Europe were forced to wear yellow stars to show that they were 'different.'

Stage 3 - Dehumanisation
Those who are perceived as 'different' are treated with no form of human right or personal dignity. During the Rwandan Genocide, Tutsis were referred to as 'cockroaches;' The Nazis referred to Jews as 'vermin.'

Stage 4 - Organisation
Genocides are always planned. Regimes of hatred often train those who are to carry out the destruction of a people.

Stage 5 - Polarisation
Propaganda begins to be spread by hate groups. The Nazis used the newspaper Der Sturmer to spread and incite messages of hate about Jewish people

Stage 6 - Preparation
Victims are identified based on their differences. At the beginning of the Cambodian Genocide, the Khmer Rouge separated out those who lived in cities and did not work in the fields. Jews in Nazi Europe were forced to live in ghettos.

AUSCHWITZ-BIRKENAU

Stage 7 - Extermination
The hate group murders their identified victims in a deliberate and systematic campaign of violence. Millions of lives have been destroyed or changed beyond recognition through genocide.
Stage 8 - Denial
The perpetrators or later generations deny the existence of any crime.

(Reference from *Genocide Watch*)

Of course, racial, religious, ethnic, or other hatred and intolerance does not immediately or automatically lead to genocide, or even to lower levels of physical violence, but the risks of some stages developing into all eight stages must always be accounted for. Societies need to be alert to the dangers of escalation from the key stages of dehumanisation and polarisation. The observations of *Genocide Watch* are retrospective, and based on historical evidence. They are designed to warn of the ingredients and indicators of potential and actual genocide.

On 10th December 1948 the United Nations General Assembly adopted the Universal Declaration of Human Rights. This arose as a direct consequence of the horrors of the Second World War and was an international statement of intent that certain rights applied across national and international borders and laws. The UN recognised that what the world, and particularly Europe, had just witnessed and combated should not be allowed to occur again. It was a declaration by the UN General Assembly that was well meant, and based on the experience of the worst genocide the world had seen. The Articles or statements of the Declaration are:

Article 1
All human beings are born free and equal in dignity and rights. They are endowed with reason and conscience and should act towards one another in a spirit of brotherhood.

Article 2
Everyone is entitled to all the rights and freedoms set forth in this Declaration, without distinction of any kind, such as race, colour, sex, language, religion, political or other opinion, national or social origin, property, birth or other status. Furthermore, no distinction shall be made on the basis of the political, jurisdictional or international status of the country or territory to which a person belongs, whether it be independent, trust, non-self-governing or under any other limitation of sovereignty.
Article 3
Everyone has the right to life, liberty and security of person.
Article 4
No one shall be held in slavery or servitude; slavery and the slave trade shall be prohibited in all their forms.
Article 5
No one shall be subjected to torture or to cruel, inhuman or degrading treatment or punishment.
Article 6
Everyone has the right to recognition everywhere as a person before the law.
Article 7
All are equal before the law and are entitled without any discrimination to equal protection of the law. All are entitled to equal protection against any discrimination in violation of this Declaration and against any incitement to such discrimination.
Article 8
Everyone has the right to an effective remedy by the competent national tribunals for acts violating the fundamental rights granted him by the constitution or by law.
Article 9
No one shall be subjected to arbitrary arrest, detention or exile.

Article 10

Everyone is entitled in full equality to a fair and public hearing by an independent and impartial tribunal, in the determination of his rights and obligations and of any criminal charge against him.

Article 11

(1) Everyone charged with a penal offence has the right to be presumed innocent until proved guilty according to law in a public trial at which he has had all the guarantees necessary for his defence.

(2) No one shall be held guilty of any penal offence on account of any act or omission which did not constitute a penal offence, under national or international law, at the time when it was committed. Nor shall a heavier penalty be imposed than the one that was applicable at the time the penal offence was committed.

Article 12

No one shall be subjected to arbitrary interference with his privacy, family, home or correspondence, nor to attacks upon his honour and reputation. Everyone has the right to the protection of the law against such interference or attacks.

Article 13

(1) Everyone has the right to freedom of movement and residence within the borders of each state.

(2) Everyone has the right to leave any country, including his own, and to return to his country.

Article 14

(1) Everyone has the right to seek and to enjoy in other countries asylum from persecution.

(2) This right may not be invoked in the case of prosecutions genuinely arising from non-political crimes or from acts contrary to the purposes and principles of the United Nations.

Article 15

(1) Everyone has the right to a nationality.

(2) No one shall be arbitrarily deprived of his nationality nor denied the right to change his nationality.
　Article 16
(1) Men and women of full age, without any limitation due to race, nationality or religion, have the right to marry and to found a family. They are entitled to equal rights as to marriage, during marriage and at its dissolution.
(2) Marriage shall be entered into only with the free and full consent of the intending spouses.
(3) The family is the natural and fundamental group unit of society and is entitled to protection by society and the State.
　Article 17
(1) Everyone has the right to own property alone as well as in association with others.
(2) No one shall be arbitrarily deprived of his property.
　Article 18
Everyone has the right to freedom of thought, conscience and religion; this right includes freedom to change his religion or belief, and freedom, either alone or in community with others and in public or private, to manifest his religion or belief in teaching, practice, worship and observance.
　Article 19
Everyone has the right to freedom of opinion and expression; this right includes freedom to hold opinions without interference and to seek, receive and impart information and ideas through any media and regardless of frontiers.
　Article 20
(1) Everyone has the right to freedom of peaceful assembly and association.
(2) No one may be compelled to belong to an association.
　Article 21
(1) Everyone has the right to take part in the government of his country, directly or through freely chosen representatives.

(2) Everyone has the right of equal access to public service in his country.
(3) The will of the people shall be the basis of the authority of government; this will shall be expressed in periodic and genuine elections which shall be by universal and equal suffrage and shall be held by secret vote or by equivalent free voting procedures.
   Article 22
Everyone, as a member of society, has the right to social security and is entitled to realization, through national effort and international co-operation and in accordance with the organization and resources of each State, of the economic, social and cultural rights indispensable for his dignity and the free development of his personality.
   Article 23
(1) Everyone has the right to work, to free choice of employment, to just and favourable conditions of work and to protection against unemployment.
(2) Everyone, without any discrimination, has the right to equal pay for equal work.
(3) Everyone who works has the right to just and favourable remuneration ensuring for himself and his family an existence worthy of human dignity, and supplemented, if necessary, by other means of social protection.
(4) Everyone has the right to form and to join trade unions for the protection of his interests.
   Article 24
Everyone has the right to rest and leisure, including reasonable limitation of working hours and periodic holidays with pay.
   Article 25
(1) Everyone has the right to a standard of living adequate for the health and well-being of himself and of his family, including food, clothing, housing and medical care and necessary social services, and the right to security in the event of unemployment,

sickness, disability, widowhood, old age or other lack of livelihood in circumstances beyond his control.

(2) Motherhood and childhood are entitled to special care and assistance. All children, whether born in or out of wedlock, shall enjoy the same social protection.

Article 26

(1) Everyone has the right to education. Education shall be free, at least in the elementary and fundamental stages. Elementary education shall be compulsory. Technical and professional education shall be made generally available and higher education shall be equally accessible to all on the basis of merit.

(2) Education shall be directed to the full development of the human personality and to the strengthening of respect for human rights and fundamental freedoms. It shall promote understanding, tolerance and friendship among all nations, racial or religious groups, and shall further the activities of the United Nations for the maintenance of peace.

(3) Parents have a prior right to choose the kind of education that shall be given to their children.

Article 27

(1) Everyone has the right freely to participate in the cultural life of the community, to enjoy the arts and to share in scientific advancement and its benefits.

(2) Everyone has the right to the protection of the moral and material interests resulting from any scientific, literary or artistic production of which he is the author.

Article 28

Everyone is entitled to a social and international order in which the rights and freedoms set forth in this Declaration can be fully realized.

Article 29

(1) Everyone has duties to the community in which alone the free and full development of his personality is possible.

(2) In the exercise of his rights and freedoms, everyone shall be subject only to such limitations as are determined by law solely for the purpose of securing due recognition and respect for the rights and freedoms of others and of meeting the just requirements of morality, public order and the general welfare in a democratic society.

(3) These rights and freedoms may in no case be exercised contrary to the purposes and principles of the United Nations.

Article 30

Nothing in this Declaration may be interpreted as implying for any State, group or person any right to engage in any activity or to perform any act aimed at the destruction of any of the rights and freedoms set forth herein.

(References from UN Documents)

It is also worth considering a piece of legislation that is much derided by some politicians and elements of the press in the UK. It is hated by some, and valued and welcomed by others. The Human Rights Act 1998 enshrined into UK law the key principles of the European Convention on Human Rights. The European Convention arose directly as a consequence of the horrors of the Second World War, and was adapted from the Universal Declaration of Human Rights. The full Act is large and complex, but the key articles and protocols are as follows:

Article 2 Right to life

Article 3 Prohibition on torture or inhuman or degrading treatment or punishment

Article 4 Prohibition on slavery, servitude and forced or compulsory labour

Article 5 Right to liberty and security of the person

Article 6 Right to a fair trial (in the determination of civil rights and obligations, or of any criminal charge)

Article 7 Prohibition of punishment without law (protection against retrospective criminal proceedings or penalties)

Article 8 Right to respect for private and family life (and one's home and correspondence)

Article 9 Freedom of thought, conscience and religion

Article 10 Freedom of expression subject to licensing of broadcasting, television, or cinema e

Article 11 Freedom of assembly and association (protest etc)

Article 12 Right to marry and found a family according to national laws

Article 14 Prohibition of discrimination in the enjoyment of rights and freedoms set forth in the convention, on grounds such as sex, race, colour, language, religion, political or other opinion, national or social origin, association with a national minority, property, birth or other status

The First Protocol

Article 1 Right to peaceful enjoyment of possessions

Article 2 Right to education

Article 3 Right to free elections

(http://www.legislation.gov.uk/ukpga/1998/42/contents)

Is it merely coincidence that those who seek to remove the Human Rights Act from the statutes are generally (but not solely) nationalistic in political thinking, or from elements of the press that traditionally intrude on privacy, or seek to demonise others, or perceive laws as being impotent, or from outside influence, or unfair to the press, or as being unworkable? The Act defines freedoms and rights that are universally recognised and are as much an obligation to a civilised society as the Geneva Conventions are on the rules of war. Should a signatory nation wish to depart from obligations to the European Convention of Human Rights, or in the case of some in the UK, remove the Human Rights Act from the law, they would still be obliged under the Universal Declaration of Human Rights. The only states that do not adhere to that, or who would seek to depart from its principles, would want to do so if there was an intention to deny such fundamental rights to its citizens, or to some within its population.

An argument often put forward in the UK is that the Human Rights Act is a 'criminal's charter' - that it somehow protects the rights of wrongdoers over rights of law-abiding citizens. It clearly does no such thing, and cannot be shown to do so. It accepts the absolute right to a fair trial with due process and this is an essential in a free and democratic society. A society can be defined by how it treats criminals. A presumption of innocence until proven guilty is of paramount importance, as is the right to a fair, public, balanced, and legally controlled trial without undue influence from the state. That criminals are unpopular and cause harm, does not deny those suspected of, or convicted or crime, from key legal rights. As soon as the state decides who can and cannot be treated fairly - or dictates the role and decisions of the judiciary - the rule of law and justice diminishes. Examples of this can be found in every modern totalitarian state and dictatorship. Such reductions or removal of basic freedoms can also be found in every state where genocides have occurred.

The rights protected by the Universal Declaration of Human Rights, the European Convention on Human Rights, and the Human Rights Act are fundamental to a free, just, and democratic society. Resistance to the Declaration, Convention and Act, and the rights they enshrine in law, is resistance to key freedoms that are recognised internationally. Why would any state wish to withdraw from such rules and undertakings, unless it was to ensure power being returned to a more local or central governmental level, without being overseen by international legislators, or a nationally independent and lawful judiciary? The need for such power can only be to ensure the reduction in freedoms and rights for citizens, whether they are law-abiding or criminal, politically active or not, placid or argumentative, or of any minority or potentially 'undesirable' group. A reflection back to the Nuremberg Laws of 1935 shows just what happens when the state dictates laws and removal of freedoms to suit the needs of those in power.

In England and Wales legislation exists which defines hate crime. This was designed to protect all potential victims of hate crime and to ensure that offenders were prosecuted. The Crown Prosecution Service defines racial and religious hate crime as:

'Any incident which is perceived to be racist or religiously motivated by the victim or any other person.

An offence is racially or religiously aggravated if:
At the time of committing the offence, or immediately before or after doing so, the offender demonstrates towards the victim of the offence hostility based on the victim's membership (or presumed membership) of a racial or religious group; or, the offence is

motivated (wholly or partly) by hostility towards members of a racial or religious group based on their membership of that group.'
(*Crown Prosecution Service*)

The Home Office statistics in October 2014 for hate crime in England and Wales for 2013/2014 state that:

'There were 44,480 hate crimes recorded by the police, an increase of five per cent compared with 2012/13, of which:

37,484 (84%) were race hate crimes;

4,622 (10%) were sexual orientation hate crimes;

2,273 (5%) were religion hate crimes;

1,985 (4%) were disability hate crimes; and

555 (1%) were transgender hate crimes.

It is possible for one hate crime offence to have more than one motivating factor. There were increases in all five of the monitored hate crime strands (race, religion, sexual orientation, disability and transgender identity) between 2012/13 and 2013/14. Much of the increase in race and religious hate crime is likely to be due to a rise in offences in the months immediately following the murder of Lee Rigby in May 2013*. Additionally, the police may have improved their recording of crime, and the identification of motivating factors in an offence over the last year. It is less clear whether the increase in sexual orientation, disability or transgender identity hate crime reflects a real rise in hate crime or improved police identification of these offences. The increase across all three strands may suggest improved identification is a factor.'

(UK Government Hate Crime statistics 2013 – 2014)

*(Lee Rigby was an off-duty soldier savagely murdered in London in a high profile and very public offence that received international attention. It was an horrific and brutal killing that was condemned across all elements of society. There is no conceivable justification for what happened. The men convicted of his killing claimed a religious and military motivation for their crime. The trial court did not accept this motivation as a defence. The convicted men claimed to be Muslims. Most other Muslims disowned them and their crime. Sadly, some in British society saw the actions of these two criminal fanatics as a reason to demonise and target other Muslims who had no responsibility for this criminal act. The offenders admitted the deed, but disputed whether it was a crime, and gave their own sham reasons for it. They were rightly convicted and, as they were filmed in the act, there is no doubt as to their guilt. But a small number of people in the UK actively targeted Muslims as a result of this crime, and many in the UK accepted without question, that this act was proof positive of the dangers Muslims as a whole posed to British society).

In history there are examples where a minority community has become victimised because of alleged (and sometimes not proved) crimes. Kristallnacht on 9th November 1938 occurred in part on the premise of revenge and anger after a Jewish student called Herschel Grynszpan was alleged to have killed a German diplomat, Ernst von Rath, in Paris. In Rwanda the spark that lit the touch paper of genocide was an assassination attributed to the minority Tutsi population. Few questions were asked before the riot of mayhem, slaughter, and revenge ensued. Evidence and proof is not always needed for violence, vilification, demonization and anger to explode.

Of particular note in the overall hate crime figures is that 39,757 or 89% of those hate crimes recorded were racial or religious crimes. The figures are alarmingly high. They do not specify which racial or religious groups have been identified as being offended against. It does not need specifics. The law states that it merely needs to be perceived as racist or religiously motivated by the victim or another person. There has undoubtedly been an increase in Islamophobic and anti-Muslim sentiments since the terror attacks on New York in 2001, and the terror attack on London in 2005. The military campaigns in countries with a predominantly Muslim population will have added to hostility towards Muslims, and anger from some Muslims who may believe that others of that faith are being harmed. But other religious groups have been targeted (including Jews), and there is hate crime against other minority communities and individuals because of their race, language, or perceived ethnicity.

Political groups on the extremes campaign using language that often remains just the right side of legal; but in remaining within the law, the leaflets, speeches, websites, and social network pages are designed to inflame and potentially to incite hatred. Elements of the mainstream press contribute to hate through alarmist headlines and articles that few people challenge or seek to contradict. Politicians in all parties could do more to pour oil on potentially troubled waters of anger, fear, and hate, but instead they compete in using language of tough rhetoric that simply reinforces an acceptance, or provides some legitimacy to the idea that many of society's basic concerns and fears are justified.

In most of Europe in the first half of the twentieth century Jews were an established and settled part of communities. Of course there was anti- Semitism, but there was also tolerance and acceptance. Most Jews were part of the society they lived in. They spoke the same language, went to the same schools, and worked in the same factories. Apart from Orthodox Jews with their traditional hair, beards and dress, it would have been impossible to tell who was and who was not Jewish unless it was already known, or faith was discussed. There was no obvious 'ethnic difference', and indeed one of Hitler's problems was trying to find a way of defining Jews as a race rather than a religious group.

In 2016 anti-Semitism is still a problem. Jews in France and the UK have expressed fears for their safety, and have questioned whether they should remain in those countries. Those fears in part follow the attacks in Paris in January 2015 when a satirical magazine was targeted and then people were killed in a kosher market. The perpetrators of those crimes were identified as Islamist fanatics, but the events revealed that anti-Semitism was a concern beyond just the actions of a few criminally-minded religious fundamentalists. Those same fundamentalists and others of their ilk have caused the majority Muslim population to be blamed for their actions, and as a result hatred has been directed towards those who are Muslim, even if they are totally innocent of crimes supposedly done in their name. Anti-Semitism and Islamophobia (amongst other hate crimes and harmful attitudes) are equally wrong.

In Europe and elsewhere today many of those targeted for hatred and intolerance can appear to be different from the majority population. Minority groups often have origins linked to former European colonies in Africa, Asia, Australasia and the Americas. Some of these people may be darker-skinned, and may have a first or second language not shared by the majority population of the country they live in. Some modern migrants do not physically differ from the country they have moved to but as well as language they may have cultural and religious practices that help some single them out as 'others'. Many victims of hate crime are targeted purely because their physical appearance or dress may suggest they belong to a particular cultural or religious grouping. For far right groups the ability to scapegoat others is made easier by simplistic categorising based on these apparent 'differences.' It is not always the far right extremists who hate and promote intolerance: it is often the accepted norm.

In modern parlance the words 'asylum-seeker' and 'refugee' are synonymous not with those who are desperate and fleeing horror and oppression: they are words associated with a generic group of undeserving wrongdoers. Migrants are not those seeking opportunities in foreign lands; they are scroungers and criminals, and people who take jobs, and housing, and school places and hospital beds (those who object to migrants deny racism yet rarely raise objections to white migrants from countries with English as a first language, or where the predominant religion is supposedly Christianity). Such attitudes to our fellow human beings are widely accepted without question. And when politicians or elements of the press publicly share such attitudes they give them a perceived moral and social validity. This is exactly what happened prior to the Holocaust. It has happened with all genocides since that time. The extremists do not create hate: they merely exploit and expand upon hateful and prejudiced thinking. Holocaust survivor, author, scholar, and lecturer Kitty Hart-Moxon points out that there have always been 'tribes' singled out for hate (in a conversation with the author). It does not make such hate right or acceptable, but it is an uncomfortable reality. Primo Levi observed: 'Nevertheless, perhaps for reasons that go back to our origins as social animals, the need to divide the field into 'we' and 'they' is so strong that this pattern, this bi-partition – friend-enemy – prevails over all others.' (Primo Levi *The Drowned and the Saved* p. 22)

Post 9/11 the prevailing attitude in the west has been anti-Muslim. It matters not a jot that most Muslims pose no danger to western society (and apart from their faith they are no different to that society, where, indeed, many millions of Muslims live). It has become acceptable to casually adopt Islamophobic attitudes. That is not to dismiss harm caused by Islamist terrorists, or religious fundamentalists who use faith as a rationale for violent behaviour. Of course that exists, but it needs to be seen in context - it needs to be seen against the attitude of the whole Islamic community, and it needs to be seen against the bigger social, economic and other factors that contribute to war and civil unrest in some parts of the world. Wherever there is extreme poverty, economic meltdown, loss of government, and the collapse of social institutions, the fanatics or criminals will fill the void. In the Middle East and some other areas at present the void is being filled by religious fundamentalists, absolutists, literalists, fanatics, and extremists. In a different time it could just as easily be filled by violent criminals with no religious affiliation, or by political groups and revolutionaries seeking to create an environment in which their ideology could thrive. Context and perspective are required in analysing and responding to these areas of violence and unrest.

Generalised blame directed at Muslims is probably misguided for many reasons, not least of which is a failure to understand the many branches and roots of that faith, but also the many differences of those who adhere to Islam – the majority of whom will want no more from life than peace, comfort, and opportunity. Of course there are those in the Muslim world that many westerners disagree with, or find elements of faith, tradition, and culture incompatible with their own beliefs or standards. Those who offer generalised hatred and mistrust of all Muslims, who see that faith as being one practised only by terrorists and criminals, are proving themselves to be no better than the Nazis and their sympathisers who made similar sweeping, and ultimately fatal, judgements about Jews, Roma, Slavs and others.

A scan through the online editions of popular daily newspapers in the UK will be guaranteed to produce stories citing Muslims, or more recently 'migrants', in an almost entirely negative way. In 2013 and 2014 in the UK the possibility of increased migration and cross-border movement by citizens of Bulgaria and Romania was met by alarming levels of scaremongering, debates in parliament, and extremely provocative press headlines. Mainstream political parties in the UK compete to issue the toughest-sounding rhetoric with regards to immigration. In the UK the rise of the far right political groups (some with popular votes at elections) is in part due to these fears. Some of the most popular Facebook pages in the UK are avowedly right wing, and are openly supported by those who are racist and religiously intolerant. The tabloid press will regularly run stories citing migrants, asylum-seekers, and Muslims in negative articles. In so doing they conveniently generalize whole communities, and whether the intention is there or not, the result is that minority groups, often not in a position to defend themselves, are blamed for society's ills, and demonized. The most vulnerable – those who flee horror to seek asylum in other lands – are seen as enemies rather than fellow human beings in need of help, support, and compassion. One could argue that the words 'asylum seeker' have taken away the reality of 'refugee' in best describing these men, women and children. The 'others' have been defined in their entirety as homogenous groups, with negativity being the prevailing and often the unchallenged attitude towards them. Whilst intolerant attitudes and even hatred do not automatically signify a precursor to genocide or mass harm, they are part of a bigger picture that has a proven historical consistency in previous genocides and crimes of racial, religious, and other hostility.

In the United States a number of far right groups have been linked to crimes of violence. Many people express views some would find distasteful, but they cite the protection of the First Amendment guaranteeing freedom of speech. In continental Europe far right parties have gained electoral success in recent years whilst promoting clear ideas of racial and religious intolerance, including anti-Semitism.

There is an historical precedent in early twentieth century Germany where news media was used as a means of promoting a sense of superiority and intolerance. The weekly paper *Der*

Stürmer only had a circulation of about half a million, and yet it greatly influenced many into believing Nazi propaganda about Jews. Its editor Julius Streicher rightly earned the nickname 'Jew Baiter Number One'. The Nazis used news media and film to sell their ideas of hate to a public already predisposed to believing such concepts. When anti-Semitism was promoted as a constant and consistent message from the top to the bottom of society it became increasingly difficult for others to challenge it. They merely took anti-Semitism to another level with tragic, brutal, and fatal consequences.

As Nazi influence spread across Europe it was an ideology that was not always met with resistance. When we ask if it could happen again we have to consider many factors. Social media, communication, and news networks ensure that information can be spread readily without the need for feet on the ground in conquered lands. This can be positive in that ideas can be more readily challenged. This can be negative in that ideas can rapidly gain a popular and widespread footing over many lands and people without the need for military conquest or huge electoral success. Many who would not vote for far right parties may still share much of their world view. This must potentially be as dangerous for racial, religious, and other minority groups as would be a vast conquering army. In modern society, as in the early twentieth century, intolerance is an acceptable norm. And those who challenge intolerance are seen as fair game for critical attack. In the parlance of today the defenders of minorities are accused of being part of some liberal élite (as if this is a flaw) and their stance is seen as some form of weakness supported only by an out-of- touch intelligentsia, and a populist clique. When the Nazis rose to prominence in the 1920s, and to power in the 1930s, they promoted themselves as being different from the established political classes and as being representative of the people. That same approach is taken by the far right of today. They claim to be part of the working masses, and to be detached from the established political élite. Indeed, they dismiss others as having no knowledge of the concerns of 'real people'. That message shouted loudly and often enough becomes plausible to those who see themselves as disaffected, unrepresented, and downtrodden. And as in the 1920s, 1930s and 1940s in Germany and elsewhere in Europe the leaders of far right parties are generally charismatic, articulate, engaging, populist, and fiercely determined in conveying their views of society's problems and in their ideas of simplistic solutions. Those solutions of course will always seek a cause or an enemy that does not belong to that nation, or more alarmingly does not belong to that nation's historical bloodstock, ancient heritage, or religious background. The consequences – should such thinking gain a truly popular foothold – are always damaging to those least able to defend themselves.

Many religious and ethnic minority groups are threatened, attacked, isolated and targeted. At times of economic recession and hardship, with populations struggling financially, with high unemployment, lack of housing, and conflict in lands near and far, it is easy to find a convenient scapegoat. Throughout history blame has been apportioned to minority groups – religious, linguistic, ethnic, or other – even when the bulk of evidence suggests more complex factors are involved. It is ironic that in Europe, one of the highest profile and most eloquent voices against the rise of far right politics, and the public face of an effective online campaign in 2014 encouraging people to vote, has been Rainer Hoess, grandson of Rudolf Hoess, the Commandant of Auschwitz.

Some might argue that intolerance and hatred – as attitudes – are not illegal. And to a degree this is true, in most societies. People can think unpopular or unpleasant thoughts and break no laws. People can voice opinions others may find offensive, and are perfectly within their rights to do so as long as no crime, such as incitement, is committed. Indeed it could be argued that comedy thrives on the potential to offend and insult, and that the possibility of being offensive is a right in a free country. It could be argued further that as long as one acts within the law one is doing no wrong. Such arguments are used by far right (and far left) political parties in ensuring that their leaflets, posters and campaign slogans do not lead to arrest and prosecution. It is also offered as an opinion that those who feel offended against are at fault (rather than those who cause offence) and that they need to toughen up, or even leave, if they don't like it. How strange society would be if such an attitude was promoted with regards to other crimes and victims.

The Reverend Martin Luther King (Junior) raised the subject of acting within the law as a discussion point in his letter from Birmingham Jail of 16th April 1963. Colleagues had written to him, calling for an end to demonstrations. He responded at length, and discussed the nature of just and unjust laws. He also mentioned:

'*We should never forget that everything Adolf Hitler did in Germany was "legal" and everything the Hungarian freedom fighters did in Hungary was "illegal". It was "illegal" to aid and comfort a Jew in Hitler's Germany. Even so I am sure that, had I lived in Germany at the time, I would have aided and comforted my Jewish brothers. If today I lived in a Communist country where certain principles dear to the Christian faith are suppressed, I would openly advocate disobeying that country's antireligious laws". He goes on to elaborate further. "I must make two honest confessions to you, my Christian and Jewish brothers. First I must confess that over the past few years I have been gravely disappointed with the white moderate. I have almost reached the regrettable conclusion that the Negro's great stumbling block in his stride towards freedom is not the*

AUSCHWITZ-BIRKENAU

White Citizen's Counciler (sic) or the Ku Klux Klanner, but the white moderate, who is more devoted to 'order' than to justice; who prefers a negative peace which is the absence of tension to positive peace which is the presence of justice; who constantly says: "I agree with you in the goal you seek, but I cannot agree with your methods of direct action"; who paternalistically believes he can set the timetable for another man's freedom; who lives by a mythical concept of time and who constantly advises the Negro to wait for a "more convenient season". Shallow understanding from people of good will is more frustrating than absolute misunderstanding from people of ill will. Lukewarm acceptance is much more bewildering than outright rejection.' (*The Autobiography of Martin Luther King Junior* p.195)

In this much misquoted and misrepresented letter King is clearly not advocating that Hitler was right. He is pointing out that the actions of Hitler, and therefore the Nazis, were within the laws of Germany as they stood at the time, even though morally and ethically they were wrong, and they were not laws that conformed to standards held elsewhere. As such, merely acting within the law does not make an action right, and that there must be scope to break laws in the interests of good, or to stand up to those who cause harm within the bounds of some current legal framework.

There are some modern experimental points of reference that may help us to understand the easy predisposition of people towards cruelty and prejudice, and how those who are being subjugated, even in safe and controlled conditions, can readily become subservient and fearful.

The Stanford Experiment in 1971 involved giving students the role of prisoner and jailer. It had to be halted after only 6 days of the planned 14 days due to the brutality of the 'jailers', and the distress of some of the 'prisoners.' The Stanford University Website about this experiment states:

'What happens when you put good people in an evil place? Does humanity win over evil, or does evil triumph? These are some of the questions we posed in this dramatic simulation of prison life conducted in the summer of 1971 at Stanford University. How we went about testing these questions and what we found may astound you. Our planned two-week investigation into the psychology of prison life had to be ended prematurely after only six days because of what the situation was doing to the college students who participated. In only a few days, our guards became sadistic and our prisoners became depressed and showed signs of extreme stress.'
(*The Stanford Prison Experiment - A Simulation Study of the Psychology of Imprisonment Conducted at Stanford University*)

In 1968 Jane Elliott, a Third Grade teacher in the US, first did her blue eyes and brown eyes experiment. She did it immediately following the assassination of Dr Martin Luther King. It was repeated a couple of times, and is readily accessible on the Internet. She convinced her young subjects that those with blue eyes were superior to those with brown eyes. There is obviously no truth in this, but as the children were categorised according to eye colour they readily conformed to their perceived type. A brief summary is available online from the BBC. It states:

'In 1968, Jane Elliott was just another American schoolteacher. She taught third and fourth grade (eight to nine-year-olds) children at a school in Riceville, Iowa, which was a very typical, all-white, small American town. Jane had tried to introduce her students to the idea of racial equality. She had even appointed Martin Luther King as the class's 'Hero of the Month.'

But she struggled to explain what racism was really like to the all-white class. They seemed keen to learn, but had never seen a black person in real life.

After the assassination of Martin Luther King, Jane tried a more direct exercise to bring the truth home about racial discrimination. It was an exercise which was to change her life. Jane Elliott told her pupils a pseudo-scientific explanation of how eye-colour defined people: blue eyes showed people who were cleverer, quicker, more likely to succeed. They were superior to people with brown eyes, who were described as untrustworthy, lazy and stupid. She then divided the class according to who had brown eyes and who had blue eyes. To ensure clarity of divisions - given that some eye colours might be subject to dispute - she used ribbons to mark out the 'inferior' brown-eyed children (those with clearly different eye colours acted as bystanders). To reinforce the situation, she gave the superior group extra classroom privileges, and would not let the brown-eyed children drink from the same water fountain. She made a point of praising the blue-eyed children, and being more negative to the browns.

Jane Elliott was amazed at the speedy transformation in her class. The superior blue-eyed children became arrogant, and were bossy and unpleasant to their brown-eyed class mates. The brown eyes quickly became cowed and timid, even those that had previously dominated the class. But what really astounded Jane was the difference academically. Blue-eyed children improved their grades, and managed mathematical and reading tasks that had proved out of their grasp before. Brown-eyed high-flyers stumbled over simple questions.

A few days later, Jane Elliott told her class that she had the information about melanin the wrong way round, and swapped the colour superiorities over. The brown-eyed children tore off their now-hated ribbons, and the situations quickly reversed.

Jane Elliott had proved - more dramatically than she had ever thought possible - how much discrimination is soaked up subconsciously, by both the oppressor and the oppressed. She had not told her pupils to treat each other differently, only that they *were* different; and yet they developed the characteristic responses of discrimination. Jane Elliott felt that they did this because they had already absorbed discriminatory behaviour from their parents and other adults. On the plus side, she had also proved that racism can be unlearnt as quickly as it can be learnt. She had also found an excellent way of demonstrating what it feels like to be the subject of discrimination.'

One of the most notable experiments regarding man's capacity for inexplicable and unnecessary cruelty is the Milgram Experiment on Obedience to Authority, conducted by Yale University Psychologist Stanley Milgram. This experiment was first described in 1963 in an article in the *Journal of Abnormal and Social Psychology* and then later in 1974 in Milgram's book *Obedience to Authority, An Experimental View*. The experiments began in July 1961, just three months after the start of the trial of Adolf Eichmann in Israel, which was of clear and obvious significance. They were designed to answer the question, 'Could it be that Eichmann and his million accomplices in the Holocaust were just following orders? Could we call them all accomplices?'

The experiment involved three individuals. One was running the experiment, one was the subject of the experiment (a volunteer), and one was a confederate pretending to be a volunteer. Only the volunteer did not know what was involved. Each of these individuals fulfilled distinctive roles. The experimenter was authoritative, the teacher was intended to obey the orders of the experimenter, and the 'learner' was to receive a stimulus from the 'teacher'. The subject of the experiment and an actor both drew slips to determine what their roles would be. Unknown to the subject both slips read 'teacher' but the actor always claimed that their slip said 'learner'. This ensured that the subject of the experiment was always the teacher.

The teacher and the learner were placed in separate rooms where they could communicate, but could not see each other. The subject of the experiment (in the role of teacher) was given a small electric shock from a machine referred to as 'an electroshock generator', and was told this was a sample of the shock that the learner would receive during the experiment.

The teacher was given a list of word pairs to teach the learner. The teacher began by reading out the list of word pairs that he wanted to teach the learner. The teacher then read out the first word of each pair with four possible answers. The learner pressed a button to indicate the response to the question. If the answer was incorrect the teacher administered a shock to the learner. The voltage increased by 15 volts with each incorrect answer. After a number of voltage increases the actor playing the learner began to bang on the wall and complained. In some versions the actor playing the learner had claimed to have a heart condition at the start of the experiment. Some subjects expressed a desire to stop the experiment. Some paused at 135 volts (or what they believed to be that voltage) and questioned what they were doing. Most continued to increase the voltage once they were assured they would not be held responsible. They were encouraged by the experimenter to continue. Twenty six out of forty participants (sixty five percent) administered the maximum required 450 volt shock – a fatal level.

The Stanford and Milgram experiments clearly show the potential for supposedly decent people to act in cruel and potentially harmful ways when given assurances that they would not be held responsible (in the Milgram Experiment), or when believing that power gave them a right to do so (in the Stanford Experiment). The Stanford Experiment also demonstrated how quickly subjugated people could bow to oppressive behaviour. Jane Elliott's test showed quite alarmingly how easily prejudice can be promoted and believed from different viewpoints, even if they are young children. None of these experiments seeks to justify prejudice, cruelty, violence, or oppression; nor do they seek to make the role of those oppressed seem legitimate. But they do show how easily thoughts, ideas, and behaviours can be promoted, established and normalized. We see in many societies today how a minority view can receive popular or populist support – as happened in Germany. And once a view is seen as validated by many, or by those in power, it becomes difficult to challenge it, and those who are most vulnerable, or are a convenient target, become at risk of harm.

Returning to the earlier question of could it happen again? It is hopefully unlikely, but not impossible, that modern Europe, with the ready access to information, with the loss of imperial ambitions, with an increasingly informed and historically-aware population, and with superior communication facilities, would allow industrial slaughter on the scale of the Holocaust to occur again. Europe today is a hugely different continent from the one that existed in the first half of the twentieth century. Policy throughout Europe since that time has been more about trade and cooperation than the overt hostility of earlier years. There is still disagreement between nation states, but there is little prospect of that spiralling to war. And the civil unrest and other factors that led to the Holocaust are not as extreme or uncontrolled.

Sadly, genocides have happened since the 1940s – including in Europe - and continue to take place now. Civil unrest, for many reasons, often results from poverty, and leads to social instability and upheaval, conflict, and the rise of radical political, criminal, or religious groups that appear to provide ready, simplistic, absolutist, or hostile solutions. Always those solutions will include blaming a convenient enemy, within the state or external to it. And ultimately these radicals will seek to destroy and eradicate such enemies. Today we can switch on a television, or log on to an Internet site, or purchase a newspaper with up-to-date information. We can readily access live images of war zones, famine and human suffering. People can see these images and choose to help, or they can ignore them as being irrelevant, and change the TV channel. Supposedly decent people can dehumanise others based on where they live, the colour of their skin, or the religion they practise. Those in most dire need become worthy of help or compassion based on the ability or decision of a viewer to press a button on a remote control. We can see today how refugees fleeing warzones and famine are seen as an enemy rather than people deserving help. When far right politicians suggest boats of refugees should be sunk to put others off travelling, we are rightly shocked. When mainstream politicians across Europe suggest refugees in dangerous and unseaworthy boats should not be helped, in order to deter desperate people from making the same journey, few raise a concern. Whether a boat is deliberately sunk or merely capsizes, the occupants are still human beings as deserving of life as anyone else. That they travel to lands far from home should be understood – work, money, safety, opportunity, refuge, close to extended family, etc – not condemned as some enemy incursion into sovereign territories. Are those who ignore the suffering of people in greatest need really any better than those who ignored train loads of people en route to death camps, or who ignored the obvious suffering and slaughter occurring in their midst?

We must never permit ourselves to excuse those who seek to harm, scapegoat, or kill others purely because of their faith, language, ethnicity, sexuality, gender, politics, or limitless other differences. But we need to understand why such attitudes and behaviour develop when left unchecked, how we can challenge the proponents of hate, and how we can seek to prevent societies walking blindfolded into situations with potentially terrible consequences. We must also learn to empathise with those who are the targets of hate, to recognise them as our fellow human beings, and to seek always to protect and nurture them as we would our own kith and kin.

There are lessons to be learned from the Nazis and individuals such as Auschwitz Camp Commandant Rudolf Hoess. As we reflect on and consider the seventieth anniversary of the liberation of Auschwitz, we who live today are custodians of history and of the future, who are honour-bound to do our duty to survivors, and those who suffered and died in the Holocaust. We must strive as individuals and as members of communities, to ensure that attitudes of hate and intolerance do not prevail, and do not become the accepted norm. And we must stand up to other societies that dehumanise fellow human beings as a means of making harm and cruelty acceptable. The consequences of what can happen are evident in the crumbling remains and the human ash pits of Auschwitz.

Kitty Hart-Moxon in *Return to Auschwitz* reflects on going back to the camp in 1993 to contribute to a television programme (*Another Journey By Train*) in which four young Nazis were persuaded to visit Auschwitz to meet her:

"In spite of all the evidence, they continued to declare their admiration for Hitler, shouting at me, 'Who cares today?' One even proudly declared, 'I'm a racist. Absolutely. And an anti-Semite.' Incapable of considering anything which clashed with their views, they finally refused further discussions." (*Return to Auschwitz* p. 239)

Kitty very eloquently observes, "The story of the Holocaust can never fully be known. Too many witnesses perished. But provided we survivors continue to tell it as fully and as honestly as we can, it will not become just some blurred image in the dim and distant past. 'Who cares today?' yelled those neo-Nazis. A careless remark, but it made me remember that for almost two generations this part of European history was largely ignored. We must care today and always. And make sure that future generations learn from our experience. Could it happen again? Only if the past is forgotten." (*Return to Auschwitz* p. 241)

Kitty's words have a power to them. They have the power of survival, of one who was there, of one who has thrived beyond Auschwitz, and of one who has dedicated a lifetime to informing, challenging deniers, and educating the young and adults of today. The wisdom of what Kitty says, needs no further elaboration.

Could it happen again? The answer is, of course, yes. It has happened since, and the potential for further genocides in the future is there. It needs merely for the majority in a society, supported or encouraged by elements of the press and by those in power, to identify a group within (or outside of) that society as wrongdoers, as dangerous, or as less worthy; and for the evidence to back up that perception to be no more than that group's difference, or a belief that the entirety of that group have the potential to cause harm to everyone else based on the reality or false belief of harm done by a minority, and a universally-held conviction that some mythical and homogenous whole are responsible. From there it is no great leap to isolating these others in specific areas (ghettoising), or ensuring they are identifiable (wearing symbols or carrying passbooks), or internment to contain known, proven, unproven, or potential wrongdoers (imprisonment or use of concentration camps), through to eliminating some of their number for the greater good of the majority (genocide). Germany, for the majority of its recorded history was a civilised land of culture and supposed decency. Most of continental Europe was similarly viewed. And yet these lands of culture readily bought into an ethos of hate and extreme cruelty that matches and in many ways surpasses anything man has encountered before or since. And at Auschwitz in particular, the bestial cruelty and slaughter was taken to a level never encountered elsewhere in history.

The ingredients of unrest that led the Nazis to power are still present in modern continental Europe and even in the UK. And once more it is racial, religious, cultural, and other minorities that are targeted for hate, vitriol, animosity, and blame. Those in power need to be seen to be acting in the interests of the electorate and of the nation. The masses need to feel protected. For these two to maintain some form of tribal and national loyalty, to work together for the common good, and to apparently protect the interests of everyone, they readily, and often without question, resort to identifying simple causes and reaching simplistic solutions. An enemy, a threat, or a danger, is all actually good for the unity of society and the state (although of course the preference would be for no danger or threat). How real those enemies, threats and dangers are does not need to be explored much or questioned if the message is being delivered without challenge at all levels. As Goebbels observed, the Nazis merely needed to ensure they went at the speed of the slowest vessel in the convoy before the majority would catch up with their ideas. Modern societies need to remain alert to such convoys, to who or what is leading, and in which direction the convoy is heading. For the safety and good of everyone, society must be prepared to slow the convoy down, redirect it, or to bring it to a halt.

There are protective factors. In Europe today most countries class themselves as operating some form of democracy. The rule of law includes international oversight and the influence of the United Nations. The Universal Declaration of Human Rights, The European Convention on Human Rights, The Human

Rights Act in the UK, and The United Nations Convention on the Prevention and Punishment of the Crime of Genocide are all safety nets to help prevent further genocides in Europe and elsewhere. Unfortunately there are currently some volatile, unstable, and largely lawless societies – particularly in parts of Africa and the Middle East – where no external influence such as the UN is recognised, and where minorities of many faiths and cultures are oppressed and face the real risk of extermination. In the UK hate crimes are defined in law and can be prosecuted. The Press, which in history has contributed to genocide, is also a medium that can publically challenge and question the promoters of hate. In the democracies of Europe and elsewhere the Press is largely free from government interference and control. The press is bound by law and regulated to try and prevent inappropriate behaviour. The laws on press freedom are largely respected, and the press does seem to exercise some self-control over what is and is not acceptable. In most European countries and in the UK too, there are elements of the press and news media that may seem to agitate or inflame intolerance, but those branches of the Press are counterbalanced by other more moderate publications and news outlets. The same restraints and alternatives seem to apply in the US, Australasia, and elsewhere. But they are not guarantees that the unimaginable cannot happen again. The best guarantee and the most effective safeguard is people, and their willingness to question, to challenge, and to stand up to those who would gradually and insidiously lead nations into the abyss of bestial cruelty that can be brought about by uncontrolled hatred. And when people in such nations cannot safely or constructively resist, we must rely on the powers of other lands to intervene for the greater good.

**

CHAPTER TEN
REFLECTIONS AND HOPE

"History, despite its wrenching pain, cannot be unlived; but if faced with courage, need not be lived again."

Maya Angelou

The children and adults of today, who did not live through the genocide in Europe, are the custodians of history. We are honour bound to preserve not just the physical premises and remains of sites such as Auschwitz-Birkenau; we also have a duty to those who lived, suffered, and died there and elsewhere across Europe. We even have a duty to the descendants of those who committed atrocities in that we must ensure the thinking, attitudes, intolerances, and accepted norms of that time are never allowed to go unchallenged when they reappear in bold ugliness today.

As we reflect on the Holocaust we are fortunate to have an immense volume of work produced by scholars, historians, and of course many survivors. A lot of survivors are still alive, and can give first hand personal accounts to families, friends, and audiences around the world. Those accounts are an essential opportunity that should not be missed by any who are interested in this subject. We are fortunate that many survivors see it as a personal duty to inform younger generations through writing and public talks. But there is a sad and harsh reality that we must accept – the survivors are now elderly. It is 70 years since the liberation of Auschwitz and other camps. Unfortunately the survivor numbers are becoming fewer, and in not too many years none will remain to talk to us in person. We must ensure that their history, their experiences, and their accounts of the truth are not lost and that they do not merely become diluted and sterile words on pages in books.

Reflecting back to those ghostly, tormented, shadows of humanity this author first met in 1980, some thirty five years after the liberation of Auschwitz, it is impossible not to consider 'what if' questions. What if they had grown up in a world without the bile of hate and prejudice that led to their incarceration and pain in concentration camps? What if they had lived their lives in peace and hope, as all should be able to do? What if the promoters and proponents of racial and religious hatred had been confronted by others willing to say no? What if they had not seen and experienced the death and destruction of camp life? What if they had not lost those they loved and cared about most? What if, on being liberated, and developing mental health problems, they had encountered a more caring system that tried to understand their emotional torment rather than just labelling them as mad? What if? What if? What if?

We cannot change the past. We can, however, learn from it and do something to address the potential for future harm. A simple tool used in helping survivors of childhood sexual abuse is the image of a tree. This visual tool uses the roots as the causes, the branches as the emotions, and the leaves as the presenting symptoms or diagnoses. It is effective because of its simplicity. It can be elaborated on by comparison to a real tree that loses its leaves in autumn, or that can be chopped down. The leaves and the body of this virtual tree can be removed only with time, support, and therapy. The stump and the roots may remain as a reminder of the past that will always have happened, but the impact of that pain can be reduced. Another way of thinking about it would be an abscess. It can merely be dressed with a plaster and remain a painful infection, or it can be lanced. The lanced abscess will leave a scar, a physical reminder that it was once there, but it will lack the pain and discomfort. In a similar way we must address the past, not merely cover it up.

With hatred and the potential for harm we can either let the roots develop into large trees with multiple branches and leaves, or allow the small infected pore to become an inflamed abscess. Or we can nip the trees at the root, or train the branches to our preferred shape, or treat the infection before it becomes too painful and requires more drastic intervention. It is surely better to act early rather than to respond later to a problem that may be more difficult to manage.

Hate will always be there. Perhaps people are by nature tribal and form strong allegiances towards a family connected by blood, nationality, faith, language, or place of birth. Tribalism is of course natural, and largely a positive thing. It ensures that we all act for the greater good of our immediate and wider community - whether that is a family group, a town, city, region, country, linguistic, religious, or other shared similarity. Perhaps that same tribalism leads to the demonizing of others, and the need to see threat and danger from those outside of the immediate tribal group. But surely part of the reason for humanity's success is also due to the ability to cooperate, to trade, to engage, to learn from each other, and to form relationships across perceived differences and boundaries. If all 'others' are perceived as harmful or potentially dangerous the consequences are conflict, lack of social stability, and disharmony for everyone. The Holocaust, and the genocides in Cambodia, Bosnia, Rwanda and Darfur, demonstrated the ultimate negative consequences of tribalism and hate when taken to its extreme. There have been countless slaughters across the world of 'others' who were deemed lesser human beings and unworthy of life because in some way they were different. Whenever a group – due to nationality, language, faith, race, ethnicity, age, gender, sexuality, education, employment, sickness, mental illness, mental incapacity, poverty, homelessness, or even wealth – is perceived to be superior or inferior to another there is the potential for harm. When any groups view others as being less deserving of basic human rights, then the same attitudes that led to the Holocaust can re-emerge. We owe it to those who suffered and died in the Holocaust to always learn the lessons of history, and pledge to prevent the past being repeated.

For two thousand years anti-Semitism has been a feature of life in Europe and elsewhere. There have been many times when that has led to violence, aggression, and slaughter of Jews and their sympathizers. There has been a convenience for the majority population in many countries to find a common enemy amongst a minority group. That group has been perceived as being different for no other reason than their faith.

We still see today the tribal propensity for seeking a convenient scapegoat. It can be religious groups – Jews, Muslims, Jehovah Witnesses, Catholics, Protestants, Sikhs, Hindus, Buddhists and others – or it can be racial groups – Asian, West Indian, African, Eastern European, Roma, or specific nationalities. It can even be communities seen merely as being 'different' such as travellers, gays, migrants, asylums seekers, refugees, and others. The common factor is the vocal and often unchallenged hostility towards another group. There will be recurring themes, including: they're criminal; they're lazy; they're dishonest; they're sexual predators;

they're lacking in morals; they're stealing our jobs; they're taking our housing; or that our hospitals, schools, and economy cannot cope; or even the more simplistic - 'We're full, and we don't want them here.' The language used seeks to dehumanise people into convenient groups. As such, 'asylum seeker' whilst it adequately describes a person's status, also has negative connotations that the word 'refugee' would not have, even though it refers to the same person. There is a socially acceptable disregard for the welfare or needs of others, and this disregard is found across societies right up to the higher levels of politics. The parallels with Europe in the first half of the twentieth century are too clear and obvious. Yet communities and those that govern them still fail to read or heed the warning signs.

Yet there is hope. Modern information and communication technology means that thoughts and ideas can be shared readily and rapidly at the press of a button. Negative thinkers may see this firstly as an asset to those who intend harm, but it is a powerful asset to the forces for tolerance and good. Those who promote intolerance through the use of flawed, misinformed, or limited messages can find that they are challenged more readily. People can check the truth of information through typing a few key words into an Internet search engine. We have, at a click, access to the greatest library the world has ever known. Political leaders at all levels are less able to sell a distorted idea to a population who will accept propaganda without question. The popular press in most democracies is a force for good. It feels a duty to stand up to those in power, and to make them answerable not just to the news media, but to the population who access that source of information. Conversely, when elements of the press behave in ways that may be harmful, the political classes and the public are better able to demand proof and an explanation of any hidden or alternative agenda. The power and availability of the Internet and social media ensures that even in totalitarian or authoritarian societies the people can access information that is supposedly forbidden.

People today – even though most have not lived through global conflict, war, or genocide – are more aware of the potential harm that can be caused from doing nothing. Society is more able and more willing to challenge than perhaps previous generations were. There will be very few people today who do not know at least something of the Holocaust, or the genocides in Cambodia, Bosnia, Rwanda and Darfur. And people are immediately informed or able to gain information about the true brutality of war in current conflicts. There is no reliance on a sanitised version being made available through official reports. Indeed the power of the Internet is such that brutal and depraved images from war zones can be accessed by a few clicks, and some terror groups use social media as a means of spreading their poison and fear.

There are reasons to be hopeful and optimistic. The hope is in the youth of today being willing to learn the lessons of the past and being prepared to do something about the future. Any talk by a Holocaust survivor is notable not so much by the interested older adults who attend armed with knowledge of the subject, but by the avid attentiveness of young people and parties from schools who hang on to every word. They are the hope for the future, and that hope is reinforced by the majority of people being decent, fair minded and caring, with multiple means of communicating with each other. Whilst 'never again' may be too optimistic, it is at least a goal that can be aimed for – but the world must always remain alert to the dangers of allowing hate and intolerance to be acceptable norms.

***

CHAPTER ELEVEN
AUSCHWITZ-BIRKENAU TODAY

P ictures alone can never convey the reality of Auschwitz-Birkenau. For visitors they serve as a reminder of what was once there. For those seeking to understand the camp they give a visual perspective that imagination on its own cannot create. For survivors they represent memories of places steeped in horror and personal trauma.

For many of us who are not survivors of the brutality of camp life, our knowledge of it, and how we perceive the environment, is in grainy black and white wartime images. The reality is that all the horrors of Auschwitz occurred not in photographs or flickering ancient film, but in colour, in actuality, in sound, in smells, in physical pain, in emotional trauma, in loss, in grief, in terror, in hunger, in disease, in cruelty, and in death. It all occurred in living memory. There are people alive today who were there, and for whom Auschwitz is part of their very existence. No photograph, no matter how well taken or skilfully produced, can ever tell the stories that need to be told.

Auschwitz-Birkenau is now a national museum. It is a heritage site of international importance. It is preserved for posterity so that survivors can visit in safety, and so that this and future generations can understand the enormity of the industrial slaughter that was the Holocaust.

The entrance sign, the brick barracks, the pathways, the electric fencing, the guard towers, the gas chamber and the gallows of Auschwitz I are maintained as a living museum. The barracks contain displays charting the activities of the camp, the cruelties that occurred there, the lives of inmates, and the record-keeping of the Nazis. Artefacts, hair, and personal effects of some who died there are contained in large rooms as a sobering and chilling reminder of the pointlessness and loss of life the camp was dedicated to in its purpose. For the visitor today there is a sense that no matter how awful the reality of Auschwitz, at least in this part of the camp it feels clean, preserved and safe.

Auschwitz II or Birkenau provides an entirely different experience. It has some immediate familiarity which is at once reassuring – 'I know this place'; and distressing – 'because I know this place'. The vastness of Birkenau is overwhelming. It is huge. Some of the brick blocks or barracks remain intact. Some of the wooden blocks have been rebuilt or maintained. Much of the original wooden material was stolen by the local population after the war. Where a barrack block once stood there remains only a chimney and a few bricks outlining the former existence of a building. Those crumbling chimneys stretch far into the distance beyond sight. Each chimney signifies a place that once held hundreds of people in conditions of unbelievable suffering and discomfort. Those blocks that remain intact contain row upon row of bunks. The conditions within are sparse. It is immediately apparent that nothing could have made this place comfortable or tolerable to any standard most people could recognise.

In between the camp sectors are the endless rows of barbed wire that would have been electrified when the camp was in use. And strategically placed at regular intervals are the guard towers from which heavily-armed and hate-filled men could shoot at will any who tried to escape or rebel.

SIMON BELL

The train tracks and the ramp are a chilling reminder of the time when millions of tired, starved, confused, bewildered, and terrified people arrived at the camp. The ramp will forever be the site of the selections when the fate of so many was decided by a cursory look and a casual flick of a hand. To the right or left was immediate death; or labour and slow death. And the visitors, tourists and pilgrims who walk in this place tread on the same stones and earth that so many did previously in a crueller, almost unbelievable time in human history.

A short walk from the ramp are the remains of the gas chambers and crematoria in which so many died; where slaughter and cremation occurred on an industrial and organised scale the world has never seen before or since; where after death the bodies of men, women, and children were stripped of clothing, before they were intimately searched for concealed valuables, and then had their jewellery and gold fillings removed. Those recently slain bodies would then be burned in their thousands in the purposely-built crematoria. And when the crematoria were too busy to cope, bodies would be thrown into pits and burned there. And when the gas chambers and crematoria were both overwhelmed people would be burned alive in pits. And the ashes from the wholesale and wanton slaughter would be spread on roads between the camps, or made into fertiliser, or scattered in the river, or just dumped in ponds that still exist there now.

For the visitor today the camp is a place to view, to ponder over, and to quietly reflect in. In summer the weather is very hot and pleasant. In winter it is bitterly cold, and even with modern clothing and a nourished, healthy body, it is uncomfortable. Birds fly and sing (it is a myth that they do not). The grass is green and plentiful. Wild flowers grow, and pollinating insects go about their daily activity. When the camp was a prison there was no grass or flowers. The inmates would have eaten even a single green blade or leaf. The place was awash with mud. The mud was everywhere, and got into everything. The bitter cold of winter had to be suffered when wearing thin pyjamas and clogs. Inmates were starved and diseased. They were weakened by overwork and physical cruelty. Most died. But some – incredibly and fortunately - survived.

For the Auschwitz visitor now, or the person viewing pictures, there needs to be a realisation that each brick, each stone, the soil, each piece of barbed wire, each blade of grass, the nearby trees, and even the air itself, are all laden with the pain, the hopelessness, the terror, the distress, the screams, and the death that once permeated the very being and essence of this place.

Tourists visit Auschwitz-Birkenau in their hundreds of thousands every year. They come as individuals, small family or social groups, organised visits, and dedicated pilgrimages. Most who visit are respectful of the camp and what its place in history signifies. A small number are blissfully unaware, or merely see the visit as something to tick off a bucket list. Some loudly laugh and joke while posing for pictures. Some, undoubtedly, visit in an effort to prove some abstract Holocaust denial theory. Most visitors - the vast, vast majority - leave Auschwitz having been personally changed forever, and hopefully for the better, by the experience.

***

CHAPTER TWELVE
ANNIVERSARY OF
THE LIBERATION

Early in 2014 a small group of people discovered each other through the wonders of social networking and electronic communications. This was no accident in the true, random sense of the word as, for different reasons, they had shared interests. The main interest undoubtedly was the Holocaust and all that it entailed. There was also an interest in understanding history, learning from the past, and promoting tolerance and understanding for now and the future. We all brought a personal perspective to these subjects for a variety of reasons: Simon Bell – an aspiring first time author with a passion for challenging hate, and for promoting lessons from the past; Jessica Clark, a student and teacher with an interest in Dr Mengele and the other Nazi Doctors; Debbie Callahan-Sepper, a newly-published author and teacher with a family link to the Holocaust; Rainer Hoess, grandson of Auschwitz camp commandant Rudolf Hoess - a man dedicated to challenging the far right, and to eradicating some of the shame of his family name.

Some readers will be aware of Rainer from the 2011 television documentary *Hitler's Children*, in which he and other descendants of senior Nazis detailed the difficulties of their heritage. Rainer's tears during the film, and the forgiving embrace of a survivor, were powerful images. The images and tears conveyed to the viewer the assumed guilt for the sins of a man he never knew, but with whom he shared a name and genetics. Some of the Hoess family remained sympathetic to the Nazis long after Rudolf had been hanged; but Rainer felt shame, and blamed himself for the crimes committed in the surname he was born with.

Since that time Rainer has campaigned tirelessly against Nazi ideology, the far right, and all forms of hate. This has alienated him from many of his family, and has resulted in hostility and animosity from many including the Far Right, and even some one would presume would be allies and supporters of his work. In 2014 he was the public face and voice of a campaign called *Never Forget to Vote*.

Through Rainer I was put in contact with fellow-writers and students of the Holocaust. Initially this small group exchanged messages and thoughts. Gradually we offered support to each other in various personal projects. Eventually we planned to meet in Poland for the seventieth anniversary of the liberation of Auschwitz. The anniversary in 2015 was going to be significant for many reasons, not least of which would be the attendance at that event of many survivors - possibly the last time significant numbers would gather together at the site of their own personal torment and triumph.

As the anniversary approached, for each of us, a range of emotions became increasingly intense. For the author these emotions included excitement, anticipation, humility, and some trepidation at being involved in something so important. There was also anxiety. It is ironic that seventy years after Auschwitz was liberated, the Far Right, and popular intolerance, are on the rise across Europe. Anti-Semitism, Islamophobia, and racial hatred are common, and prevalent attitudes that have some popular acceptability, and are even defended as 'rights'. It does not matter which individual or group is targeted, the sentiment of hate is just the same. Within this month of celebration and commemoration there were acts of barbarity in Paris, marches of Far Right activists in Germany, synagogues and mosques being attacked, and minority groups living in fear. However, there were also marches of hope and voices of tolerance being loudly heard.

Prior to arriving in Poland we set up a Facebook group called *Footsteps*. The name of the group was intended to remember the millions of innocent footsteps that walked towards death in the gas chambers of Auschwitz and other camps. In recalling those footsteps we pledged to walk forward in their memory to challenge hatred and intolerance in all of its forms, and to help ensure the Holocaust is not forgotten. In due course Rainer Hoess hopes to set up the *Footsteps Foundation* to promote these concepts in a more structured, broader, and high profile format. Whether a Footsteps Foundation will be created remains to be seen, but it is a positive ideal.

Rainer Hoess is a high profile man within what can best be described as the 'Holocaust industry.' The demands placed upon his time and energy are immense, but he seems incapable of declining an interview or an invitation. He does, however, refuse to participate in any event or activity that may distract from survivors, or cause offence to them and those who care about them.

Meeting Rainer in person one is struck immediately by how likeable, approachable, decent and caring he is. He appears to have no false airs or pretensions. Although he is clearly not responsible for the crimes of his grandfather, he is determined to make amends in whatever way he can for wrongs done in the name of Hoess. His sincerity is such that Eva Mozes Kor, a survivor of the Mengele twins' experiments, 'emotionally' adopted Rainer as her grandson.

The Holocaust industry is a big business. There are many individuals, groups, organisations, and parties that benefit greatly from it. Most, with certainty, are involved for good reasons. The Auschwitz Museum stands out amongst those dedicated absolutely to maintaining the history of the place and what happened there. There are some elsewhere, undoubtedly, who have less than noble motives, including self-promotion and financial gain.

As a nurse and first time writer I had never encountered before the pressures, reality, and intensity of the news media. At the liberation anniversary – probably the major news event at that time – seeing the media in full flow was alarming. We (our small group) met Rainer in Krakow early in the afternoon of 25th January. This was meant to be a quiet time, to socialise and plan the activities of the next few days. Plans – I quickly realised – mean nothing during a major news event. Within minutes of greeting each other we were whisked by car the 40km to Auschwitz, for Rainer to be interviewed by Polish TV. In between takes, and once the interview was completed, he was accosted by news teams from across the world. He willingly gave time to answer their questions and cooperate with filming. It was after 9.00 p.m. before we got back to Krakow to unwind and relax. The following day we left Krakow at 6.30 a.m. for Rainer to do more interviews. We were introduced to the press as writers and board members of *Footsteps*, but the news crews had no interest in us, nor did they need any. I realised Rainer's world is so different from mine. At the conclusion of another interview an Auschwitz survivor interrupted. He recognised Rainer and had been following him around the camp. He wanted only to talk. The meeting of the survivor and the grandson of the commandant was full of warmth.

After several interviews we left Auschwitz main camp. Rainer had more interviews to do. The press wanted him to attend an event at the library in Oświęcim at which survivors were talking to the media. Rainer declined as he knew his presence would distract from survivors. I recorded my thoughts about this in an email to a friend. 'One of the most moving things was an event at the library in Oświęcim the day before the ceremony. About a dozen survivors were telling their stories. We got there in time to listen to a man called David Wisnia. He spoke articulately and powerfully to the assembled masses of the world's press. The place was packed with more cameras and journalists than I have ever seen. He mentioned that following liberation he wrote a song called 'Oświęcim'. As questions were being asked some journalists were ignoring him and doing their pieces to camera. A journalist asked if he would sing his song. He cleared his throat, and gave a rousing, if shaky, rendition. It was in Polish, with only the word Oświęcim being familiar to me. The place was stunned. Those who were doing their recordings to camera stopped and turned around. Others rushed to start recording. You could hear a pin drop. At the end everyone stood and applauded. And all I could think of was how, 70 years ago, he and the others were liberated into a world where they had nothing; where loved ones had been killed, homes were lost, and they lacked a country to call their own. They were physically and emotionally on their knees, having suffered and witnessed unbelievable horrors. And when they relocated they were voiceless through choice, or because others did not want to hear. And yet there David sat and sang his song. And at last the whole world was listening to him and the other survivors. He, and they, finally had a voice. I cried buckets.'

Several press interviews later we became the focus of attention for a pleasant group from New York. They had an art event at a local venue and wanted us to attend. As nothing was immediately planned we agreed. We were provided with food (an occasional luxury during a media storm) and they tried to arrange a meeting between Rainer and a survivor. Unfortunately the survivor had left in distress, having been led to believe that

Rainer is a Nazi who profits from the Hoess family history and by selling property associated with his grandfather. Of course this is verifiably untrue, but once a myth has been started it is difficult to disprove. Although there was no hostility, and polite apologies were offered profusely, the atmosphere felt strange and strained. One of their group – an artist – did eventually agree to see us, and show us her fantastic pieces of work. We were given a guided talk and tour of a display at a local synagogue. We left in time for a final interview at Auschwitz.

Our last activity of that day was a visit to the Hoess villa on the edge of Auschwitz main camp. No photographs of inside the villa will appear in this book. It is now a family home and it is only right and proper that some privacy is respected. We were welcomed warmly and openly by the lovely young couple who live there. They gladly allowed us to briefly invade their home and showed us all that we might want to see. Most of the interior is reasonably modern in décor, with no indication of the property's history. The space inside the door has a 1937 mark signifying when it was built. The stairs include intricate iron work done by inmates of the camp. The only place unchanged is the bunker beneath the house. It is a dilapidated basement area that actually extends into the camp. The gas chamber at Auschwitz I is less than two hundred metres from the villa. From the upstairs windows of the villa the view into the camp is clear and almost unbroken. The wall of the large garden does not provide a significant barrier. The Hoess family would have seen – indeed they could not have missed – the horrors taking place so nearby. In fact, when they lived there, fruit and vegetables grown in the villa garden, had to be cleaned thoroughly, to remove ash from burning human bodies.

Our group returned to Krakow for a meal and a relaxed but brief chat. We were none of us up for too much jollity. The day had been exhausting, and at times heavy going. And the major event, the seventieth anniversary of the liberation of Auschwitz, was the next day.

Before discussing the liberation ceremony it is worth talking about the impact of Auschwitz itself at this time. We were fortunate to be given virtually free rein to walk around the camp at our leisure, either with Rainer, or on our own whilst he did interviews. One cannot walk around Auschwitz in January without contemplating the enormity of what happened there. The camp has an unusual mystique. It was eerily quiet during the day. Visitor numbers seemed to be few. Small groups of press moved about seeking the best shot to broadcast, or to set up a piece to put on camera. Due to the lack of people the deep snow was often pristine, without a footprint visible. The quiet was strangely deafening. As dusk and then night-time fell, the atmosphere changed even more. The buildings, guard towers, and barbed wire fences, were shaped and emphasised by the brilliant whiteness of the snow, the darkness of the sky, and the piercing rays from the lights that are strategically sited. Auschwitz has a haunting quality even for those who are familiar with it. The gas chamber is quiet. Entry to that place of mass murder is unchallenged, and adds to the sense of empty and silent futility. The scratches on the walls made either by visitors or by dying inmates seem all the more powerful in the hush of a camp without the sound of tourists. The barrack blocks, the gate, the gallows from which Hoess was hanged, and the paths upon which human ash was scattered in winter, all take on a different quality. Seventy years ago when the nearby guns of the Soviet army would have been heard, most of the guards had left, senior officers were long gone, and many inmates had been transported westwards in what became known as death marches. Very few surviving souls remained to be liberated at this bleak and frozen place on 27th January 1945.

We were picked up from a central Krakow hotel early on the morning of the ceremony. Originally it had been hoped that we would have passes allowing us admission to the VIP tent to watch the formal ceremony close up. Those passes were not forthcoming, so we made plans to be in the main public area, which actually felt more acceptable and appropriate. Far better to be outside in the bitter cold, than enclosed in the sanitised environment created around the main entrance. That warm environment was better used for dignitaries and elderly survivors.

We had also expected early access to the Birkenau site on the day of the ceremony. We planned a private and quiet visit to the selection ramp and Kanada camp areas to offer personal thoughts for those who suffered and died, and to make a pledge to humanity on behalf of our group. As before, in the security and media maelstrom of this event, plans meant nothing. The levels of security were so high that there was no way they were letting four people wander around with or without supervision. Access was denied.

We assembled at the main camp for Rainer to do yet another interview. He would do more interviews after the ceremony. The camp was all but deserted apart from the press and security staff. Then we noticed small groups of no more than thirty people, walking slowly to lay wreaths. Some were elderly and clearly survivors. Some of the survivors actually wore striped pyjamas. We stepped quietly to one side to let them past. This was their moment of private and very personal homage.

There was a surreal eeriness to Auschwitz on this day. The snow was falling, and a bitter cold had descended. Thoughts immediately reflected that on this exact day seventy years ago the weather was colder, the conditions were harsher beyond belief, and a few thousand terrified and vulnerable souls finally met an army of liberation rather than an army of destruction.

To the front of the main camp and beyond, the activity was fevered and frenetic. Convoy after convoy of police vehicles with sirens wailing accompanied heads of state and various dignitaries as they arrived. More security escorted them through the main entrance. The press corps was held back far away whilst we – because we were with Rainer – were allowed to wander around quite freely near to this activity.

At Birkenau the main celebration had been planned for months quite meticulously. The huge main entrance gate – so symbolic of that place – had been enclosed within a vast tent-like structure. The VIPs would travel there in luxury. So too would approximately three hundred survivors - undoubtedly the most important people there. Those of us not permitted in the main event were taken to a large car park. We were loaded (in fact crammed) onto buses. Around us were groups of many ages and nationalities. Some were draped in flags. Some sat quietly. Some chatted excitedly. Some sang songs. There was an abundance of languages and palpable differences, but we all shared a common reason for being there. As we waited uncomfortably on the bus it occurred to me that we were in a modern version of a transport to Birkenau. But this transport served only to convey us to celebrate and commemorate. How different from seventy years ago! There was a vocal music of a unified people. We were none of us different here. Even the famous and immensely wealthy would travel to the ceremony in the same manner. This transport – as was the case all those years ago – did not recognise social boundaries.

As we arrived at Birkenau we were taken well away from the main event. The security fears were clearly much heightened. The gate, in the distance, so familiar to everyone and synonymous with this place, was hidden beneath its vast temporary dome. Much of the camp was fenced-off, and inaccessible to the public on this day. We walked between chilled (and chilling) barrack blocks to an area a few hundred metres away from the International Holocaust Memorial. Through the snow and dimming light we could see that vast concrete monolith, with flags blowing in the winter breeze. It blended into the wooded area behind. We could see the ruins of the crematoria and the stones that mark the pits where human ash was stored before being scattered and distributed. We could see the cattle truck on the selection ramp – lit up for the ceremony. It stood alone as an isolated and stark symbol of man's inhumanity to man.

We were guided between more barrack blocks towards a big screen. It was the only way we would see the ceremony. In the gathered crowd were rich and poor, famous and unknown, people of many lands, genders and ages. We chatted to a young man who survived the Rwandan genocide. All of us were nameless here. We noticed a couple of men, well-dressed, and of senior years. They were twins. We wondered about the experiments and horrors they endured at this place. There were descendants of senior Nazis, unknown to most, but recognised and known to our friend. They quietly paid their respects to the dead and the survivors. It felt as if all humanity was represented here – in this bitterly cold, snow-covered and windy place – by the presence of a few hundred pilgrims.

Seventy years ago those who were liberated were starved, diseased, and weakened. Many were broken, but many were determined, despite the odds, to survive. The conditions then were much worse than this day. Appropriately, the weather changed for the event of commemoration. The camp was already covered in deep snow, but the snow began to fall heavily once more, the wind picked up, and the temperature dropped dramatically. It was bitterly and painfully cold. We stood as well-nourished and healthy observers clothed in modern winter garments, but we struggled with the conditions for these few hours. Of course we were not miserable or complaining. After all, our discomfort – relative as it was – would not last long before we returned to the warmth of hotels and homes. Those who were here seventy years ago had no such luxury. They suffered and endured, or they died, falling to the ground with the look of a Muslim at prayer - a Musselmann. That was a sobering thought to hold on to.

The ceremony ran its course with the planned formality and gravity. We were glad to be in this isolated spot and to observe from a distance. The day was about survivors and those who had died. It was about history. It was not about us. Gradually the crowds drifted away, and the dignitaries were transported in their loud, police-escorted convoys. And later, no doubt, Auschwitz-Birkenau was left in icy, snow-swept silence, unchanged by the grandeur and events of the day, and left to continue to hold memories in the vastness that made it the most significant place of extermination in human history.

I pondered later that evening in the warm loneliness of a Krakow hotel room. 'I am so honoured to have been there today. We were dressed in good winter garb, but the cold bit its way through to the point of pain. Hard to comprehend how it was for survivors on this day 70 years ago. My trip to Poland was mainly for this event and all that it signifies. Never again should we allow the bringers of hate to prevail or accept intolerance and scapegoating as a social norm. I will reflect long and hard about these last few days. History is not just a series of events, dates, names and places. It is a living entity that needs to be fully understood in all of its aspects, whether they are good or bad. I have been fortunate to witness history, and today I have been within history; but I am not part of that event. I am instead a custodian of what I have seen, heard, perceived, and know. To honour the Holocaust we must truly learn from it, otherwise we will allow similar horrors to happen again in our life time. Racial, religious, and other hatred is not acceptable in any form. This, to me, is the greatest lesson.'

Dignity, respect, compassion, and caring are basic and fundamental human traits, as natural to mankind as breathing.

They do not need to be dictated to us, or taught, or rationed, or to be based on any political, cultural, or religious framework. They are traits for which we all bear responsibility. Failure to aim towards such simple ideals leads ultimately to suffering and the hell of genocide, but aspiring to achieve them gives us hope. This book is ultimately dedicated to the principles of decency and hope over hatred and intolerance, using the lessons of one period of history as a warning and guide for the future.

***

EPILOGUE
DARKNESS OR LIGHT?

Seventy years after the liberation of Auschwitz and other camps, the world has cause to reflect and consider how it deals with modern crises. There have been other genocides recognised by the United Nations – Cambodia, Darfur, Bosnia and Rwanda – and other conflicts that may in due course be seen as genocides, even if they are not currently acknowledged as such. The world today is a place where strife and discord have had dire consequences for those who are vulnerable. Following the terrorist attacks on the U.S. in 2001, and London, Madrid, Paris, Nice, Berlin and elsewhere since, there has, for many people, been a sense of unease and danger.

Military interventions in Iraq, Afghanistan, Libya, and to a degree Syria, have been led by western powers, often in coalition with more local regional forces. The civil war in Syria escalated in 2016 with the intervention of Russian forces assisting the government regime. The siege of Aleppo horrified the on-looking world as images of death and destruction filled news outlets. Civil wars and oppressive regimes wreak havoc in other countries. The hopes of what was known as the 'Arab Spring' did not bear fruit as expected. Islamist terror groups have filled power vacuums with barbaric brutality beyond the comprehension of most decent people. Established networks such as Al Qaeda, although weakened, remain dangerous. In Nigeria and neighbouring countries Boko Haram operates over large areas with impunity. Al Shabaab attacks government and western interests in East Africa. The Taliban seek to regain control of Afghanistan and parts of Pakistan where previously they had imposed a strict and harsh version of Islam, and had harboured groups seen as terrorists to most other nations. Most notably we have seen the emergence of a group that calls itself 'ISIS'.

These groups are Islamist. They have a strictly literalist and fundamentalist interpretation of Islam and the words of the Qur'an as they choose to interpret them. They impose rules that are totally alien to the vast majority of the world's Muslims. They torture, subjugate, and murder at a rate not seen so widely (probably) since the Second World War. Public executions are commonplace, and as a terror tool many of these are filmed and broadcast on social media. The people of the West are understandably horrified and outraged when citizens of their own countries are harmed. There is less outrage at the killing of tens of thousands of innocent Muslims by these groups.

Some citizens of westernised nations, bloodied by a few awful acts of terror, have come to see all Muslims as a danger. The reality that most who follow that faith are perfectly peaceful and law-abiding is not accepted or understood. The fact that the vast majority of those harmed and killed by Islamist groups are Muslims is seen as an irrelevance. In the eyes of some, all Muslims are terrorists, even if they flee such terror to save their lives.

In 2016 the western world has become increasingly perplexed about the issue of refugees from the civil war in Syria, which is now in its sixth year. According to the United Nations Refugee Agency - UNHCR - in July 2015 the Syrian refugee crisis was the single largest refugee crisis under its mandate in almost a quarter of a century. Countries neighbouring Syria have taken a total of over four million refugees, and almost eight million are displaced within the borders of Syria. Many hundreds of thousands have travelled further afield, including to Europe.

The conflict in Syria shows no signs of ending. Opposing sides are entrenched in a brutal war, and as is always the case, most victims are civilians. It is currently estimated that well in excess 200,000 have been killed. The regime of the government (and its Russian ally) is held responsible for many of those killed, and for the hardships others have experienced. But the insurgent groups fighting the government are a mix of what some may call 'freedom-fighters', or a legitimate opposition, and also some who would be deemed extremists. In neighbouring Iraq a power vacuum exists in large areas where the government has not had control since the departure of U.S led forces. Over a vast swathe of Iraq and Syria (and possibly elsewhere) ISIS have taken control. They adhere to a fundamentalist and literalist version of Islam with roots in Wahhabiism and Salafism that is unfamiliar to most of the world's Muslims. They have brutalised, raped, enslaved, tortured, and murdered tens of thousands of people. They have tried to eradicate established communities, including Christians, Yazidi and Muslim. They may also be responsible for attacks on countries outside of their control or at least inspiring such attacks.

Away from this region there is the chaos and civil unrest in Arab lands that sought liberation from old totalitarian regimes; there is the continued danger of a conflict in Afghanistan and Pakistan; there is the brutality of life in Eritrea and other East African countries; there is the brutality of Boko Haram in Nigeria; and in the Far East the Rohingya people are suffering and fleeing the regime in Myanmar.

Terror groups claiming an adherence to Islam make up a miniscule representation of the world population of Muslims.

Yet in the westernised countries it has become acceptable to demonise all Muslims, and tar them with the brush of 'terrorist'.

As millions flee the horror and uncertainty of these brutal lands they travel in search of refuge, safety, and sanctuary in other countries. By and large, support and assistance has been offered. There is a certain irony that in Europe it has been Germany that has led moves to provide homes to the dispossessed. Other European countries have followed suit with popular support. Some countries, due to internal problems, or due to the volume of refugees arriving, have struggled to cope. And some countries, despite wealth and the facility to assist, have shown intense reluctance.

Those people who are fearful and desperate to the extent that they risk their lives in the hands of criminal traffickers, who put their loved ones on unsound boats to cross seas, who travel through hostile lands with little means of support, should, if humanity prevails, receive unfettered support and assistance. But many, in the lands of supposed safety, offer only hostility. The vulnerable have become the enemy. The generalised animosity seeks not to understand the individual stories, or the circumstances that led to flight; it seeks only to find reasons to refuse and block those in need. It is a fair observation that despite these people being the victims of the horror the West fears, they are seen as being part of the danger. Mainstream elected politicians in parliamentary democracies have even advocated placing all refugees in offshore processing centres to establish the validity of claims, and to isolate and remove those deemed unworthy. In another time such establishments were called 'concentration camps'. In 2016 in Europe and elsewhere, there has been a marked rise in extreme and populist far-right groups (and far-left as well as religious conservatism), supported by elements of the press. The rhetoric of intolerance and hate may be directed towards different targets, but it is as poisonous and potentially harmful as any intolerance in history.

Sadly there is a reality: the refugees of 2016 are mainly brown- skinned, Arabic-speaking Muslims. They have been dehumanised in the same way that Jews were in the first half of the twentieth century.

We need to get back in touch with our humanity, and consider the lessons we thought we had learned from the brutality of Nazism. Do we allow the beams of hopeful light to shine, or do we allow them to be dimmed by the darkness of hate and intolerance? The choices are ours to make.

THE END

References

Hoess, Rudolf. *Commandant of Auschwitz.* Phoenix Press 2012 edition
IBSN: 978-1-8421-2024-8

Hitler, Adolf. *Mein Kampf.* Pimlico London 2014 edition
IBSN: 978 0 7126 5254 4

ICD-10 Classification of Mental and Behavioural Disorders. Clinical descriptions and diagnostic guidelines. World Health Organisation Geneva
IBSN: 92 4 154422 8

Harding, Thomas. *Hanns and Rudolf. The German Jew and the hunt for the Kommandant of Auschwitz.* William Heinemann 2013 edition
IBSN: 978 0 434022 36 6

Owen, James. *Nuremberg, Evil on Trial.* Headline Publishing Group 2007 edition
IBSN: 978 0 7553 1545 1

Rees, Laurence. *Auschwitz the Nazis and the Final Solution.* Ebury Publishing 2005 edition.
IBSN 978 0 563 52296 6

Sweibock, Teresa and Henryk. *Auschwitz, The Residence of Death*
IBSN: 978-83-6029-245-7

Rees, Laurence. *The Nazis, A Warning from History.* Random House Publishing 2005 edition
IBSN: 978 0 563 49333 4

Asking the Question About Violence and Sexual Abuse in Adult Mental Health Assessments. Department of Health and National Institute for Mental Health in England

Lekarski, Przeglad. *Auschwitz Survivors Clinical Psychiatric Studies*. Wydawnictwo Przeglad Lekarski, Krakow, 2013 edition
IBSN: 978-83-918170-0-1

Levi, Primo. *If this is a Man. The Truce*. Penguin Books, 2011 edition
IBSN: 978-0-349-10013-5

Levi, Primo. *The Drowned and The Saved*. Abacus Books, 1988 edition
IBSN: 0 349 100470

Pivnik, Sam. *Auschwitz, The Death March and my Fight for Freedom*. Hodder & Stoughton, 2012 edition
IBSN: 978 1 444 75837 5

Hart-Moxon, Kitty. *Return to Auschwitz*. The Holocaust Centre, Laxton, Notts, UK. 2010 edition
IBSN 978-0-9555009-0-9

Survival. Holocaust Survivors Tell Their Story. Quill Press and Holocaust Centre, Laxton, Notts, UK, 2004 edition
IBSN: 0-9543001-1-4

Venezia, Shlomo. *Inside the Gas Chambers. Eight Months in the Sonderkommando of Auschwitz*. Polity Press, Cambridge, UK
IBSN: 978-0-7456-4384-7

Mozes-Kor, Eva. *Surviving the Angel of Death. The True Story of a Mengele Twin in Auschwitz*
Tanglewood, 2012 edition
IBSN: 978-1-93718-57-6

King, Jr, Martin Luther. *The Autobiography of Martin Luther King, Jr.* Abacus Books, 2000 edition
IBSN: 0 349 11298 3

Weisenthal, Simon. *Justice Not Vengeance.* George Weidenfeld & Nicolson Ltd, 1989 edition
IBSN: 0 297 79683 6
Mandela, Nelson. Long Walk to Freedom. Abacus Books, 1999 edition

Czech, Danuta. Auschwitz Chronicle 1939-1945. From The Archives Of The Auschwitz Memorial And The German Federal Archives. Henry Holt and Company.Inc. 1997 edition
ISBN 0-8050-0938-8

Jewish History in Germany – Jewish Virtual Library
http://www.jewishvirtuallibrary.org/jsource/vjw/germany.html

The Roma and Gypsies in German and Auschwitz – Jewish Virtual Library
http://www.jewishvirtuallibrary.org/jsource/Holocaust/gypsies.html

Adolf Hitler – *Basic biographical information*
http://www.jewishvirtuallibrary.org/jsource/Holocaust/hitler.html

Rudolf Hoess – *Basic biographical information*. Jewish Virtual Library
http://www.jewishvirtuallibrary.org/jsource/biography/Hoess.html

Adolf Eichmann – *Basic biographical information*. Jewish Virtual Library
http://www.jewishvirtuallibrary.org/jsource/Holocaust/eichmann.html

Heinrich Himmler – *Basic biographical information*. Jewish Virtual Library
http://www.jewishvirtuallibrary.org/jsource/Holocaust/himmler.html

Joseph Mengele – *Basic biographical information*. Jewish Virtual Library
http://www.jewishvirtuallibrary.org/jsource/Holocaust/Mengele.html

Hans Frank – *Basic biographical information*. Jewish Virtual Library
http://www.jewishvirtuallibrary.org/jsource/biography/Frank1.html

Joseph Goebbels – *Basic biographical information*. Jewish Virtual Library
http://www.jewishvirtuallibrary.org/jsource/Holocaust/goebbels.html

Reinhard Heydrich – *Basic biographical information*. Jewish Virtual Library http://www.jewishvirtuallibrary.org/jsource/Holocaust/Heydrich.html

Herman Göring – *Basic biographical information.* Jewish Virtual Library
http://www.jewishvirtuallibrary.org/jsource/Holocaust/goering.html

Rudolf Hess – *Basic biographical information.* Jewish Virtual Library
http://www.jewishvirtuallibrary.org/jsource/biography/Hess1.html

Julius Streicher – *Basic biographical information.* Jewish Virtual Library
http://www.jewishvirtuallibrary.org/jsource/Holocaust/Streicher.html

Nazi Concentration, Death, and Labour camp numbers
https://www.jewishvirtuallibrary.org/jsource/Holocaust/cclist.html

Berlin-Wannsee Jewish Populations List
http://prorev.com/wannsee.htm

Abraham Maslow. 1943 paper '*A theory of Human Motivation*' (http://www.simplypsychology.org/maslow.html)

The Stanford Prison Experiment - A Simulation Study of the Psychology of Imprisonment Conducted at Stanford University (http://www.prisonexp.org)

BBC Online *Jane Elliott and the Brown Eyes Blue Eyes Experiment*
(http://www.bbc.co.uk/dna/place-devon/plain/A1132480)

The Milgram Experiment – Various online sources but for simplicity of access to information Wikipedia
http://en.wikipedia.org/wiki/Milgram_experiment

Genocide Information. Holocaust Memorial Day Trust
http://hmd.org.uk/page/holocaust-genocides

Heinrich Himmler Posen Speech. Jewish Virtual Library
(https://www.jewishvirtuallibrary.org/jsource/Holocaust/HimmlerPosen.html)

The Path to Genocide. Genocide Watch
(www.genocidewatch.org)

Universal Declaration of Human Rights
(http://www.un.org/en/documents/udhr/index.shtml)

Human Rights Act 1998
(http://www.legislation.gov.uk/ukpga/1998/42/contents)

CPS Hate Crime Statistics
(http://www.cps.gov.uk/publications/equality/hate_crime.html)

Also Recommended:

Ancona-Vincent, Victoria. *Beyond Imagination*. Quill Press, 2004 edition
IBSN: 0 9543001 6 5

Ligocka, Roma. *The Girl in the Red Coat*. Delta Books, 2003 edition
IBSN: 0-385-33740-X

Rees, Laurence. *The Dark Charisma of Adolf Hitler*. Elbury Press, 2012 edition
IBSN: 978 800919 176 54

Schloss, Eva. *After Auschwitz*. Hodder & Stoughton, 2013 edition.
IBSN: 978 1 4447 6068 2

Schloss, Eva. *Eva's Story*. W.H.Allen & Co. Plc. 2014 edition
ISBN 0-95237169 3

Keneally, Thomas. *Schindler's Ark*. Serpentine Publishing, 2007 edition
IBSN: 978 0 340 93629 0

Collins, Matthew. *Hate. My Life in the British Far Right*. Biteback Publishing, 2012 edition
IBSN 978-1-84954-327-9

Cywinski, Piotr. *Epitaph*. Auschwitz-Birkenau State Museum, 2015 edition
IBSN: 978-83-7704-084-3

Weinberg, Felix. *Boy 30529 A Memoir. Verso*, 2013 edition
IBSN: 978-1-78168-078-0

Callahan, Debbie. *Lest We Forget: Lessons From Survivors of the Holocaust*. Bruske Books Publishing, 2014 edition
IBSN: 978-0-692-24284-1

SIMON BELL

Rusesabagina, Paul. *An Ordinary Man. The True Story Behind 'Hotel Rwanda'*. Bloomsbury Publishing, 2006 edition
IBSN: 0 7475 8304 8

Wachsmann, Nikolaus. *KL - A History of the Nazi Concentration Camps*. Little, Brown. 2015 edition.
ISBN 978-0-316-72967-3

Stone, Dan. *The Liberation of the Camps. The End of the Holocaust and its Aftermath*. Yale University Press. 2015 edition
ISBN 978-0-300-20457-5

Printed in Great Britain
by Amazon